DO DOGS GO TO HEAVEN?

Eternal Answers for Animal Lovers

Jean Holmes

JoiPax Publishing
A division of JoiPax, Inc.
P.O. Box 701252
Tulsa, OK 74170-1252

www.joipax.com
e-mail: jean.holmes@joipax.com

Do Dogs Go To Heaven? Eternal Answers for Animals Lovers

ISBN #0-9676218-0-1

Cover illustration from an original oil painting by Lee Shortridge, M.F.A. Assisted by Seth Jensen (illustration), and Jason Graham (layout/ research). © 1999 Joipax, Inc.

Published by:
JoiPax Publishing
a division of JoiPax, Inc.
P O Box 701252
Tulsa OK 74170-1252

DEDICATION

I dedicate this book:

To God, our Creator,
— Father, Savior-Son, and Holy Spirit —
who loves all His creation
and has eternal plans for the good of all.

To the animals who have loved us, taught us,
cared for us, even given their lives,
and who patiently await our enlightenment.

To Irene Hume Holmes, my witty wonderful Mom,
for her courage in asking a question
every dog lover, every animal lover, wants to know,
who loved all God's creatures without fear,
who taught me to love truth, and to enjoy the sunshine
and rain equally.

To John M. Holmes, D.V.M., my beloved "Doc,"
my shy, brilliant father, who first assured me
that there was a heaven for dogs, and lived
rightly without boasting.

Both now enjoy heaven, and
know the answer to this book's question.

To those people who love animals and
need to know about their eternity.

ACKNOWLEDGMENTS

There are many who deserve thanks and acknowledgments who have played a part in this book. I cannot think of how many. May God richly bless each one!

Special recognition and thanks go to the following persons and dogs:

Thanks to my patient editor and friend, Norma Jean Lutz, of Notations un-limited. To Elsie Sommers, my roommate, friend and, with her experience in the book printing business, a guardian angel. To Paula and Sharon for the typing services they've added. To the Tulsa Christian Writers Club for encouragement and sponsorship.

Special thanks to the dog models which Lee Shortridge used for the oil painting which is the basis for the book cover:

Toy poodle: Steve & Gwen Alley and family for "Bambi"

German Shephard: Geri Hibblen Jackson's dogs: Kingfield's Starlight CGC, HIC, TDI ("Angie") and Ch. Summitwood's Everready, CGC, TDI (Reggie)

Thanks to Winters, King & Associates, Inc., my law firm, for the prayers, patience and support in the long process of writing and publishing this book.

Thanks to Pat, Pam & Allen at SunTech, and Mike & Cindy at Banner Media, Elsie, Curtis and those at Regent Printing, Doug at Paragon Communications Group and lots of others who've helped get this book in print, many thanks.

Thanks to those who have prayed and believed this would happen, and helped me through the hard times when I was too tired to move: Mozelle Babin, Oonchor & Pearl Khoo, Angela Hendrix and her family, Eric & Anna Ewing, Dick & Pat Peterson, Eric & Anna Ewing, John Venturella, Bobbie Taylor, Geraldine Boyle, Terri Steinmetz, my priest, Vic Smith, and members of Church of the Holy Spirit in Tulsa, and too many others to name and remember as I press on to get this into the hands of readers!

CONTENTS

Preface i

1 *Mom's Question* 1

2 *Is It Okay To Love Animals?*...9

3 *Dogs and Cats In The Bible* 25

4 *Do Animals Have Souls and Spirits?* 41

5 *In Awesome Wonder*
or Animals At Creation 73

6 *The Naming of the Animals*...85

7 *The Fall of Man and the Animals* 101

8 *Who Were the First* 131
Animal Sacrifices?

9 *Covenants: Beginning with Noah* 143
and the Ark

10 *Job and Other Old*...165
Testament Nuggets

11 *Jesus Christ and Animals*...177

12 *What Parts Do Animals Play?*...................................193

13 *Eternity: Two Destinations*..209

14 *The Restoration of All Creation* 227

15 *Hope of Resurrection!* 253

PREFACE

This book came about because my Mom, Irene Hume Holmes, asked the question which is the title, "Do dogs go to heaven?" During her lifetime, Mom had many animal friends — a lot of them were dogs.

Mom's question strikes a nerve in animal lovers. Heaven for us means our animals will be there, too. This book is for adults, like Mom. It does not treat Mom's question as something "just for children." It is a thorough study of her question which took me years to research and write.

Mom went to heaven in 1988, having lived almost nine decades. For her the question is settled. She knows the answer. But Mom's question launched me on a quest to find true answers. Not just glib, pat, surface answers, but answers with substance. In the 1990s the search became a fire in my bones.

I determined to have a proven answer, one based in Scripture, and substantiated by research and evidence. To honor Mom and our Lord, I wanted the full truth. There are some "hard" questions about the role of animals here and in the hereafter. I wanted the answer, even if I didn't like the answer. And I *knew* I would find it.

THE IMPORTANCE OF ANIMALS

Animals, both wild animals and domestic, play tremendous roles in our lives, and have done so since the dawn of creation. Animals provide companionship, do work, become food and clothing, and are vital players in the diverse interconnected ecologies of our world. Pets give us unconditional love and faithful companionship. From aardvarks to zebras, elephants to trained mice, animals enrich our lives. Animals as diverse as reindeer, oxen, horses, camels, llamas, cats, dogs and parrots, have worked with us and for us. Today a variety of animals are serving in therapy roles to young and old. History is replete with examples of animals who have been friends, rescuers, healers, and calming influences.

The pet industry in the U.S. alone, is a multibillion dollar industry.[1] In 1995, a newspaper reported in France there were some nine million dogs. (That didn't include cats, birds, and other pets.) Egyptians have bred and kept dogs, and other domestic animals, for thousands of years. Friends in South America tell me of the pet lovers they know there. Among the oldest house-dogs and cats are Asian breeds. The whole world is full of animal lovers. Since time began, animals and humans have shared bonds of affection.

Modern animal behavior studies now show that animals (including insects) display intelligence, moral choice and various skills. "Moral choice" includes honesty, responsibility, bravery, loyalty, love, and grief — as well as their opposites. Play and humor are evident. Animals have acted, even died, heroically or sacrificially for others. Animals solve complex problems, use tools, and communicate. Some have complex social structures. There is increasing medical evidence of animals as human healers. We humans study, exploit, revere, fear, love, hate, document, film and write about animals both domestic and wild.

QUALIFICATIONS

What are my qualifications to write this book? My heritage, my experience, and my training have all prepared me. Most important, finding an answer has become a kind of calling, driving me to research, observe, pray and work until Mom's question, with all its implications, had a well-documented answer.

My heritage is that I've been surrounded by animals from infancy. Caring for animals was a requirement; cruelty was not an option. My parents, my older brother, Jim, and I are all animal people.

Mom was an incredible woman and a great Mom. Irene Holmes had poise and pluck, grace and wisdom. She also had a tongue as sharp as her mind, but she chose to use it to love and protect. Whether Mom was in the kitchen, before the fireplace, in the barn, or in the fields, she made life — even its challenges and hurts — fascinating and funny. Mom was fearless and adventurous. I gained a great deal from her, not the least of which is my intense love of and admiration for animals. Mom is the reason for this book. (Thanks, Mom!)

My late father, Dr. John Marshal Holmes, D.V.M., was a brilliant veterinarian. He graduated from Ohio State University with honors. He had a large and small animal practice in Hagerstown, Indiana, during my childhood. Through him and his practice I was exposed to a wide variety of animals — some tame, some wild.

Mom raised pedigreed standard dachshunds and enjoyed all creation. From her I learned to view nature with all its humor and grandeur, with awe and wonder. Understanding and respecting all living creatures was a requirement in her presence. Mom taught me that each animal had its own unique personality, its own strengths and weaknesses, its own purpose and value.

My parents modeled intelligent curiosity, responsible caring service, dedication, and a love of excellence. Mom was especially patient, gentle, and just — although she could be a "she-bear" when protecting others from harm. My parents showed me a passion for truth and integrity, for justice and right — even when it kills you. While my parents were far from perfect, I saw in them the basic moral values which make a person a good citizen of the world. Caring for animals is part of that citizenship.

Because of my parents, I come by the love of animals naturally. My experience with animals is reasonably broad. I cannot remember being without one or more pets. Horses, dogs, cats, birds, and other critters filled my childhood days. I've enjoyed reading about and listening to other people's experiences with animals. Animal stories and science are areas I can interface with. Throughout my life, I've learned to remain curious and ask questions. Logic, and other mental and emotional disciplines, were part of my education.

Currently I practice law. Having practiced many years, my skills in research and communication are honed. I am accustomed to gathering evidence and legal authorities. Having focused for years on doing appeals of cases from trial courts, I "try cases" on paper. You might say I research and write legal briefs for a living.

Another important qualification is that God, our Creator, is real to me. I know Him experientially. No one can take that from me. I know God is real and that He loves me. For many years I explored the world's religions and philosophies. For several decades, I have been "at home" with Jesus [or Yeshua] of Nazareth, as my Lord and Savior. and confidante. The promises that the Holy Spirit (Spirit of the Lord) will guide me into all truth and will teach me all things, have been real to me many times over. [John 14:26 & 16:13] As an avid student of the Bible, I use both Christian and Jewish sources in every search for truth.

Last, but not least, more than just caring, I love animals — especially ones who have been my friends, companions, and teachers. Mom's question has become my question, too.

The views expressed here are my own. By choice a long-time member of one denomination, I have explored practices and doctrines from Catholicism to Pentecostalism. I have been enriched by the different experiences of all Christians. If my interpretations of Scripture offend your beliefs or your church's doctrines, please accept my statement that I do not intend to offend, only to challenge. (Please take it to the Lord. Where I am in error, I know He will correct me.) I have worked hard to try to accurately handle God's Word, to state the truth.

MY QUEST

Mom's question inspired my own "need to know." I, the lawyer and veterinarian's daughter who loved God's Word, didn't have an answer for her. I didn't know what the Bible said about animals going to heaven. I wasn't even sure it said anything. But I had acquired a reputation for being able to find answers in the Bible. It was a challenge for me to find answers to the difficult questions. If the Bible had an answer, I'd find it. Mom's question caused a spark to be kindled inside me. That spark would smolder and finally burn hot until I found the answer.

The quest for an answer to Mom's question has taken a lot of prayer, work, and thought. What began as a fun project to honor Mom, became a serious project which took years of discipline and careful listening. Johann Wolfgang von Goethe's words on seeking truth are apt:

It is easier to perceive error than to find the truth, for the former lies on the surface and is easily seen, while the latter lies in the depth, where few are willing to search for it.

This book came about because I asked the Lord God to show me, in His Word, the Holy Bible, *His* answer to my mother's question. I am confident that He has indeed shown me.

And what I have learned has been staggering. Come with me as we explore the Bible, and other sources to find answers to Mom's question. Do dogs go to heaven? There is an answer! A Bible answer of tremendous import. Join me in the search for truth that brings freedom! God will be with us. I pray your questions will be answered here. If you have questions or comments after reading this book, feel free write or e-mail me. I'll make every effort to respond.

May our Creator, the Lord God Almighty, bless you as you join me in examining Bible evidence which answers the question, "Do dogs — and other animals — go to heaven?" Mom's question does have an answer.

Jean Holmes
Tulsa Oklahoma,
November 1999
e-mail: Jean Holmes@joipax.com

CHAPTER 1

MOM'S QUESTION

I think I could turn and live with animals, they are so placid and self-contained;
I stand and look at them long and long.
They do not sweat and whine about their condition; ...
Not one is dissatisfied — not one is demented with mania of owning things;

Walt Whitman, "Song of Myself"

The most predictable thing about my Mom was that you never knew what would come out of her mouth next. My Mom, Irene Hume Holmes, was a master at asking probing questions and making life fun and interesting. Some eight years before her death — when she was in her 70s — Mom asked a series of ministers the question which became the title of this book: "*Do dogs go to heaven?*" She asked it of pastors and priests, all men of the cloth. Each gave a different answer. None gave the same one.

THE DEATH OF MOM'S CHOC

Mom asked her question after Choc died. Choc was the last of Mom's dachshunds. Choc was a rare chocolate point, marked like the black and tan dachshund, except the black was brown.(She was the only one I had ever seen.) Naturally, "Choc" became her nickname. Choc was born just months before my father (whom we called "Doc") died. After more than twenty-five years of raising pedigreed dachshunds, this pup was from Mom's last litter. Choc was special to Mom.

Choc died a horrible death. Mom and I were living together in Madisonville, Kentucky, and our house had no fenced yard. When we went shopping for the day, we simply tied up the dogs. One day we returned to find Choc had strangled when her long chain became entangled around a bush. We were devastated.

MOM'S QUESTION

Sometime after Choc died, Mom and I were chatting with the man who delivered our newspaper. He was also a country preacher, and while not well educated, he was a hard-working fellow who appeared to love the Lord. Mom and I both liked him. Suddenly Mom asked this preacher:

"Do dogs go to heaven?"

The question took me off guard. Looking back I wonder if Mom was thinking of Choc. Instantly, I was curious as to how the preacher would answer. He looked surprised. He paused and thought. Then he said, "Well, in the Book of Revelation, it says that Jesus is coming back on a horse. So there are horses in heaven." He paused and thought some more.

From the look on his face, it was obvious he was searching his mind for Bible verses. "It also says, 'without the gates are the dogs.' So, dogs aren't in heaven." He paused again. Then his face brightened as he stated with confidence, "There are horses in heaven, but there are no dogs in heaven!" He beamed — proud that he'd found a Bible answer. He did not realize how that answer struck a dog lover.

Actually, the man's answer hit my funny bone. I couldn't laugh, however. Mom required us to be polite. His answer seemed logical. The preacher didn't know that the term "dog" in that passage is a slang expression. I knew, but remained quiet. Mom did not show her reaction.

DIFFERENT ANSWERS

Because I was very active in Christian service in Madisonville, we knew many of the ministers, priests and preachers there, from the Roman Catholics to the Pentecostals. Some were highly educated; others were nearly illiterate. Some obviously cared for people and others seemed to treat ministry like a tiresome job.

Within days, Mom asked the same question of the next minister we encountered. As I recall he was pastor of a large church. This second man of the cloth answered stiffly, "I don't know. The Bible doesn't say." It was clear from his tone and body language that Mom's question made him uncomfortable. The subject was quickly changed and he made his exit.

For several weeks, each time we ran into a minister, Mom would ask her question. Most seemed stunned or taken off guard by the question. One said, "God is love, so surely He will let you have your beloved dogs in heaven."

Another said, "No, there's nothing in the Bible that says animals go to heaven." Yet another said, "I don't think so. The Bible is silent about it." And another, "I don't know that the Bible says — but I'm sure God would let you have your pet in heaven if you wanted it."

The answers ran the gamut from negative to positive. One gently replied, his voice full of love, "If you want them to be there, I'm sure they will be."

Of all the pastors, priests and ministers who answered the question, no two answered the same. Most seemed to be voicing an opinion. No one quoted or referred to Scripture, except the country preacher.

The more Mom asked her question, the more my amusement died. I winced inside. It occurred to me that I had never, in all my years of church attendance, ever heard a sermon on animals going to heaven. No seminary or Bible school offers courses on it. Where would ministers look for answers? I began to wonder why the topic is so ignored. And what message does this convey to animal lovers?

Most ministers love God and people. Most love animals, too. Most struggle to please God and do right by people. Such men and women work hard to serve. Many ministers have few resources or little time to seek an answer to such a question. My purpose is not to fault such men and women. It is Mom's question that is the focus here.

That question was important to my mother. Hers was no ordinary poll. She loved dogs. Mom had given her heart to Jesus and knew she was going to heaven when she died. She was in her 70s and had no fear of death. But would her dogs be in heaven? She truly wanted to know the answer. It was a very important question to Mom.

I believe it's a very important question for many people.

PIECING TOGETHER THE PUZZLE

"Do dogs go to heaven?" is a question not directly answered in the Bible. It must be searched out. The pieces have to be patiently gathered, carefully laid side-by-side, then prayerfully interpreted. Mom's question requires a look back at the history of Christianity and its diverse theologies. The ministers Mom asked were uninformed or confused about this question. My research helps us to understand why that is so.

MY APPROACH

I approach the evidence on Mom's question as a lawyer. (Scientific methods[2] obviously don't work well on questions like Mom's.) Attorneys rarely have the luxury of direct, scientific proof. We are accustomed to using circumstantial evidence. A trial attorney's job is to reconstruct past events to prove a case. We also have to reconcile conflicting laws and authorities. Our stock and trade is gathering evidence and authorities to prove our cases. Whether we need to prove something "by a mere preponderance of evidence," "by clear and convincing evidence," or "beyond a reasonable doubt," if we find enough law and evidence, we make our client's case. Thus the legal method is useful in examining spiritual concepts. The Bible is both a law book and is full of circumstantial evidence about animals and heaven.

In my search, I have examined theological writings, scholarly dissertations, scientific, and popular resources. Even though I am accustomed to the sometimes dry subject of law, most theological works are very arid and not fun for me. They make me wonder about theologians who seem to believe that complicating simple things is a mark of genius! I believe the opposite: true genius makes complicated things simple. Jesus did that. This is what I attempt to do in this book.

This project has been a journey of faith for me. Faith is still "the substance of things hoped for, the evidence of things not seen." [Hebrews 11:1] Faith empowered me to find answers. It gave me the focus, the calling, and vigor to work until I had answers. Someone said, "Faith builds a bridge from this world to the next." You might say, this book is a bridge for us to take.

You, the reader, must draw your own conclusions. It is your duty and right. May God give you His faith for the task ahead, as He did me.

NO EXTREMES

The polarization in Christianity between animal lovers and animal users is disturbing. At one end of the spectrum, St. Francis of Assisi called animals "brother" and "sister." Christians, who believe as St. Francis did, are the ones who often sacrifice and work for the humane treatment of all animals. I understand that the SPCA (Society for the Prevention of Cruelty to Animals) and other humane societies have roots in Christian revivals of the past.

At the opposite end of the spectrum are the exploiters of animals. Often, in the name of God, they treat all creation as if it were made for man to do with as man pleases. Such persons interpret the Genesis 1:28 "dominion" to mean that humans may freely use animals — without reservation — for sport and experimentation. They believe it is their right to destroy animal habitat with impunity.

I want state up front that I am not an "animal rights" activist. Most extremes make me uneasy. (Only simple Biblical truths are the extremes I strive to adhere to — like loving your enemies, being generous to all, being sober and faithful.) On the other hand, I hold to the belief that good stewardship and kindness to all living things is mandated. Cruelty in any form is a violation of God's law and nature. The Bible tells us how animals are to be treated. Whether or not they have God-given rights is not an issue which this book is meant to address.

The question of animals going to heaven certainly raises ethical and moral dilemmas for the here-and-now. This includes the treatment of animals for work and food, the use of animals for research, the destruction of animal habitats for commercial gain, hunting for sport and the like. While some questions must be addressed, it is not the purpose of this book to join these debates. We address such questions solely for the sake of finding the pieces to our "animals-in-heaven" puzzle.

THE FUN PART

The fun part of writing this book was when I discovered that there are hundreds of people who also want to know the answer to Mom's question. A lot of folks love their dogs, cats, horses, goats, pot-bellied pigs, hamsters, parrots, canaries, ferrets, and dozens of other various types and breeds of critters. They too want to know if those departed pets will be waiting for them in heaven.

YOUR SEARCH

You may have your own personal reason for wanting to know the answer to Mom's question, "Do dogs — and other animals — go to heaven?" Perhaps you've known the attentive love of an animal. Perhaps an animal has been a helper, healer, or rescuer for you or your loved one. You may be upset because someone told you that "this life" is all there is for your pet. You may have a close friend or relative who is grieving over the loss of a pet. You aren't sure what to say to comfort him or her.

On the other hand, your reasons may be none of the above. Instead, you may have a simple childlike curiosity to know the truth, whatever it is.

Whatever your reasons, welcome to these pages. The Lord promises that those willing to do the will of God, shall know if the teaching is truth. [John 7:17] If we abide in His Word, we shall know the truth and the truth will set us free. [John 8:32]

CHAPTER 2

IS IT OKAY TO LOVE ANIMALS?

I cannot but have a reverence for all that is called life. I cannot avoid compassion for everything that is called life. That is the beginning and foundation of morality. ... It is our duty to share and maintain life.

* * *

The ethic of the Reverence for Life is the ethic of Love widened into universality. It is the ethic of Jesus, now recognized as a necessity of thought.

Albert Schweitzer

"Then I don't want to go there!" Trish (not her real name) responded hotly. This teenager had just asked her minister if her beloved horse would be in heaven. His answer was an unequivocal no. "Without my horse, heaven won't be heaven to me," Trish retorted.

I met Trish's parents in a church group. When I mentioned I was writing a book entitled, "Do dogs go to heaven?" I noticed this couple's look of astonishment. Later, cautiously, they approached me to tell me about Trish's experience with her minister, explaining their daughter's vehement reply.

Once they felt safe, these parents freely talked to me. They reminded me of skittish, abused horses themselves! I watched their expressions of anxiety, and heard it reflected in their voices. As we visited, they identified themselves as animal lovers. They spoke in detail of their pets — each one special — then went on to explain that they'd been accused by some church folk of loving animals "too much." The solution to the problem, Trish's parents discovered, was never to speak of their animals while at church. They assured me, however, that they would never stop loving their animals.

They were delightfully surprised when they learned the subject of my book. They had felt alone, outside church doctrine, and therefore they welcomed a kindred spirit. Once they knew I wouldn't condemn them, they opened up to me. They loved God and were truly concerned about their horse-loving daughter. Trish had been crushed by the minister's harsh answer. Her relationship with the Lord had not been the same since. I hope this book comes into the hands of Trish and her parents — and all those like them.

LIFE-CHANGING ANSWERS

Never having met Trish's pastor, I have no idea where he got his theology (although I could guess), nor why he believed it. It caused no small problem for this couple and their daughter Trish. Too bad he didn't remember this passage:

> *Then I saw heaven opened, and behold, a white horse. And Him who sat on him was called Faithful and True, ...*
>
> Rev. 19:11 [NKJ]

From Mom's experience, I knew there were at least six answers ministers gave when asked if animals go to heaven. What a recipe for confusion! When adults in authority give an answer to a young person, it can be a life-changing moment. A minister stands as God's representative, and thus his words, tone, and deeds have a strong impact and can cause a dramatic change in a person's beliefs. For that reason, the Bible says not many should be teachers, for teachers will bear a stricter judgment with God. [James 3:1] Jesus emphatically stated that causing a child to "stumble" isn't a smart thing to do. [Matt. 18:6-7]

IDENTIFYING OBSTACLES TO ANSWERS

Good questions are the key to getting good answers. The

question of animals going to heaven begins with identification of obstacles which stand in the way to receiving good answers. Also, true debate dispels bad premises but does not attack people. God sent His Son to die for people not principles. I am a lawyer skilled in advising people of the law, but not the judge of anyone. We seek to understand the problem, which is the first step to finding the solution.

HARSH REACTIONS — MY OWN EXPERIENCE

Like Trish, and like my mom, I too have experienced harsh reactions to this subject. One reaction was not from a pastor, but a man in a leadership position in a church. This incident occurred when I was well along in writing this book.

I was a first-time visitor at the church. After the service, I was chatting with several people when the subject of my book came up. This leader immediately took issue with me. He seemed compelled to straighten me out. "Animals cannot go to heaven, because they don't have souls or spirits," was his emphatic retort. Frankly, his forcefulness took me aback.

Because I was a guest, and because I did not wish to offend, I tried to answer gently but firmly. Everything I said he disputed vigorously. My replies seemed only to incite further anger and argument. He was on a crusade, bent on correcting me. He didn't know nor seem to care that I'd spent almost twenty years studying and praying about this subject. He seemed more eager to prove me wrong than to hear truth.

I held my tongue. Something inside me wanted to ask him why he didn't love animals — but I refrained. What a stark contrast this was to other conversations I'd had that very day with people eager to know the answers I'd found in the Bible. Thankfully I've met more like the latter than like this church leader!

As the word has spread among my friends and acquaintances regarding this book project, I have received phone calls from Christians grieving over the death of a beloved pet. Many have been devastated by people like Trish's pastor and the church leader described above. Their hope of ever seeing their pet again has been shattered or damaged.

Some who have heard of my project phone me, desperate for comfort from the Bible.

Harsh words heap additional grief and condemnation on animal lovers. Some state in no uncertain terms that the pet lover must give up the belief that animals go to heaven. The pain this inflicts is appalling.

Is it foolish to love and grieve for a departed pet when the bond of love was so sweet and strong when they were alive? How can the love just stop?

I know that having your love of animals brought into question by the teachings and actions of religious leaders and church members can be very intimidating. I was taught to respect authority, especially religious authority. It requires a good degree of confidence and a strong foundation of Scriptural knowledge to overcome such intimidation. I have not always had either, but I refused to stay that way!

OTHER QUESTIONS

Before asking *if* animals go to heaven, we need to address some myths about loving animals and wanting them to go to heaven. Can we love an animal "too much"? Is it okay to want that animal to be in heaven with you?

A lot of folks think not. Others aren't really sure. Others have been frightened into avoiding the question altogether. Let's look at some of the myths, attitudes, and problems which cloud the issues and make it more difficult to find answers.

MYTH #1: "ONLY A CHILD WOULD ASK SUCH A QUESTION"

Ever hear that one? Many people react to my book topic, as if the question were only for children. "It's cute," they might say, "but not a topic for serious Biblical study or scholarship." They see it as trite rather than a serious theological issue. Perhaps they have never known the love of a special dog, cat, or horse.

Even if it were a question only a child would ask (which it is not), the fact is children ask very important questions. Children have an uncanny way of asking profound questions. I like to be around children for that reason. Why are some adults uncomfortable about such questions? Is it because we have no answers?

Sometimes a child exposes the fact that our long-held beliefs are wrong, or at best, inadequate. Sometimes we get "conned" into believing a lie. Hans Christian Anderson's tale about "the emperor's new clothes" is our story, too. Cheating weavers convinced this emperor they had exquisite cloth, and embarrassed everyone who couldn't see it. The emperor commissioned new clothes from this cloth, and paraded through town. A child asked why the emperor had no clothes on. The "suit" didn't exist. Adults may be afraid to expose a lie, but not a child. Why are we afraid?

I'm not sure why Mom's question is treated as one that only children would ask. But that point is not nearly as important as finding the right answers. I believe adults and children deserve to know the truth.

MYTH #2: "THE BIBLE DOES NOT SAY"

This is a common reply to Mom's question among evangelicals and Bible believers. While the reply is often given lightly, almost without thinking, this is a serious statement. The Bible is our authority. If the Bible does *not* say, then Christians have no basis for a belief that there will be animals in heaven.

At first, I too did not think the Bible said much about animals and heaven. In fact, I began my search prepared to accept that where animals were concerned, this life was all there was. Frankly, I have been astonished at how much the Bible *does* say about animals and their roles in God's Kingdom — both in this life and the next. Indeed, the Bible says a lot!

Now there is not one Scripture that simply says, "Yes, Mom, dogs do go to heaven!" Like many Bible doctrines, the answer is not spelled out in one clear statement. But when different Scriptures are lined up and put together, a clear picture or answer emerges.

Whether there are horses in heaven is easy to answer. Elijah and Jesus both travel to and from heaven via horse power. [II

Kings 2:11; Revelations 19:11-14] So there *are* horses in heaven. Trish and her parents will be delighted! (The next question is whether these horses ever lived on earth or if they were heaven-born.) Throughout the scriptures, other animals play both large and small roles in God's plan.

In fact, we find very little in Christian literature about God's plans and purposes for animals — and less about their eternity. English translations, from the King James to the more modern English versions, are largely silent on whether animals have souls or spirits. Man's duty of stewardship over the animals is the issue that is most often addressed.

Most Christian theologians believe that since God is Spirit, a soul or spirit must be present in order to live in God's presence. Heaven is a spiritual place ruled by God who is spirit. Some people reason that since the Bible doesn't clearly say, then animals must *not* have a soul or spirit.

Those theologians who have addressed this question, believe that animals perish when they die. Later we will trace the origins of this idea. Perhaps the concept is rooted in guilt over treatment that animals have received at human hands. If they have no souls or spirits, and if they perish at death, the conclusions is, it doesn't matter how they are treated.

Cruel people often cover their cruelty with the cloak of religion — whether it is treatment of enslaved men, women, children or animals. Animals throughout history have been tortured and killed for sport and food, and have been abused as beasts of burden. The Society for the Prevention of Cruelty to Animals, and other humane societies are relatively new in history — although kind people have always been around.[3] Guilt and fear do strange things to people.

MYTH #3: "LOVING ANIMALS TOO MUCH IS PAGAN IDOLATRY"

Perhaps Bible scholars have not searched the answer due to a fear of violating the Ten Commandments which teach against worshiping other gods and against making idols.[4] [Exodus 20] The Bible makes it abundantly clear that God hates idolatry.

Other Mosaic laws declared that spirit or soul transfers between men and animals is witchcraft, punishable by death. [Exodus 20:3-5; Deuteronomy 5:7-9] Israel got into a "heap of trouble" when they made a golden calf and worshiped it. [Exodus 32] Idols come in all forms, human, animal and imagined. It should be noted that loving a person or an animal is not the same as worshiping it as an idol.

Ancient Egyptians and other nations during Bible times worshiped all kinds of creatures from beetles to cats. Idolatry still plagues this earth, even in the Lord's church. God is just in His love. His hatred of idolatry is very rational when you understand it. That is why devout Christians take pains to avoid non-Christian beliefs — including those regarding animals. Sometimes because we fear sinning, we err by being too rigid.

Knowing the truth is complicated by the fact that the Biblical God has not left Himself without a witness in any nation or people. [Acts 14:17] All religions contain some measure of truth. Otherwise no one would believe them. Sorting out the truth from error is therefore not always easy. In other words, counterfeits can look very much like the real thing. (You have to know the real very well to recognize a good counterfeit.) We must examine what in our Christian theology of animals is true and what is not. That's why we have the Bible.

For example, I know most Native Americans (or Indians) believe or believed that humans and animals are "brothers;" and that one's human spirit can be intertwined or linked with that of a particular animal or animal species. I used to be concerned that this belief was idolatry. I had to lay aside my fear to examine this. It was alien to the Bible teaching I'd received. While there are still elements which make me uncomfortable, I have come to understand that believing an animal is your "brother" is not worshiping the animal. Rather, it is but a statement of respect for another intelligent being with whom we can share a kinship relationship. If my understanding is correct, the Indian belief then is not idolatry but friendship with God's animals.

It is challenging to honestly search Scripture to discover what it said on a subject. To accurately handle or divide the Word of God, as 2 Timothy 2:15 admonishes, we have some work to do.

MYTH #4: "ANIMAL LOVERS ARE IMBALANCED"

We've all heard it. An owner spends several hundred dollars on a sick pet dog, and someone remarks, "Why spend so much? It's just a dumb dog!"

From the facial expression, it's obvious the speaker thinks it's crazy to spend so much money on "a dumb animal." There are some people who regard animals as they would furniture — disposable items with no feelings. Since they believe that animals are to be used and discarded, they view those who love animals as imbalanced.

If you have ever been treated that way, you know. It can mangle your self-image. Many of us animal lovers have learned to stifle our exuberance for pets — especially around religious types. Like Trish's parents, we let our love for animals show only if we feel the listeners are of kindred heart. We don't want to appear out-of-balance or ungodly in this love.

There are theologians and ministers who teach that loving an animal "too much" is wrong. Carried to its logical conclusion, it means: "Do not love animals — exploit them." I've heard sermons which condemn spending money on pets because children are starving somewhere. What a guilt trip! Are we supposed to let animals starve, too? Do such ministers fear that loving animals leads to bestiality (sex with animals) prohibited by Scripture? That's absurd! Anyone who really **loves** their pet is **not** interested in sex with that animal nor the animal with them — no more than a loving parent is interested in incest. What is "loving too much?" Isn't there enough love to go around?

Jesus identified God's Great Commandment as all-encompassing love! [Mark 12:29-31] I'm talking about the God-kind of love. Not a "codependent love," but a rich, caring, giving-and-receiving love which becomes a good relationship between two living beings. Can you love God too much? Can you love your spouse too much? Or your child? Or other people? Did Mother Theresa of Calcutta love too much? Absurd! How can anyone really love an animal "too much?"

Unfortunately, this thinking has caused some people to emotionally withdraw from animals. That deprives us of something wondrous. We are expected to ignore animals who have shown us more love and forgiveness, more loyalty and constancy than most humans. If we allow such religious ideas to influence us, we tend to withdraw our affections from our animal friends. That must confuse and hurt them, just as we would be hurt if a person we cared about refused to commit in a caring relationship. Both parties suffer.

Some of us "rebel" and continue to love our pets "too much." This can produce feelings of guilt. Such thinking puts the animal lover between a rock and a hard place — with no apparent means of escape.

MYTH #5: "ANIMAL LOVERS ARE A LUNATIC FRINGE"

Have you ever known or heard of a person (usually a woman) withdrawing from society and living with dozens, even hundreds, of cats, dogs, or other animals? Usually the home or apartment is in unsanitary squalor with animals everywhere! This type person is sometimes thought to really **love** animals. Animal lovers are often grouped with these types of people, and called "the lunatic fringe."

In truth, people who withdraw from society, living in squalor with lots of animals, are mentally ill. No one who loves animals would cause them to live in squalor. True animal lovers are responsible, caring individuals. They don't lock dozens of animals together in small spaces without adequate hygiene, food or proper exercise. Nor do they purposely avoid healthy human relationships.

If there is a "lunatic fringe" with regard to animals, it is those who practice animal cruelty. Some by neglect or mental illness. Others, such as serial killers and other violent criminals, enjoy the torture of animals, usually from childhood.

These are both kinds of "imbalanced" people who do not or cannot love.

MYTH #6: "ANIMALS ARE NOT IMPORTANT IN GOD'S PLAN"

This myth is based on several assumptions: (1) Man is the only living thing created in God's image, so next to God, we have supreme importance; and (2) Animals cease to exist at their death, and are therefore "temporal" not "eternal." [2 Cor. 4:18] Temporal things have no eternal value. Another way of putting it, things with short "lives" have little value. To illustrate the difference, consider that a piece of paper is worth pennies, while gold is valuable. One is "temporal" and easily destroyed; the gold has lasting value. If animals perish with this life, then what value have they? Even if it's only implied, the message is: "Animals are not important in the great scheme of things." It is like an old fable:

> *A dog, that had been sold by his master, broke his chain, and returned to the house where he had been born. Judge his surprise, when, as a reward for his zeal, he was soundly beaten, and taken back to his new residence. An old cat of his acquaintance, observing his extreme surprise, said to him; "Poor fool! did you imagine that we were prized for our own sakes?"*[5]

The minister who told Trish that horses would not be in heaven, conveyed this message to the teenager. The person who is disgusted because someone else spent hundreds of dollars on a veterinary bill for a sick pet, believes this.

I know many who have closed their hearts to loving an animal because it hurts too much when they die. They never want another pet. To pour your heart into a temporal thing seems foolish. It also hurts when you lose that animal to death.

God created and preserves even the smallest sparrow. [Matt. 10:29] How can a person be certain he or she knows the whole plan of God? How can anyone say that animals are unimportant to our Creator God? Animals **are** important. I'm not sure any of us realize how important.

MYTH #7: "YOU ARE ANTHROPOMORPHIZING"

"Anthropomorphism" is a fancy word which simply means ascribing human characteristics, motivation, or behavior to inanimate objects, animals, or natural happenings. We see this in cartoons, in children's storybooks, and in animated movies. Animals and inanimate objects are portrayed as acting like humans — trees dance, bears hold conversations, dogs drive cars, teacups sing.

The academic world has long believed that animals lack such human abilities as thought, reason, motive, and emotion — although that is changing. To be accused of anthropomorphizing is an insult. You are (or were) not a "true intellectual" if you believe that animals think, communicate, or have moral values. Some Christian theologians and clergy also use the term as an insult.

Nonetheless, animal lovers, including the best trainers, have long observed that animals display distinct personalities. "Personality" includes the ability make choices, to reason, and to feel emotion. Animals have been known to show courage and cowardice, unselfishness and jealousy, love and cruelty, deceit and loyalty.

There is nothing quite like the disdain of a proud academic or theologian. Their confidence in their being right usually overwhelms all but the most confident. I have enough higher education to have experienced those types. (Thank God, all academic and theologians are not like that!) But attitudes about animals are changing. Time magazine, in 1993, stated anthropomorphism is no longer a sin. Now it's okay to say animals think and hope, and are puzzled; that animals have expectations, are disappointed; and that some make their own little plans in a time scheme of their own.

The term anthropomorphize makes man the center— which is the first mistake. As a disciple of Jesus Christ, I believe attributes of personality, motivation, and other characteristics, originate with God Who has all such qualities in perfect goodness. Therefore, I have no trouble with "theo-morphizing" the behavior of animals which God made. (When we study a person's art, we glimpse the artist.) Animals are God's art, masterpieces each one.

Spend time around animals. Observe their behavior with an open mind. You will see character traits, personality traits, language, emotions, the ability to make moral choices — all quite like God, and like man who is made in God's image. Accusing people of anthropomorphizing comes from intellectual pride, not wisdom.

MOM'S QUESTION IS IGNORED

Another obstacle is silence. The question is simply brushed off or ignored. The second preacher Mom asked did that. Only a few preachers ever touch the subject of animals in heaven, let alone their role on earth. Have you ever heard a sermon devoted to the place of animals in God's kingdom? God loves all of His creatures. So why is a huge part of this world is simply ignored in the pulpit?

The silence is deafening.

I'm not talking about Biblical animal illustrations to teach us about ourselves. Jonah and the Whale, Daniel in the lions' den, and Balaam and his donkey, as well as the colt Jesus rode on as he entered Jerusalem, are used in lessons for children or to illustrate adult sermons. But the animals themselves are not important. The lessons and sermons are not about the animals themselves.

I'd like to know what God did to have that whale where Jonah was tossed in the sea. Was this a special whale who volunteered or what? And what did the whale think about swallowing a man and keeping him alive inside its belly[6] until the prophet repented? A rebellious man of god had to be troublesome cargo. Talk about indigestion! How did the whale do it? What praise did the Lord have for that "great fish," do you think?

Other than Saint Francis of Assisi (who is thought of as a bit strange because he referred to the animals as his "brothers" and "sisters"), no one else is lifted up by Christian leaders as a lover and advocate of animals.

To be ignored is to be treated as valueless. It's been my experience that the place of animals in God's kingdom has been ignored. Except when children and old women ask about animals going to heaven, the question has been given little or no thought. Only in recent years has that been changing. Many are uncomfortable with the question, which is a message in itself.

GIVEN A GUILT TRIP

Have you ever felt guilty just because you enjoyed something? Maybe you didn't know why you felt guilty — you just did. While any of the things listed here can produce guilt, sometimes a feeling of condemnation creeps in like a fog from nowhere. If there is no truth behind the fog, it may be the condemnation which is not from God. [Romans 8:1, 31-35]

Most of us have experienced feelings of being unworthy, unloved, or falling short. I've struggled with depression a few times. Life is rough sometimes. I suspect all of us have those days, even years. It's a cruel world sometimes. Yet when humans ignore or disdain us, a dog — or cat or horse or other animal — will love us like we're the best! How do we handle that? Guilt? Or acceptance?

Christians have often been taught — directly or indirectly — that every pleasure and joy we experience in this world is "worldly" and "sinful." If you have believe that, then the *joie de vivre*, i.e., the joy of living, which all healthy animals exhibit, probably makes you uncomfortable.[7] Every animal I know enjoys being alive. Most animals are masters at living in the moment to the fullest. If this life is all there is for them, why are they so happy? Mine always try to get me to join in the joy. Enjoying the animals may make you feel guilty because it's so much fun.

Animals can teach us how to enjoy every moment. My Gretchen made every walk in the park an exuberant adventure. Daily that German Shepherd ran the same circuit of trees chasing squirrels, but always with great pleasure. My cats play with the same toys, like they'd never played that game before, and each insect is a new discovery. My horses clowned and teased. Even training is something an animal must enjoy or they are difficult to work.

I know Christians who would never feel right about enjoying themselves as much as my animals do. That's "dead religion" to me, but I sympathize with the guilt trip it produces.

I'm sure I have not covered all the reasons people feel guilty about loving animals. We humans are very creative in how we condemn ourselves. It doesn't help to overcome guilt that we tend to follow Adam's example of rationalizing our behavior. We make excuses and blame others instead of facing the truth in a responsible manner. We are too susceptible to the lies of the devil about God, His nature, and His plans. Please note that I said "we" — for I've done these things as well.

We may feel we aren't worthy of the unconditional love our pets shower on us — and it may be true. (If we feel more love from our dog than Christians, our family, friends, or minister or priest, that unworthy feeling can take hold of us.) Dogs treat us like gods, even if we abuse them. Maybe the name "dog" — which in English is "god" spelled backwards — is a message. Dogs do love us "too well." My animals are not guilty about loving me, why should I hold back from returning their love?

It is so easy to give and receive love from these little friends. Is it Godly to love a pet more than people? Or is it sin? Doesn't the Bible command us to love God and man? It doesn't tell us to love animals, does it? Is loving an animal wrong?

GATHERING PIECES TO A PICTURE PUZZLE

Finding answers to Mom's question has taken me through many steps. In exploring what the Bible says, we will address many questions. First, we must address the question: do animals have souls and spirits — believed to be a prerequisite to eternal life or heaven?

We'll look at the roles animals play in God's kingdom throughout history and now. We'll finally line up the evidence of animals in eternity and address the question of whether our particular animals will be in heaven.

Like pieces to a giant puzzle, there are verses of Scripture which, when laid together, present quite a picture.

I look to the Bible for answers in much the same way that I practice law. When a client first presents a problem, I don't know what evidence will turn up. First, evidence must be gathered from all sides. Then we prepare the case and estimate what chance the client has of winning in court.

Gathering evidence is like finding pieces to a puzzle. Until you have the pieces, you don't know how the picture will look. If you cannot find certain key pieces, then you have no case. If key pieces favor the other side, you will lose. Only if you find key admissible evidence to prove your client's version of the facts, do you have a chance at winning the case.

The Bible passages about animals are much like pieces of evidence or pieces of a puzzle. Separately, the pieces hold little or no importance. Only when I placed them in order did an image appear. Why others have not done the same, I have no idea. My legal training helps, but that is not critical to good Bible study. Primarily it involves work, albeit a work of faith. All I know is that Mom's question has an answer.

CHAPTER 3

DOGS AND CATS IN THE BIBLE

In the beginning God created the heavens and the earth, the animals and man. Daily God walked with man in intimate fellowship. When God got very busy, man became downcast. When God asked why, the man said he missed spending all his time with God and was lonely. After pondering this, God made a companion for man. It wagged its tail. Man was happy, but asked God what to name it. God said, "This animal is a reflection, a mirror image, of my love for you; so it will be called "dog." The dog and man became great friends. After a while the man changed under the worshipful love of the dog. The angels came to God and said, "Man has lost his humility due to this dog's worship of him. You must do something." God thought, and then He made another animal. It became another companion of man and taught him humility. Man was happy, the angels were pleased, God was satisfied, the dog wagged his tail, and the cat didn't give a d__. [8]

Dogs and cats have long been the most popular domestic pets. Some of us love dogs; some of us cats, and some of us both. I prefer a home with both species myself. It is safe to say God did not inspire those who wrote the Holy Scriptures to say much about dogs or cats.

Perhaps a lesson can be drawn from two trees in the Garden of Eden, the tree of life and the forbidden tree of the knowledge of good and evil. [Genesis 2 & 3] While the forbidden tree receives all the attention, the tree of life is hardly mentioned. We don't speak of being "tempted to do good." In this upside-down world, the good often goes unheralded, while the bad makes up the daily news. Likewise, good dogs and cats are unheralded in God's Word. For those who love dogs and/or cats, it may be disturbing.

After all, it is like pointing out the obvious. The value of a good dog is apparent to all who have experienced a dog's loyalty, affection and intelligence. A cat's entertaining cleverness and calming effects aren't mentioned either. If you consider the purpose of the Bible, then it makes sense. The good Lord did not have to instruct humans in the Bible about the dog's worth or the cat's value. Their value is apparent to those who spend time with them.

While I wanted to cover what the Bible does say about cats and dogs in depth, there is only one Bible passage that must be addressed to answer Mom's question. That is the one our country preacher quoted from the Book of Revelation. Of course as a prelude to that verse, I will cover more. (The lawyer in me must build a case.)

DOGS IN THE BIBLE

To err is human, To forgive, canine.[9]

The one absolutely unselfish friend that man can have in this selfish world, the one that never deserts him, the one that never proves ungrateful or treacherous, is his dog. When all other friends desert, he remains.[10]

Robert Louis Stevenson was remonstrating with a man in the street ill-treating a dog.

"What business is it of yours?" the man said. "He ain't your dog."

"No, but he is God's dog," said Stevenson, "and I'm here to protect him."[11]

The more I see the representatives of the people, the more I admire my dogs.[12]

There are about forty references to dogs in the Bible, most of which do not treat dogs with favor. (Of course, there are many wicked *people* mentioned in the Bible as well.) Two different kinds of dogs are mentioned: feral or half-wild dogs that were ownerless and scavengers; and working dogs who helped man herd and protect their livestock. (These may also have been hunting dogs.)

Biblical references support a long relationship between man and dog. In the Old Testament we learn that Job kept herd dogs. [Job 30:1] In the New Testament it says that small dogs — which must have been pets — ate under the tables. [Mark 7:24-30] Archeology and history provide references to dogs as house pets in the Near East. Most historians agree that dogs were among the first domesticated animals. Personally, I vote that dogs became man's friend in the Garden of Eden.

To those who have taken time to be kind to them, dogs have been wonderful companions and heroes. While writing this book, I happened to catch a TV program called, "Miracles." The show related how a Rottweiler seemed to know her fireman master was having a heart attack, drew him into the house and when the man collapsed, got the portable phone and put it by his hand, so he could call 911. It is one of many remarkable stories I have heard and read about animals.[13] Dogs outnumber the other animals in acts of heroism toward humans.

Who knows but what man's best friend may have tried to draw Adam away from the serpent and prevent him from eating the forbidden fruit! It wouldn't be the last time a dog tried to warn its master or mistress of danger!

O, DESPISED DOG!

Dogs, as we all know, have a dark side. As a lawyer, I am aware of the legal issues dogs can bring about. These include aggressive attacks, noisy barking, and diseases such as rabies, are all very real hazards. Dogs often destroy property or injure other pets. Barking dogs can be a real and a legal nuisance.

Homeowners' insurance generally covers damage or injury by pets, which is a reason people buy the coverage. And last but not least, for city dwellers, there is the problem of dog waste.

Scriptures about dogs indicate the ancients had a low esteem for the animal. For example, "Better is a live dog, than a dead lion" (which means it's better to be alive and despised than dead and respected) [Ecclesiastes 9:4]. "Like a dog that returns to its vomit, is a fool who repeats his folly" [Proverbs 28:11]; "Like one who takes a dog by the ears is he who passes by and meddles with strife not belonging to him." [Proverbs 28:17]

This attitude makes sense when we consider conditions existing when the Bible was written. The ancient world was an unsafe place. Packs of half-wild, half-famished dogs often roamed towns and villages[14] [1 Kings. 14:11; 16:4; 2 Kings 9:10] People around the world still despise feral dogs. Wild dogs and half-wild dogs can maim and kill, and also carry communicable diseases.

Ironically, some of these qualities make dogs useful. Then, as now, dogs were useful around the towns and villages as garbage disposals and as guard dogs against strangers, robbers, and wild beasts. Consider this Bible passage:[15]

At evening they return,
They growl like a dog,
And go all around the city. Ps. 59:6 [NASV]

Packs of dogs are extremely dangerous. Much of the world today is the same for dogs and humans as it was in Bible times. The fear of dogs is understandable. Some dogs were vicious; some had rabies or other diseases. As a child, I saw rabid dogs quarantined by my father. Rabies strikes a healthy fear in the heart of anyone who has seen the ravages of that terrible fatal disease.

The fearful, however, never know the love and loyalty which dogs, when healthy and well cared for, are capable of giving. The fall of man, which brought the curse of sin on the whole world, separated man from animals.

The Lord God, in love, warns us about many dangers which occur in this fallen world. It does not mean that the animals, which are subject to the effects of man's sin, are evil. We can enjoy the love of dogs, while acting wisely to protect ourselves from the risk of poorly trained, mean, and diseased animals. Thank God for modern medicine and the wisdom to live better than our ancestors ever dreamed possible. God's kingdom blessings are being tasted here and now.

WHAT "DOGS" ARE OUTSIDE THE GATES OF HEAVEN?

Let's look at the Bible verse that Mom's Kentucky preacher referred to when he stated that "Dogs are outside the gate, so there are will be horses, but no dogs, in heaven." It reads thus:

> *Blessed are those who wash their robes, that they may have the right to the tree of life, and may enter by the gates into the city. Outside are the* ***dogs*** *and the sorcerers and the immoral persons and the murderers and the idolaters, and everyone who loves and practices lying.*
>
> Revelation 22:14-15 [NASV]

When we study Scripture, it's important to study it in the context of where it is found. Otherwise we may misinterpret the meaning. It's also important to understand that Scripture contains many metaphors and similes.

Another key is to allow Scripture to define Scripture. In this technique, we compare as many verses as possible using the same term to shed light on how the Spirit and the Lord inspired its meaning. Applying these rules of interpretation to this Scripture in Revelation we can clarify the passage.

First of all, if dogs got inside the gate they would not have "robes" to wash! Dog paws just were not designed for buttons or zippers! If they had clothes they'd need also to operate a washing machine. (I want that dog!)

Secondly, being a "canine" is not a sin in the same sense as the other things listed. "Sorcerers," "immoral persons," "murderers," "idolaters," and "liars" describe humans. While an animal might deceive or commit murder, the other things cannot apply. I've never seen a dog telling a fortune, casting a spell, or worshipping an idol. A literal "dog" does not fit in this context.

From this we must assume that the Scripture is referring to

people not animals. The terms in Revelation 22:14-15 describe human behavior. If the term "dogs" is taken literally, the passage makes no sense.

In the next verse, the Lord speaks of Himself as "the bright and morning star." That certainly appears to be a metaphor. This section of Scripture may have other metaphors. The whole book of Revelation appears to be full of metaphors! Sorting them out can be a challenge.

Are there other Scriptures in which the word "dog" is used metaphorically to describe people? Yes, there are:

> *Beware of **dogs**, beware of evil workers, beware of the false circumcision.*
>
> Philippians 3:2 [NASV]

> *For **dogs** have surrounded me; a band of evil doers has encompassed me; They pierced my hands and feet . . . Deliver my soul from the sword, my only life from the **paw of the dog**.*
>
> Psalm 22:16 & 20 [NASV]

> *And the Philistine [the giant Goliath] said to David, "Am I a **dog**, that you come to me with sticks?" And the Philistine cursed David by his gods.*
>
> 1 Samuel 17:43 [NASV]

When the country preacher answered Mom's question by referring to this passage in Revelation, he evidently was not aware that the word "dog" in Scripture is used as a slang term. "You dog," is an age-old insult. (It may be so the world over.) It is not to be taken literally.

In the Bible, "dog" is sometimes a slang term of deepest scorn. The label described three kinds of people: (1) people who were cruel, (2) despised, or (3) homosexual[16] The behavior of dogs accounts for this: First, dogs may attack without provocation or take down animals in a hunt in a manner which looks cruel. Secondly, dogs are unclean animals, garbage-loving, disease carrying, animals. They can appear groveling and therefore too easily abused — behavior despised in men. Thirdly, dogs "mount" each other indiscriminately, males on males, and females on females, in the appearance of aberrant sexual behavior. So the slang term, calling humans "dogs" has its origin in common doggy behavior.

Fierce and cruel men are sometimes called *dogs*.[17] Examples of human "dogs" being cruel include Psalm 22 which describes men surrounding the psalmist like a pack of wild dogs, attacking the psalmist or the person he describes prophetically. Psalm 22 is believed by Christians to describe Jesus' death at the hands of Jewish leaders and Romans. [Ps. 22:16 & 20] The term "dogs" in Psalm 22:16, is obviously a metaphor for wicked people.

THE TEST OF GOD'S LOVE

Lastly, it is best to measure one's interpretation of Scripture against what we know of the character of God. If the interpretation agrees with His holiness, His purity, His nature as love, wisdom, truth, and righteousness, then it is likely correct. If it violates any part of God's nature, then it is questionable or may be in error. Mom taught me that, "God is love, and if it isn't love, it isn't God."

The term "dog" in Revelation 22 must refer to a type of human behavior which is being condemned. Our loving God would not condemn an entire species of animal unless all members were rotten to the core! There are too many good dogs for that conclusion to be correct.

Without this understanding, one can make the mistake our Kentucky preacher made in interpreting Revelation 22:15. That mistake produces the incongruous conclusion that "there are horses in heaven but no dogs." When we use Scripture to interpret Scripture — a practice that requires some work — the results are far more accurate. Don't you think this is a piece of the puzzle — the answer to Mom's question? If there are horses in heaven, why not dogs? Why not a lot of animals? We will talk more on this issue later on.

Back to the subject of dogs, Mom would have heartily

agreed with George Vest's description, and would have argued that dog's goodness alone might be its ticket to heaven:

> *The one absolute, unselfish friend that a man can have in this selfish world — the one that never deserts him, the one that never proves ungrateful or treacherous — is his dog.*
>
> *Gentlemen of the jury, a man's dog stands by him in prosperity and in poverty, in health and in sickness. He will sleep on the cold ground, ... if only he can be near his master's side. He will kiss the hand that has no food to offer, he will lick the wounds and sores that come in encounter with the roughness of the world. He guards the sleep of his pauper master as if he were a prince. When all other friends desert, he remains. When riches take wings and reputation falls to pieces he is as constant in his love as the sun in its journey through the heavens. ... And when the last scene of all comes, and death takes the master in its embrace, and his body is laid away in the cold ground, no matter if all other friends pursue their way, there by his grave side will the noble dog be found, his head between his paws, his eyes sad but open in alert watchfulness, faithful and true even to death.*
>
> Hon. George G. Vest[18]

Many of us totally agree with Mr. Vest. My dogs have been some of my most faithful friends.

WHAT ABOUT CATS?

When God made the world, He chose give each animal whatever it wanted. All the animals formed a line before His throne. The cat went quietly to the end. To the elephant and the bear God gave strength; to the rabbit and the deer, swiftness; to the owl, the ability to see at night; to the birds and the butterflies, great beauty; to the fox, cunning; to the monkey and chimpanzee, intelligence; to the dog, loyalty; to the lion, courage; to the otter, playfulness. These were things which the animals begged of God. At last He came to the end of the line, and there sat the little cat, waiting patiently. "What will you have?" God asked the cat.

The cat shrugged modestly, "Oh, whatever scraps you have left over. I don't mind."

"But, I'm God. I have everything left over."

"Then I'll have a little of everything, please."

And God gave a great shout of laughter at the cleverness of this small animal. He then gave the cat everything she asked for, adding grace and elegance and, only for her, a gentle purr that would always attract humans and assure her a warm and comfortable home.

But He took away her false modesty[19]

Cats make me laugh. Mine are such monkey-like clowns! At this writing, my house is the playground of three Siamese. I love all animals, but there have been special friends among my cats. Except for lions, the Bible makes no mention of cats. I found myself at a loss when I searched the Bible for references to cats. Lions are mentioned with some frequency in the Bible. I counted over 150 references.

All of God's creatures are fascinating, but cats retain a position of special magnetism. People tend to be polarized about them, loving or hating them. Few creatures beat a cat for graceful movement and a sense of elegant mystery. Someone said that God created the cat and keeps to Himself the reason for it.

Perhaps the reason is that God likens Himself to the lion. The Bible says that the Lord God acts like a lion at times of judgment. [Hosea 5:14] His Cherubim, which are in His presence constantly and represent the Almighty, have four faces. One is the face of a lion. [Ezekiel 1:10; 10:14; Rev. 4:7] One of the descriptions of Jesus of Nazareth, the Messiah, is that He is the "Lion of tribe of Judah." [Rev. 5:5] Ponder what Jesus Christ as "the Lion of the tribe of Judah" means. If we are imitators of Christ, we must consider the nature of the cat, particularly the big cat — the lion.

The Lord God's people also are likened to lions. Judah, one of the strongest tribes in the history of the Hebrew people, and the tribe of Dan also were called "a lion's whelp." [Gen. 49:9 & Deut. 33:22] The princes or rulers of Israel were described metaphorically as lions who learned to tear their prey, and devour men. [Ezek. 19:1-9] The description is not always good, but sometimes describes a wild rebellious people. [Jeremiah 2:30]

ATTRIBUTES OF CATS

All I know is that cats are marvelous creatures, although often frustrating to those who don't know them well. Cats have proven to be intelligent[20] and heroic[21] animals. Some animal behaviorists put cats just below chimpanzees in problem solving abilities and memory capacity. In my observation they get bored, just like humans, which means trouble.

In the opinion of many experts, all cats, both large and small, have much in common. Apparently the main difference between the cat families is one of scale, i.e., size. Perhaps in studying lions in Scripture, we can include all cats. Like dogs, the big cats get good press as well as bad in Scripture.

Those of us who attended Sunday School as children heard the stories of Samson and Daniel. Samson killed a lion with his bare hands because the spirit of the Lord came upon him. [Judges 14:5-6] Daniel was thrown in a den of lions and lived, while his accusers were eaten. [Daniel 6:22] Bible accounts about lions have lessons and insights into God's purposes for cats.

MIRACULOUS BEHAVIOR

In 1 Kings 13, we find the story of a disobedient and deceived prophet who was killed by a lion. The Hebrew people were, at the time, divided into two kingdoms. Israel had ten tribes on the north; Judah and Benjamin lay to the south. Israel had turned to idol worship in a big way. (Although Judah had its idols, too.) The Lord sent a man from Judah to Bethel, Israel, to pronounce judgment on the idolatry and sin.

This unnamed prophet had strict instructions to give the prophesy, and return directly to Judah without eating or drinking in Israel. His mission was high drama. The prophet confronted King Jeroboam and Israel alone. After he issued God's warning, the King was angry. When he stretched out his hand to harm the prophet, the Lord withered his hand and split the altar in two! Humbled, the King asked the prophet to pray for him. Also the king invited the prophet to eat, but the man refused. So far, so good.

On the way out of Israel, an old prophet went after the man, entreating him to eat and drink. When the man refused, the old prophet lied to him. He told the man that an angel told him to bring the man back and feed him. The young prophet turned aside, ate and drank with the old prophet. The Lord spoke through the old prophet, that the man of Judah would "not come to the grave of his fathers." Probably terrified, the man left and headed home. (I bet he took the back roads.)

> *So when he had gone, a lion met him on the road and killed him. And his corpse was thrown on the road, and the donkey stood by it; the lion also was stood by the corpse.*
>
> *And there, men passed by and saw the corpse thrown on the road, and the lion standing by the corpse. Then they went and told it in the city where the old prophet dwelt. So when the prophet ... heard it, he said, "It is the man of God who was disobedient to the word of the Lord. Therefore the Lord has delivered him to the lion, which has torn him and killed him, according to the word of the Lord which He spoke to him." ...* ***Then he went and found his corpse ... and the donkey and the lion standing by the corpse. The lion had not eaten the corpse nor torn the donkey.***
>
> *And the prophet took up the corpse of the man of God, laid it on the donkey, and brought it back... Then he laid the corpse in his own tomb.*
>
> 1 Kings 13:24-30a [NASV]

Look at the behavior of the lion and the donkey. They stood by the dead prophet, next to each other! The lion did not harm the donkey! The donkey did not run away! That's a miracle! That is unnatural. These animals kept that position for a long time. It must have taken hours until the body was discovered. The old prophet was notified and he came and took the corpse. This is quite a series of miracles.

I have never heard of any person walking up to a lion and taking its kill away from it. This old prophet had the Spirit of God operating in him, even though he was a deceitful old cuss. He knew the lion and the donkey were obeying the Almighty. I dare say, he knew something about animals and about God. God intended for the man from Judah to have a proper burial, since he had obeyed in confronting the King and Israel.

DOMESTIC CATS

Domestic cats are not mentioned in the canonical Scriptures, but are found in the non-canonical Apocrypha. For instance in Baruch, the writer speaks of Jeremiah's prophetic teaching that the Israelites will endure slavery or captivity in Babylon; and that these people of God will encounter sin and idolatry there. While the heathen and foreigners fear such gods, the Lord's people should not fear idols. Reasons are given, like the fact that the idolatrous priests must lock the temple doors from thieves; they light lamps to see, but the images of their sightless gods are black with smoke.

> *Bats, swallows, and birds light on their bodies and heads; and so do **cats**. From this you will know that they are not gods; so do not fear them.* Baruch 6:22-23

Animals seem to know what is God and what is from the devil.

The domestic cat was certainly known in the Holy Land. Cats were domesticated at least 4,000 years ago.[22] In rabbinic literature, there are a few references to the cat. The cat apparently was not bred to any great extent. Other animals were apparently preferred for catching mice and snakes.

The rabbis did permit the breeding of cats in Israel, as well as other animals which rid the house of rodents and snakes. Mosaics with figures of cats have been uncovered at Nirim in the Negev. This is evidence of cats being bred in Israel in Byzantine times. In Babylonia, the cat was highly regarded as a remedy to rid a house of poisonous snakes. It was considered dangerous to enter a house after dark where there was no cat.

Rabbis praised the cat for its extreme cleanliness: "If the

Law (Torah) had not been given, we could have learned modesty from the cat," one said. Even after the time of Christ, rabbis or Jewish leaders have recommended that cats, or some other domestic pet, be kept in the home to teach children to fulfill the duty or *mitzvah* of feeding animals before partaking of food oneself. Perhaps it was to teach modesty also? (I wonder if they believed dogs teach us, by example, humbleness and forgiveness?)

CAT LEGENDS

There are legends or myths about cats from Bible times. Several about the Noah's ark and the cats are amusing. An Arab legend has it that the mice on the Ark so multiplied that life was rendered unbearable; so Noah passed his hand three times over the lioness' head and she obligingly sneezed the cat. Another story has it that the monkey and lioness forgot their vows of fidelity and the cat was the result — together the spirit of such coquetry[23]

CAT HEROES

Like their lion cousins, the small domestic cat can be fierce and aggressive in the face of large or small enemies. Even in this day, domestic cats have been known to deal with snakes as well as rodents. My friend Jana was picking up a sack of grain in her barn, when her cat leaped between her and the sack. Under the sack was a copperhead, a very poisonous snake. That cat saved Jana's life.

In their book on *The Mysteries of Animal Intelligence, supra*, the Steigers describe a cat in California which prevented a rattlesnake from entering the nursery while the baby was in the room. House cats have also attacked would-be rapists and robbers[24] Like those lions, some cats serve the Lord by serving us. They do good, while executing judgment on the disobedient.

My Siamese, Kitty, however, had the snake and mouse thing backwards. Kitty was my faithful friend of 17 years. I was still in law school when Doc died, and I had left Kitty with Mom a few months at her hillside home in California. Boy, did Kitty prove to be some companion for Mom. Mom wrote me that Kitty was bringing live mice and dropping these gifts at Mom's feet. Kitty would go hunting out through the "doggie door." One night Mom went to bed before Kitty came back in the house. A quote from Mom's letter describes what happened next:

> *About 12:30 a.m., I awoke with Kitty on my chest releasing a live mouse! From there on, there can be no clear cut story. I leaped from the bed, throwing the covers over the cat and mouse. I spent the next hour looking for the mouse, mad at Kitty. She went about flicking her tail, mad that I'd rejected her mouse!*

Kitty then switched to live lizards and snakes. Fortunately Kitty never dropped them in Mom's bed. Mom was concerned that Kitty would "gift" guests with these live treats, however. Kitty never did – but maybe it was the closed doors.

As a lawyer, I was delighted to find that my profession has a patron saint, who loved cats:

> *In passing it is interesting to observe that St. Ives, the patron saint of lawyers, is represented as accompanied by a cat. ...holy men as well as devils found the cat the most attractive of animals. The profound wisdom, the concealed claws, the stealthy approach, and the final spring, all seem to typify the superior attorney. We should not be astonished, therefore, that Cardinal Wolsey placed his cat by his side while acting in his judicial capacity as Lord Chancellor.*[25]

In closing this part about cats, it seems fitting to quote a Christian pastor. More than one clergy person has written on cats, and other pets. In T*he Tiger in the House,* Carl Van Vechten explores the history, manners, and habits of the cat, including folklore or religious references, music, painting, law, poetry and fiction. Dr. Van Vechten writes:

> *The Orientals are more astute about cats than we are. They ascribe to them a language, a knowledge of the future, and extreme sensitiveness which allows them to perceive objects and beings invisible to man. ...It may be said here that an occidental clergyman has written a book*

to prove that animals have souls and will share our future existence. A heaven without cats would, of course, be deserted for a hell with them[26]

We understand. If God had not peopled the earth with our animal friends, we would not know how poor life would be without them.

Death has taught most of us how barren life is without the love of a dog, or cat, or other pet. The fact is that a heaven without our dogs, cats, parrots, horses, and other loved animals would not be heaven for most of us. The wonderful thing is that the God who is love, has a plan, a heavenly plan, for all His creation.

CHAPTER 4

DO ANIMALS HAVE SOULS AND SPIRITS?

> ***Soul.*** *1. The animating and vital principle in man credited with the faculties of thought, action, and emotion and conceived as forming an immaterial entity distinguished from but temporally coexistent with his body. 2. Theology. The spiritual nature of man considered in relation to God, regarded as immortal, separable from the body at death, and susceptible to happiness or misery in a future state. 3. The disembodied spirit of a dead human being; a ghost; shade. . . . 6. A central or integral part of something; vital core. ... 9. The emotional nature in man as distinguished from his mind or intellect.*
>
> ***Spirit.*** *1. That which is traditionally believed to be the vital principle or animating force within living beings. 2. Capital S. The Holy Ghost. ... 4. Any supernatural being, such as a ghost. 5. a. That which constitutes one's unseen, intangible being. b. The essential and activating principle of a person; the being. ...* [27]

Like many of you, I have watched a beloved pet die. I've held the still-warm corpse when the life-force left and breathing ceased. Their death appeared to be no different from that of humans. When death took my friends and relatives, their corpses looked, felt, and smelled the same. Death looked and felt no different whether it was man or beast. Suddenly they were gone. Their body was an empty shell. What left? Was it the animal's "spirit" or "soul?" Does the Bible say?

Tulsa, Oklahoma, where I currently live, has earned the nickname, "Buckle of the Bible Belt." We have a number of mega-churches, a Christian university, seminaries and Bible schools. This provides me with ample opportunity to observe the reactions to Mom's question from a variety of Christians of diverse backgrounds, both laity and clergy. Over the years it has taken to write this book, I've witnessed a number of reactions.

"Dogs are not rational beings, so they cannot have souls," has been a common response to Mom's question from a number of Bible-believing Christians. Sometimes the speaker inserts "spirit" instead of "soul."

For centuries, the prevailing Christian theology has denied that animals have soul or spirit. Roman Catholics and others hold the doctrine that animals do not have souls. Even today, well-known leaders in the Evangelical, Charismatic-Word/Faith and Pentecostal groups teach that animals do not have spirits. It appears that a majority of Christian leaders believe animals do not go to heaven. It would be interesting to know what they imagine heaven is like. Picturing a cat and mouse playing at the feet of God is very upsetting to some folks — even if only in spirit form!

Why is having a soul or spirit important to animals' going to heaven, you might ask? "Souls" and "spirits" are the stuff of eternity — the metaphysical "stuff" it takes to live with God in heaven. At death the mortal body returns to dust — the elements from which it came. "For you are dust and to dust you shall return." [Genesis 3:19] If you and I are nothing more than flesh and bone, then there is no afterlife. The same is true of animals. "You gotta have soul!"

If an animal has a mortal body only, then when it dies it is gone forever. If the animal lacks soul or spirit, there can be no heaven (or hell) for that animal. However, if animals have a soul and spirit then, theologically, a hereafter for animals becomes a real issue.

Christians are often double-minded about animals.

Strangely, some who believe animals don't have souls or spirits, still believe their pets will be in heaven. This is the same reason others give for animals not making it past this life. Isn't that confusing? We say that animals have no soul or spirit, and yet we recognize their ability to make choices, to show emotion, to problem-solve, all of which are attributes of intelligence and personality. (I, too, tended to be double-minded as well before this study.) We do this without realizing how odd and illogical it is.

If we believe an animal has no life beyond this brief span on earth, then we will tend to hold back from loving any animal. Such behavior in turn confuses the animals.

Certainly, animals don't hold back love as humans do.

POLARIZED VIEWPOINTS

People are polarized in their attitudes toward animals. On the one extreme are those who treat animals as unfeeling machines, like Pavlov's dog. B. F. Skinner, an atheistic animal behaviorist, carried Pavlov's thinking to its logical conclusion.[28] On the other extreme, are those convinced that animals do have souls and spirits. The best animal trainers tend to fall in the latter class. Trainers know that animals communicate and reason, and that animals make moral choices. The gulf is obviously very wide between the two camps.

Where did these ideas come from? Does the Bible vindicate one side or the other?

We need never be afraid to ask God to show us His truth and give understanding. [James 1:5] If we don't ask, we'll never know God's truth. [Mat. 15:2-6; Mark 7:8-13] We need never be afraid to question our "leaders in the faith." Jesus did it as a twelve-year-old boy in the temple. [Luke 2:42 & 46] Checking out a teaching to see if it agrees with God's truth, does not dishonor a good teacher. The answers found in my study do contradict long-held beliefs and that can be disturbing. If we want to really know who God is, as well as who we are and why we were created, we must ask about our companions and fellow inhabitants of this creation.

I suggest, if you haven't already done so, that you pray for God's grace to know and understand the truth. It requires an open heart and mind — not easy commodities to come by. This chapter particularly will challenge some long-held beliefs. It challenged some of mine. While I do not compare myself with those who penned the Holy Bible, God still inspires people to write and speak His truth. Otherwise, I would not be presenting these answers to Mom's question.

A LOOK AT HISTORY

> *In philosophy past and present, the prevailing attitude has been that any questions having to do with nonhuman animals are of decidedly secondary importance . . . Animals may be studied scientifically as part of the natural world, but their philosophical importance lies in what they lack. They are not just nonhuman, but less than human.*[29]

The theories that animals lack souls and spirit have their roots in early church history. Some of it is confusing. For example, according to one source, St. Augustine (354-430 A.D.) believed that animals had souls; another source said the theory that animals cannot reason or feel — and therefore are not eternal — came from Augustine.

By the end of the first millennium, Christianity had spread the Good News across Europe, but had not made the same inroads on other continents. It was gradually transforming primitive, barbaric groups of people; however, the humane treatment of slaves, women, children, and animals was slow in coming. Primarily only church leaders, such as monks and priests, could read and write; books were few, being hand-copied.

As we will discuss further in the coming chapters on heaven, by the 1200s or 1300s, European Christian theologians believed the hereafter was a place of pure light and pure spirit; and that Heaven was devoid of animals.

The Gutenberg printing press, invented in the 14th century, revolutionized the world — much like the Internet did in the 1990s. Among the first things printed were Bibles. A copy of the

1611 King James Version is instructive about the attitude toward animals. Consider the translators' introduction:

> *A man would think that Civilities, whole-some Laws, learning and eloquence, Synods, and Church-maintenance,... should be as safe as a Sanctuary, and out of shot, as they say, that no man would lift up the heel, no, nor dog move his tongue against the motioners of them. For by the first, we are distinguished from* ***bruit-beasts led with sensualities****; ...*
>
> (Emphasis supplied)

This was the common view that animals are "brute-beasts" who are ruled by base cravings or instinct. Many hold to this view today.

We tend to be products of our times. Personally I think both Bible translators and readers are products of their time. Medieval and Enlightenment Bible readers either had the Latin Vulgate or a translation based on the Vulgate. They did not use the original Hebrew or Aramaic texts, and only a few Greek texts were available. Medieval church leaders did not fellowship with Jews and did not consult rabbinical sources to interpret Scripture. Their interpretations were colored by their world view or experience.

While I don't profess to be a scholar, it appears to me that the early Bible translations set the tone for all translations since then — even though modern translators have many more ancient manuscripts available in the original Hebrew and Greek. Challenging long-held interpretations can get you labeled a heretic.

As near as I can tell, in early translations, the treatment of "soul" and "spirit" were the same. This treatment is still followed today in most translations. A translator's theology will influence him to continue interpreting Scripture one way, even when other choices are as good or better. So will a reader's world view. We all have preconceptions, preconditioned responses. I know. Many of mine have been challenged while writing this book.

The Medieval Church believed that man, who was created in the image of God (Gen. 1:28), is different from and superior to all animals. If animals are truly only “bruit beasts led with sensualities” then man has little to learn from them. Man also has nothing to lose by exploiting them. Even today, this “human superiority” colors our behavior toward every living creature.

The consequences of this thinking seems to have come into full fruit with Charles Darwin(1809-1882), an English minister and naturalist. Darwin is the “father” of evolution as a theory of the origin of life. The “flower,” which preceded this “fruit,” seemed to have blossomed in the Age of Enlightenment (16th-17th centuries). By this time the first Bible translations were available to the “masses” in England and Europe.[30]

A key figure in this “flowering” of the idea that animals lack souls and spirits was the French philosopher, scientist, and mathematician, Renee Descartes (1596-1650). Descartes is famous for his philosophy or theology expressed in the Latin phrase: “Cogito, ergo sum” (“I think, therefore I am”). Descartes viewed the material world as mechanistic and entirely divorced from the mind. He believed the only connection between the mind and the physical world was by intervention of God; therefore rationalization and logic replaced experience, since experience could be illusion. You might say the sum of Descartes’ philosophy was “mind over matter.” Logically, if the material world was mindless, then animals were like machines, totally preprogrammed, moved solely by instinct. Descartes’ influence on philosophy and religion was incalculable.[31]

Important for our study is also a protégée of Descartes, Nicolas Malebranche (1638-1715). Malebranche carried the Cartesian argument to its logical conclusion, i.e., animals are “beast-machines” which cannot feel or suffer. Malebranche was said to have kicked a pregnant dog at his feet. When the dog cried out, an acquaintance rebuked him. Malebranche replied, “Well! Don’t you know that it does not feel?” Descartes reportedly owned a dog which he treated with great kindness. Malebranche, denied animals have any conscious experience, thinking he was following Descartes’ teaching, i.e., Cartesian philosophy.[32] How ironic.

The Cartesian argument goes like this: (a) Since God is just, and (b) many innocent animals suffer, especially at the hand of man, then (c) there must be recompense to the animals; if there is a recompense, (d) it is obvious that there is often no relief or reparation in this life for many suffering animals; therefore, (f) God must reward animals in the hereafter and logically, (g) justice requires that God takes suffering animals to heaven. Therefore, (h) we must avoid the distressing consequences of attributing a rational soul to beasts.

The same minds that argued how many angels could dance on the head of a pin, must have thought up the reason given by Cartesian thinkers: "Surely heaven could not hold all these beasts and humans, too!" So Descartes' disciples argued that: (a) animals do not have true intelligence, souls or spirits; therefore (b) animals lack the ability to sin, and hence (c) are incapable of salvation or redemption; so (d) animals cannot go to heaven.

In short, Enlightenment thinkers justified cruelty to animals by rationalization. They refused to believe heaven could handle an infinite number of souls in time and infinity. They limited God.

They also got hung up on the issue of whether animals have free will and can therefore commit sin. If the animals are innocent, then likewise it follows there must be a recompense for animal suffering. So the rationalists, including Darwinists, avoid the issue of animals having souls or spirits.

Enlightenment thinkers argued that three things in the Bible support this Cartesian philosophy: (1) only man is created in "the image of God" — Gen. 1:26-27; (2) the mandate to man to "subdue the earth and have dominion" over fish, birds and every living creature — Gen. 1:28; and (3) that "sin" or "salvation" is apparently not mentioned in relation to any animal. These verses are still used today when arguing animals lack souls and spirit, and don't go to heaven.

> *Debates about animal consciousness fall into two periods: before and after Darwin. Cartesian metaphysics cast its shadow over both periods. ... The animal without consciousness — the beast-machine — was then*

preeminently a Cartesian creature . . . The Cartesian beast-machine breaks down under the weight of analysis within Descartes' own framework. The behavioral and theoretical case for it fails, and it fails for Cartesian reasons. Even the theological arguments for it are weak.[33]

WHAT IS WRONG WITH CARTESIAN ARGUMENTS?

Is the Bible discredited by the Cartesian use of Scripture? Or is something else wrong? Daisie and Michael Radner state the thinking of many who oppose Cartesian theology:

> *. . . it does not say anywhere in the Bible that animals receive compensation for their suffering. There is no reason why Scripture should provide an answer one way or the other on this matter, since nothing hinges on it as far as human salvation is concerned. It is strictly between God and the brutes.*
>
> ***The notion that God should take on some sort of obligation with respect to animals is not without precedent in Scriptures.*** *After the flood, God establishes a covenant not only with Noah and his descendants, but also "with every living creature that is with you, of the fowl, of the cattle, and of every beast of the earth with you; from all that go out of the ark, to every beast of the earth" (Gen. 9:10)....* ***It is revealing that when Malebranche discusses the covenant of the rainbow in connection with natural laws, he refers to it simply as God's covenant with man (OC 10:80). Most clergy do the same.***
>
> * * *
>
> *The choice is between two prejudices, one against animals in heaven, the other about animal suffering.*[34] (Emphasis supplied)

The Radners' observation matches my experience and research. I found nothing like Cartesian philosophy in Jewish or early Christian writings which I examined. Nor is the idea prevalent in other cultures. As we have seen, the issue of whether animals have intelligence, souls, or spirits appears to be European and relatively modern in origin.

A LICENSE FOR CRUELTY TO ANIMALS

Using these Scriptures, many ministers and theologians concluded that Descartes and his followers were right. The unfortunate natural result is that humans have abused animals with impunity. Unspeakable cruelty to animals — whether killing baby seals with clubs or dissecting animals alive to see how their organs work — was excused in "Christian" society.

Vivisection was practiced here and abroad. (Vivisection is the cutting open and examination of an animal's organs while it is still alive — without anesthesia.) Students used live cats and dogs in biology classes until recent years. This was done in the name of Christianity — because man has dominion over animals, and animals are not rational beings!

Dr. Albert Schweitzer, an exemplary Christian missionary physician, said:

> *"... thoughtless injury to life is incompatible with ethics." ... I cannot but have reverence for all that is called life. I cannot avoid compassion.*

I believe it is blasphemy to think that God of the Bible has anything to do with such cruelties. The Jews have always interpreted Scripture to condemn brutality to animals. Christians have led the drive to abolish vivisection. Humane societies were started by British and American Christians to combat animal cruelty. C. S. Lewis, scholar and Christian author, was a staunch anti-vivisectionist. (He did, however, struggle with whether or not animals have individual souls.)[35] The success of this anti-cruelty movement is felt today and undoubtedly influences animal-rights and ecology activists, whether they understand the spiritual roots or not.

No honest observer of animals believes animals neither think or feel.:

> *I have noticed that my companion animals' nerve endings react instantly to the gentlest caress, and that if I should accidentally step on the tail they react as I would if a giant stepped on my foot. Dr. Louis J. Camuti states, "Never believe that animals suffer less than humans. Pain*

is the same for them that it is for us. Even worse, because they cannot help themselves."[36]

DO ANIMALS HAVE "TRUE" INTELLIGENCE?

If a being must have "true intelligence," as well as other abilities, to have a "soul" or "spirit" does the Bible have any support for this idea about animals? In fact, Holy Scripture *does not* support the Cartesian theology or Darwinist thinking. Let's look at stories or lessons relating to animals in the Bible which treat them as having intelligence and skill.

Many passages tell us to learn from animals. For example, Proverbs 6:6-8 tells the lazy person to learn about work habits from the ant. We are instructed to learn wisdom from rock badgers (building safe homes in rocks); from locusts who advance in ranks; and from spiders (or lizards) due to their survival skills in kings' palaces. [Prov. 30:24-28] Majesty can be learned from the lion, greyhound,[37] and the male goat. [Prov. 30:29-31] The bloodsucking leech is a lesson in selfishness. [Prov. 30:15] The eagle and serpent are used to teach us about wonder and awe:

> *There are three things which are too wonderful for me, Four which I do not understand: The way of an eagle in the sky, The way of a serpent on a rock, The way of a ship in the middle of the sea, And the way of a man with a maid.*
>
> Prov. 30:18-20 [NASV]

Scripture uses animal metaphors to instruct, also. In Numbers 24:8-9, likens Israel to a wild ox and to a lion— fierce, protective and untamable. Ezekiel 19:2-3 compares Israel to a lioness who loses her young lion to captivity — an image of grief and rage.

Several Bible accounts illustrate that animals have a heart of compassion in addition to intelligence. "Compassion" and "intelligence" are components of "moral choice." Those who argue that animals lack souls because they cannot make moral choices, have never looked closely at the animals in the Bible.

BALAAM'S DONKEY

In the delightful story of Balaam's donkey (or ass) in Numbers 22, intelligence, bravery, compassion and loyalty are demonstrated. Balaam's donkey was anything but a "dumb beast!" On three occasions, that "dumb" animal faced the Lord's angel. This huge angel had an assignment to execute Balaam for disobeying God. The angel of the Lord stood in Balaam's path with sword drawn ready to do his business.

Balaam was a prophet, a respected position in ancient times. The king of Moab sent for Balaam to curse the nation of Israel. God had a covenant with Israel to give them land. The Lord had just brought Israel out of slavery in Egypt. Having been offered money and honor, Balaam saddled his donkey and along with two servants went to meet the Moabite leaders. God was not pleased and sent His executioner.

Balaam's donkey saw the Angel of the Lord with a drawn sword ahead of them. Realizing the Angel meant harm to her master, she turned off the path into a field. The prophet, blind to the Angel's presence, beat the donkey. Next, the Angel took a stand in a narrow roadway, walled on each side. The donkey seeing the Angel, pressed against the side of the wall to avoid him. Balaam, having his foot crushed against the wall, beat the donkey again. The third time, the Angel picked a place where there was no way to turn. So the little donkey lay down. This again provoked Balaam's anger.

Furious, Balaam beat the little donkey with his stick — probably a walking stick of some size. At that point, the Lord gave the donkey the power of speech. The animal asked Balaam what she had done to deserve three beatings. In anger, he replied that she was "making a mockery of him" and if he had a sword, he would kill her.

It appears the donkey didn't realize Balaam could not see the angel. But we know that animals see things in the natural realm which the human eye cannot see — just as they smell things, hear sounds and feel vibrations that we cannot. My dogs and cats have looked at me as though I were deficient when trying to get me to realize something was happening that they could hear or see. The account of Balaam's donkey shows that animals see things in the spirit which we humans do not see. How often this happens, there is no way of knowing.

Consider the loyalty and love of this little donkey. That donkey had a deep affection for her master to take what she did! Ponder her next question. "Am I not your donkey on which you have ridden all your life to this day. Have I ever been accustomed to do so to you?" Balaam had to answer, "No." She was a good donkey. She made good choices, heroic choices, to endure pain for the sake of her master's life. Even under Cartesian theology, that is clear evidence of a "soul" and of a "spirit."

Even more remarkable is the favor the Lord gave to the donkey's intercessions. Due to the donkey's efforts, the angel sent to destroy Balaam did not or could not touch the man! How could a small donkey stop a warring angel of God Almighty? We learn from other Bible passages that the Lord's angels possess awesome power. Some have single-handedly destroyed cities and armies. God permitted that not-so-dumb animal to intercede for her master. Perhaps God appointed her for that task.

Isn't it interesting that Balaam believed this donkey had the ability to mock him? If animals lack intelligence, souls, or personalities, how could they make mockery of anyone? Why would Balaam react to the donkey as though she were a person? He clearly believed the animal had a will, and therefore she possessed choice of action. He clearly felt that the two servants who witnessed the donkey's behavior would think the donkey was mocking him, or else he would not have become angry.

Before granting Balaam the ability to see the angel waiting to kill him, God honored the donkey by giving her voice. I've heard sermons about this donkey, many of which make the point: "If God used a dumb donkey, He can use anyone." Such a sermon overlooks the point that this was by no means a dumb donkey.

Any animal who challenges God's avenging angel to spare its master's life and wins, has both soul *and* spirit! If a human did that we'd call him or her a saint! Are you willing to take a beating for a disobedient preacher? How many humans do you know who would serve a greedy man for a lifetime, then take a series of beatings to save his life? Do we love those in authority over us as this donkey loved Balaam? Balaam's donkey showed intelligence, love, vision, loyalty, and perseverance. Those comprise the definition of "soul," don't they?

OTHER BIBLE EXAMPLES

Other Biblical accounts of intelligent animal behavior offer more proof of "soul" or "spirit." Most of us are familiar with the account of the ravens which brought food to the prophet Elijah for weeks, months, even possibly a year or two — "until the brook dried up." [1 Kings 17:1-7] During a severe drought, birds and animals suffer just as the humans do. If you were those ravens, would you have brought meat across drought-stricken land to a man? Only the Lord knows what those intelligent, independent birds went through to feed that prophet day in and day out. Tell me why those ravens lack souls?

Consider the unusual bovine behavior described in 1 Samuel 6. Two cows were commandeered to pull the cart holding the Ark of the Covenant from ancient Philistia back into Israelite territory. Not a difficult task? These cows had never before pulled a wagon. No human trained nor drove them. Both cows bawled loudly as they went, because they left nursing calves behind. Now that's a whole series of miracles!

Also, there is that lion who killed a disobedient prophet, and the prophet's donkey. Remember the story? The lion stood next to the corpse with the man's donkey until another prophet came, loaded the body on the donkey, and then buried the dead man. [1 Kings 13] **"The lion had not eaten the corpse nor torn the donkey."** [1 Kings 13:28b] Sounds like the lion would have even helped load the body, if given the chance.

OTHER ANCIENT SOURCES

The Greek philosopher, Aristotle wrote a *History of Animals*. He illustrated animal intelligence with several examples. He reported that when swallows have no more mud to use to make their nests, they get wet, roll about in the dust, and make their own mud.

The ancient historian, Plutarch, in *The Cleverness of Animals*, used stories from others ancients. These included such great minds as Aristotle, Aeolian, and Pliny. For example, someone observed foxes in Thrace refused to cross a frozen river upon hearing running water underneath. The ancients felt this illustrated wisdom or intelligence: (a) what makes noise is in motion; (b) what is in motion is not frozen; (c) what is not frozen is liquid; (d) liquid gives away under weight; therefore (e) what makes noise gives away under weight. Thus the ancients knew that foxes demonstrated the ability to reason or problem solve. Ancients also recorded seeing a dog on a ship putting pebbles into a half-full jar of oil until the oil rose high enough for the dog to lick the oil. Who can argue that the dog lacked intelligence? (Of course, I know some people who'd argue that grass is orange if someone else stated it is green.)

One of my favorites is the story of Thales' mule. Crossing a river with a heavy load of salt, the mule fell. The sacks of salt, upon getting wet, dissolved. Thereafter the mule, upon coming to a river or stream, lay down to lighten its load. The wise owner loaded the mule with sponges and wool. So the smart mule stopped lying down and was careful to keep its cargo out of water!

MODERN DAY EXAMPLES

Just in case ancient wisdom and powers of observation are in question, modern animal observers confirm these incidents of animal intelligence. Television, movies, books, and magazines present a variety of fictional animals or animal-like beings which match or surpass humans in intelligence and wisdom. From *Winnie the Pooh* books to the *Star Wars* trilogy, we find examples of various intelligent life-forms — some attractive, some repulsive. *E.T.* and *Teenage Ninja Turtles* are reptilian personalities of high intelligence and abilities. New ones are invented daily. Why this inclination to ascribe intelligence and personalities to such "animals"?

Good animal trainers have long related to animals anthropomorphically, i.e., as "persons" possessing intelligence with abilities to lie or be honest, to love or to hate, to be cowardly or brave. This is in spite of the academic world's disdain for such a view of animals.

> *Trainers, for example, have no hesitation in talking*

> *about how much a mare loves or worries about her foal, a cat her kittens or a dog or a horse their work. But for philosophers and psychologists to speak of love was to invoke abilities that are, for reasons I am still not clear about, as rigidly restricted to Homo sapiens as some religious doctrines have restricted the possession of a soul to members of certain races, cultures and sometimes genders.*[38]

Animal behaviorists are challenging these Enlightenment doctrines about animals lacking souls or intelligence. Scientists in recent years are challenging the traditional conclusions that animals live by instinct and reflex alone. For example, in *How Smart Are Animals?*[39] Dorothy Hinshaw Patent explores the science of animal intelligence and the difficulties of examining totally different species. As we study animals in the wild, not in artificial laboratory settings, animals are proving to be far more "mentally talented" than lab scientists ever thought possible.[40] Just browse through the animal section of a modern library or in any university and look at animal intelligence studies which have come out in the last few decades. It is awesome what they are observing and chronicling about animal intelligence and behavior.

CLEVER BIRDS

Another example, a favorite of mine, is the story of little English birds which outfoxed milkmen for years. Starting about 1921, a little bird, the blue tit or titmouse, discovered it could break the foil tops of milk bottles after the milkman delivered them to people's doorsteps in the predawn cool. (Decades ago in the U.S., milk came in glass bottles with paper or foil stoppers or lids, and in urban areas were left on people's doorstep. I assume this was true in England, as well.) The birds sipped the cream at the top of the milk. (This was not homogenized milk.) It took the humans a while to figure out what was causing the loss of cream. A war of cleverness ensued. The birds learned to follow milkmen and hammer off lids. Milkmen put rocks or other objects on the milk jars; the birds shoved them off, sometimes with several birds acting together. Finally, the milkman put the jugs in a box, turned on its side so the box top just covered the milk jug top, only to turn and see the birds in the milk wagon sipping their cream! This behavior was first seen in southern England about 1921. By 1947 the sightings had spread all over England as well as to neighboring Scotland and Ireland. Apparently this art passed by imitation from bird to bird and generation to generation. Those who enjoy home delivery still have some thievery.[41]

So much for the validity of the statement "dumb bird" and "bird brain" as demeaning terms. Recent studies reveal that "bird brained" may be a high compliment, not an insult.

> *...Parrots can deal with abstract concepts, communicate with people, understand questions, and make reasoned replies. This is amazing information. Saying that the parrot can deal with abstract concepts, listen carefully to questions, and give an answer that has been "thought out" changes entirely our whole concept of the animal kingdom.*
>
> *Linking this with the new research coming out on dolphins, whales and chimpanzees indicated that* ***we may have to rethink our position of what separates the animals from humans.***
>
> *The ability to rationalize and reason used to be one of the central and main differences that distinguished man from beast.* ***Philosophically, it was even thought that the aptitude for reasoning meant the presence of a soul*** *and was what separated higher from lower intelligence.*[42] (Emphasis supplied)

MORAL CAPACITY IN ANIMALS

Another doctrine from the medieval church was that animals lacked moral capacity — the capacity to know right and wrong and make choices. We have already addressed Balaam's donkey and other animals in the Bible which belie that Cartesian theology. Observation of animals also put that to the test. Consider the growing use of animals, dogs, monkeys, cats, horses, and birds, as service or therapy animals, as healers. Also, there are numerous anecdotes of animals which have acted as heroes or rescuers.

People magazine featured an article about heroic animals who had saved peoples lives. Cows, like dogs and horses, can do strangely compassionate things. Daisy, a 25-year-old "bell" cow, daily led the other cows to a Welsh farmer each day. When a 3,300 lb. bull, on loan for breeding, knocked the man to the ground and was stomping him, he thought he would die. The farmer lost consciousness. When he came to, he found himself in a circle of his cows. Daisy was directing them. They kept the circle around him, keeping the bull at bay until the farmer crawled home. He recovered in spite of the injuries. When asked about the "bovine intervention," the farmer replied:

> *I have treated the animals reasonably, and they have looked after me in return. People say I am too soft, but I believe you reap what you sow.*[43]

An issue of *Angels* magazine told about a large family dog who refused to get in the vehicle with the family as they left to escape a flood. The dog chose to go ahead of the vehicle down the middle of the flooded roadway. He guided the way so they would not go into either ditch — ditches which were impossible to see due to the swirling water. This family was convinced that their dog was on a mission from God. The dog certainly acted like an furry, four-footed angel of God.

The truth is, animals of various species have been observed making similar choices. A dog was observed giving the first bone he received from a butcher to a lame "dog friend," then returning for a second bone for himself. And cats have been known to act as guides for blind dogs.[44]

Aiding each other is not so uncommon, as observers note with regularity. Even wild animals show an ability to make "moral choices." Consider the accounts of a lion pulling out an antelope stuck in a mud hole and letting it go,[45] and an elephant stopping to carefully cover a sleeping infant with palm leaves which kept the flies off. Why didn't the lion kill the antelope and eat it? Why would elephants care about a human child? Are these not acts of mercy — moral judgments?

Anyone who says animals lack intelligence or the ability to make moral decisions is ignorant or blind — just as Balaam was. They are also ill-informed of the Bible and a poor observer of animals — God's creation.

Game-playing is a form of problem solving and many games involve a high degree of shrewdness, judgment, perspicacity and acumen. Would you agree that the ability to play games is a sign of intelligence and the ability to make choices?

Many of us have observed our cats, dogs, and horses playing games. The wild otter's play is well documented. A most unusual scene was a small herd of buffalo which ran and slid, spinning, across a frozen lake one after the other. When it slowed, the slider would make a sound. Each would then carefully make its way across the ice and back up the slope to repeat the action.[46] Sounds like fun to me!

While Cartesian theology attempts to tell us that animals lack souls and spirits — even lacking the ability to feel — this has no basis in truth or Scripture. Only by twisting a few verses can you believe this doctrine is Bible-based. Yet this heresy has excused unspeakable arrogance and cruelty toward animals. Such nonsense must be stopped! That is where we who have the Bible — with modern sources to better understand it, and who are believers in the Lord Jesus Christ, have an advantage.

We have much to learn from animals and about them. Since the theologians conclude that the soul is the seat of intelligence, wisdom, will, and emotions, then if animals evidence these attributes, how can we say that they have no souls? Love is an attribute of God, and God is spirit. Is it not logical that if a creature can love, it is a spiritual being? Animals evidence "spirit" because they love.

And for those who would argue that animals don't love, but are "acting instinctively," they need to get educated in the ways of animals (or go have their heads examined). "Instinct" does not explain the well documented complexities of animal behavior. Besides, there is even *more* Bible proof of animals having "souls" and "spirits."

SOUL AND SPIRIT DEFINED

What is a "soul" or a "spirit?" The dictionary definitions

(quoted at the beginning of this chapter) provide a good starting point. In the English language, "soul" and "spirit" are defined as the "animating force" of a person, the "seat of the mind, will, and emotions." We must go to the Bible to see if there is any Scripture which states that animals have either a "soul" or "spirit," i.e., that invisible "animating force."

In case you didn't know, our English Bibles are all translations. The King James Version is a translation of a translation, since the Latin Vulgate was a translation. (It is still a masterpiece of English literature.) "Even at its best, the art of translation is an inexact science," says Dr. Brad Young, (Ph.D. Hebrew University).[47] Most translations into other languages are translations from English. The miracle is that God's inspiration comes through the translations — often with remarkable clarity.

While revolutionary in its time, the 1611 King James Version is now understood to contain many errors in translation. The translators did not have the manuscripts or archeological evidence which modern translators now possess to aid in more accurate translations. The wonderful research tools available today enables anyone who is willing to study, to find answers — without being literate in Hebrew or Greek. Mom's question has required a bit of work, but I thank God for the scholars who have made it possible for me to do so.

SOUL — NEPHESH

In the English translations of the Old Testament of the Bible or Hebrew Scriptures, the term "soul" is the Hebrew word "*nephesh*" [Strong's #5315]. It means literally, "a breathing creature." In the King James Version, "*nephesh*" was invariably translated "soul" in reference to man. However, when *nephesh* refers to animals, it was never translated "soul" but only "beast" or "living creature" or "life." Are you surprised?

This matches Cartesian philosophy. Those who know Hebrew probably never question whether animals have souls, unless their thinking is contaminated by this theology.

The first few chapters of Genesis establish this pattern. Let's look at the King James Version on a series of verses:

*And God said, Let the waters bring forth abundantly the moving creature that hath life [*nephesh*], and fowl that may fly above the earth in the open firmament of heaven. And God created great whales, and every living creature [*nephesh*] that moveth, which the waters brought forth abundantly, after their kind, and every winged fowl after his kind; and God saw that it was good.*

* * *

*And God said, Let the earth bring forth the living creature [*nephesh*] after his kind, cattle, and creeping thing, and beast of the earth after his kind: and it was so.*

* * *

*And God blessed [*humans*], and God said unto them, Be fruitful and multiply, and replenish the earth, and subdue it: and have dominion over the fish of the sea and over the fowl of the air, and over every living thing [*nephesh*] that moveth upon the earth.*

Genesis 1:20-21, 24, & 28

Compare those verses with Gen. 2:7 [KJV]:

*And the Lord God formed man of the dust of the ground, and breathed into his nostrils the breath of life; and man became a living soul [*nephesh*].*

Thus animals are referred to as living "things," and man as a living "soul." Yet both are translated from the same word.

Next we move from creation to God's speaking to Noah and the animals following the Great Flood:

*Every moving thing that liveth shall be meat for you; even as the green herb have I given you all things. But the flesh with the life [*nephesh*], which is the blood thereof, shall ye not eat. And surely your blood of your lives [*nephesh*] will I require; at the hand of every beast will I require it, and at the hand of man; at the hand of every man's brother will I require the life [*nephesh*] of man.*

Gen. 9:3-7 [KJV]

The King James translators carried this distinction between man and beast throughout the Old Testament. A few examples are: Genesis 8:17 says every "living thing" was to be brought into Noah's Ark; and in Leviticus 11:46 the law was regarding every "living thing."

So the great distinction between man and animals is a translator's philosophical construction!

More recent translations correct this error somewhat but not completely. The *Open Bible* version of the King James, for example, adds "soul" as a footnote to "life" in Genesis 1:20. *The Amplified Bible* stopped using "soul" altogether, and replaced it with the term "living creatures" (animal) or "living being" (man) or "life" (as in Gen. 9:4). A similar change is seen in the *New King James, New American Standard, New Revised Standard, New International, Jerusalem, New Century Version,* to name a few.

The distinction is still there to the uninformed reader. How could you tell that "living creature" or "living thing" (used for animals) is the same as "living being" — the term used for humans? Humans are "beings" but animals are still "creatures" and "things." No modern translation uses "soul" for both man and animal. It has to be a translation compromise to find suitable terms and still give a "nod" to Cartesian philosophy.

Some modern references are correcting this Cartesian error. For example, different editors of two Bible Dictionaries use the same definition of "soul" stating it includes animals.[48] Some Christian writers are doing the same.

> *The Hebrew word for "soul," nephesh, is used 393 times. Properly it means "a breathing creature"— i.e., any "animal." In the abstract it means "vitality." Nephesh is used widely in a literal, accommodated or figurative (bodily or mental) sense. It has many meanings, including appetite, beast, body, breath and creature. Biblically, then, the soul is simply the life of a breathing creature, which departs when that living creature dies.*

* * *

The words "living soul" (nephesh chayah) were used in Genesis 2:7 when God originally gave life to man. You can read the same phrase in twelve more passages in Hebrew where, surprisingly they all refer to animals! The first five appear in the first two chapters of Genesis:[49]

I was surprised by these definitions. Aren't you?

Why would "*nephesh*" be translated "soul" only in reference to humans by English translators? The distinction is not in the Hebrew Scriptures. Why are animals only referred to as "beast," "living creature," "living things" when the Hebrew "*nephesh*" appears? It must be that the Cartesian theology was already deeply entrenched in the minds of church leaders and translators.

"SOUL" IN THE NEW TESTAMENT

What about the New Testament? In the New Testament Greek manuscripts, the Greek word "*psyche*" is the one commonly translated into English as "soul." "*Psyche*" [Strong's # 5590] means "breath," "life," and "soul, mind, or self." The Greek word is a root word for many English terms, like psychology and psychedelic (mind-altering).

The same patterns used in translating "*nephesh*" are followed in translating "*psyche*" and its relatives. For example, see Luke 6:9 and 9:24. In Acts 20:10 regarding the death of Eutychus, Paul embraced the boy's body and said, "His *psyche* is still in him." Revelation 18:13 refers to the wicked selling of human *psyche* along with slaves, animals and other merchandise. Contrast that with Revelation 8:9, the only passage which uses *psyche* in reference to animals:

*...a third of the creatures, which were in the sea and had life [*psyche*], died.* [NASV]

This passage has a familiar ring to it. Doesn't it remind you of Genesis 1:20-28? John, who wrote Revelation, would have known Genesis in Hebrew. That may be why John, when writing Revelation 8:9, used *psyche*. He could have used the Greek word "zoe" (as in "zoology") which means all living things, from amoeba, to dandelions, to whales — not just breathing "souls." Perhaps it was put there for us — those of us who want to know the answer to Mom's question.

Looking again at definitions of "soul" based on Bible sources, it becomes clear animals fit the definition. If you have an "ego" or "self" then you have a soul:

> *Soul . . . [T]he word [is] commonly used in the Bible to designate the nonmaterial ego of man in its ordinary relationships with earthly and physical things. It is one of a number of psychological nouns, all designating the same non-material self, but each with a different functional relationship.*[50]

Animals have *psyche* or *nephesh*. Observers note that dogs, cats, horses and other mammals clearly have a sense they are separate "selves" from others of their species, other animals, and humans. They hoard things showing a sense of ownership, act possessive or jealous, are territorial, act heroic and kind to others, including other species. They problem-solve and also use tools. Animals show every indicia of "ego" or "self."

All you have to do is observe animals to know what the Bible means. I have cats who look alike physically, but have strikingly different personalities. The same is true of other animals. Shepherds know their sheep by name. Farmers working with milk cows daily, can tell them apart both by looks and personalities. And the list goes on. Animals do have personalities or personhood, or "non-material egos" — just as man does. Therefore, it cannot be the soul that distinguishes man and beast.

"Soul" is a hard word to define clearly. What is a soul, anyway? The *Pictorial Bible Dictionary* definition of "soul" has this commentary:

> *The above remarks assume dichotomy, that is, that there are only two substantive entities which make up the whole man (1) the body, which at death returns to dust, awaiting the resurrection, and (2) the nonmaterial self which, if regenerate, goes to paradise or heaven; if not, to the abode of the wicked dead. There are many, however, who hold to a trichotomous view, arguing that "soul" and "spirit" are two distinct substantive entities, and the body, a third. They cite I Thessalonians 5:23; I Corinthians 15:44 and Hebrews 4:12 for evidence.*[51]

What about animals? According to Scripture, are they two-part or three-part beings? We see they are two parts, having *nephesh* and their physical bodies. In the minds of some, possessing a soul is enough for animals to be candidates for heaven or hell.

However, I suspect some will hold out: "If animals lack spirits, they cannot go to heaven, since God is spirit, and it takes 'spirit' to worship Him." [John 4:24] Are animals three-part beings, like humans? Do animals have spirits?

DO ANIMALS HAVE SPIRITS, TOO?

Would you agree that if animals have spirits, the case becomes stronger than animals **are** candidates for heaven? If so, we might answer Mom's question in the affirmative.

I was taught the Bible does not say that animals have spirits. Many Christians have repeated this lesson to me. Is it correct? What does the Bible say?

Again, we must return to the original languages to find the answer. In the Old Testament Hebrew, "*ruwach*" [Strong's #7307] is the Hebrew word translated as "spirit." *Ruwach* is the Hebrew word used for the human "spirit."

Ruwach literally means "breath." It has figurative meanings, such as: "life," "anger," "unsubstantiality" and, of course, "spirit." When you think about it, the connection between "breath" and "spirit" is no great intellectual leap. Both describe the intangible. Both describe something essential to life. When the breath leaves the body, the spirit has departed. The spirit is the core of a living being, the vital principle.

According to *Strong's Dictionary of the Hebrew Bible*, published in 1890 and part of the Strong's Exhaustive Concordance (1894), when "*ruwach*" is translated as "spirit," it denotes only "a rational being." (Do I hear echoes of Descartes?)

Gesenius' Hebrew-Chaldee Lexicon To The Old Testament, published in 1847, defines *ruwach*, similarly, adding that it is also used to describe the "wind." When describing humans Gesenius said *ruwach* means "*animus*" or "seat of the senses, affections and emotions of various kinds," as well as "the mode of thinking and acting," "will and counsel" and "intellect."

This term is used to identify the Holy Spirit of God, "*ruwach ha kadosh.*" [Ps. 51:13; Isa. 63:11-12] It is also used to identify demons, i.e., evil "spirits," which torment humans. [1 Sam. 16:15-16] That is intriguing, given our question.

"THE EXCLUSIVE RATIONAL-BEING CLUB"

This "Rational-Being Club" has been exclusively human and supernatural for centuries. Animals need not apply! *Ruwach,* the word used for "spirit" has received the same treatment as "*nephesh*" or "soul" in English translations. This is not surprising. It is consistent with the Cartesian viewpoint.

The first passage where *ruwach* is used in connection with animals is in Genesis 7. This passage illustrates a Cartesian bias affecting translation:

> *...they [Noah and his family] and every beast after its kind, all cattle after their kind, every creeping thing that creeps on the earth after its kind, and every bird after its kind, every bird of every sort. And they went into the ark to Noah, two by two, of all flesh in which is the breath [*ruwach*] of life.* Genesis 7:14-15 [NKJ]

Only in one place do translators use "spirit" when connected to an animal: Ecclesiastes 3:21. In any well-known English translation, you cannot find *ruwach* translated as "spirit" where it refers to an animal in any other verse. The only reason it is translated "spirit" in Eccl. 3:21 is there is no other way it would make sense. Consider the passage, using the New American Standard Version, one I like for its reputation of being very literal:

> *I said in my heart regarding the subject of the sons of men that God is ... trying them that they may see that by themselves ... they are but as beasts. For that which befalls the sons of men befalls beasts, even one thing befalls them; as the one dies, so dies the other. Yes, they all have one* ***breath (ruwach)****, so that a man has no preeminence over a beast; for all is vanity . . .*

All go to one place; all are of the dust, and all turn to dust again.

*Who knows that the **spirit (ruwach)** of man whether is goes upward and the **spirit (ruwach)** of the beast whether it goes downward to the earth?*

Ecclesiastes 3:18-21 (NASV)

When he wrote Ecclesiastes, King Solomon, was considered both the wisest man who ever lived and the Playboy of his world. He was learned; a prodigy. Solomon wrote Ecclesiastes under the inspiration of the Spirit of the Lord, according to both Jewish and Christian canons. Solomon's final question is a rhetorical one; it is answered in the statements preceding it. All have the same *ruwach*; all die the same. Who can say one goes up and one goes down? Can you?

Solomon observed that humans and animals die similar deaths. Whether they are killed, die of disease, disaster, or old age, there is little difference in how the physical body dies. All flesh goes the same way. No one who has witnessed the death of a human or animal can honestly question that observation. When the *ruwach* — the animating force — leaves the body of man or animal, what remains is an empty shell of clay. I've seen a number of dead bodies and I am still shocked how different a body is when empty of life.

Animals have spirits just as humans do. This is the word from the Holy Bible. This is from the inspired Word of God. Twice in this passage the word *ruwach* refers to animals. Solomon repeatedly states man and animals are no different: we both have spirits and we die the same!

Theologians, like Descartes, sidestepped the issue of animals having "spirits." They used learned sophistry and kept readers in the dark. I submit they were less than intellectually honest. Isn't it time to dismantle this cruel philosophy?

Solomon was meditating on the vanity, the futility, of humans in thinking we are so superior. He stated that we die just like animals. We go to the same place. He never questioned that animals have spirits, *ruwach*.

MORE REFERENCES

There are more references, more "witnesses." The psalmist described the provision which God makes for animals and then says:

> *You open Your hand, they are filled with good. You hide Your face, they are troubled; You take away their* ***breath [ruwach],*** *they die and return to their dust. You send forth Your* ***Spirit [ruwach],*** *they are created; And You renew the face of the earth. May the glory of the Lord endure forever; May the Lord rejoice in His works.*
>
> Psalm 104:28b-31 [NKJ]

Note the play on words which is missed in the English. The psalmist juxtaposed the spirits of animals to the Spirit of God. Animals die when their spirits leave their bodies. The Holy *Ruwach* sustains and creates animal *ruwachs*! The Holy Spirit is a Person, a part of the Godhead, the *Elohim*. God actively cares for animals! (I think the psalmist was also saying man is no different from animals — we all need God's Spirit to sustain our spirits.) The psalmist knew. Wow!

Another interesting phrase appears in Numbers 16:22 and again in Numbers 27:16:

> *...the God of the spirits [*ruwach*] of all flesh...* [NKJ]

In both of these Scriptures, the context is addressing human need. However, there is no dispute that in the Bible, "flesh" and "all flesh" are used in reference to animal as well as human flesh. The writer of Numbers also uses "all flesh" as it is used in Genesis 2:21, 23; 6:12-13; 7:15, 16, 21; & 9:15-16. The Hebrew term refers to animals as well as humans.

ANOTHER PIECE TO THE PUZZLE

Another piece of the puzzle is in the familiar phrase from Psalms:

> *Let* ***everything*** *that has* ***breath*** *praise the Lord.*
>
> Ps. 150:6 [NKJ]

This is a different Hebrew word for "breath" or "spirit." This word is "*neshamah*" [Strong's #5397]. It means "puff" as "wind."

Figuratively, it has come to mean angry or vital "breath," divine "inspiration," and "intellect." You might say it is activated spirit.

Neshamah is translated into English as the "breath" or "spirit" of life. *Neshamah* is used in Genesis 2:7 regarding Adam, and in Genesis 7:22, Deuteronomy 20:16, and Joshua 10:40 regarding all life, i.e., including animals. Let's look at Genesis 7:22:

> *All in whose nostrils was the breath [**neshamah**] of the spirit [**ruwach**] of life, all that was on the dry land, died. So He destroyed all living things which were on the face of the ground: both man and cattle, creeping thing and bird of the air. ... Only Noah and those who were with him in the ark remained alive.*
>
> Gen. 7:22-23a [NKJ]

This passage is interesting because "spirit," *ruwach,* is in ancient Hebrew texts, but is left out of the Greek Septuagint, and the Latin Vulgate translations. The Septuagint is a translation of the 39 Hebrew books of the Old Testament, prepared in the third century before Christ for Greek-speaking Jews in Egypt. The Latin Vulgate translation was prepared for the early Roman Christians by Jerome, using Hebrew and several Greek translations including the Septuagint. One of the questions I have for the Lord when I reach heaven is, why would these translators leave out *ruwach*? Was it because they did not believe animals had "spirits"?

"*Neshamah*" is also translated as "soul," as well as "spirit" — whether human, animal or divine. See, for example, its use for God's breath or Spirit in Job 32:8 and 33:4. It seems to be linked with the term for life or living. "Let everything that has breath praise the Lord," is commonly understood to mean humans and animals. But the information that "breath" also means "spirit" is hidden to uninformed English readers.

When you understand that the word "breath" — whether "*ruwach*" or "*neshamah*" — can also be translated "spirit," then you see there are multiple references in the Bible which show animals have "spirits." What was hidden, is now revealed. The Bible does say. And it says animals have spirits, too.

SPIRIT IN THE NEW TESTAMENT

The New Testament is very skimpy in speaking of animals and their natures. Perhaps this is because it is well covered in the Old Testament or Jewish Scriptures. Jesus came to fulfill the Hebrew Law, not abolish it. [Matt. 5:17]

The Greek word commonly translated "spirit" is "*pneuma*" [Strong's #4151], from "*pneu*" "to breathe or blow." This is a familiar term to English-speaking folks. We use pneumatic pumps and tires and we contract pneumonia, a disease of the "air pumps" we call lungs. It is therefore basically identical to the Hebrew "*ruwach*." "*Pneuma*" likewise means "breath" or "wind." By extension it also means "spirit," "rational soul," "vital principle," or "mental disposition."

"*Pneuma*" is used by New Testament writers to identify divine, human, angelic and demonic beings. The Holy Spirit, or Holy Ghost, is the "*Hagia Pneuma*." "*Pneuma*" is not used in the New Testament to refer to any animal's breath or spirit. But a relative of *pneuma* is.

> *The God who made the world and all things that are in it, since He is Lord of heaven and earth, does not dwell in temples made with hands; neither is He served by human hands, as though He needed anything, since* ***He Himself gives to all life and breath [*****pnoe*****] and all things****; and He made from one, every nation of mankind to live on all the face of the earth, having determined their appointed times, and the boundaries of their habitation,...*
>
> Acts 17:24-25 [NASV]

The term "*pnoe*" [Strong's # 4157], means "respiration." It is closely related to "*pneuma*" [#4151]. They share the same root word. The distinction seems to be in the activity described: "*Pneuma*" describes a current of air, i.e., breath or breeze. "*Pnoe*" describes "respiration" or breathing. Both are translated "spirit" or "wind." That makes sense in English — we are all living breathing creatures, sometimes full of wind!

The only other place this word "*pnoe*" is used is Acts 2:2 to describe the sound of the coming of the Holy Spirit on the day of Pentecost, when Jesus' disciples were filled and changed. It can be read: "And there came suddenly out of heaven a sound as a rush of violent wind" or " ... of a mighty Spirit." It is not hard to picture the Almighty — excited about the wonderful gift He was sending to believers — expelling His breath in a violent rush. It must have sounded like a tornado! Atomic breath! God's mighty Spirit came rushing to fill His disciples with power!

BOTH THE OLD TESTAMENT AND THE NEW AGREE

So we have authority in both Old and New Testaments, Hebrew and Greek, that animals have "spirits." They are tripartite beings just like humans. As we discussed above, modern scholarship agrees.

> *The time is long overdue for abandoning the anthropocentric approach to philosophy . . . So long as animals are ignored, either as objects in the world or as perceivers, they will continue to make messes. ... When the chickens come home to roost, [a contrary philosophy] silently wrings their necks at the entrance to the coop, before they can get in and cackle." ...*
>
> *Here we let the chickens cackle loud and clear. . . Certain issues in philosophy of science, philosophy of mind, even history of philosophy, take on new light when animals are given center stage.*[52]

The intent of this book is not to "give" any creature, including man, "center stage." Rather it is to find the Author's placement of animals — the place He intended and intends them to have — on His "stage" in His Kingdom. No more. No less.

The consequences of the Cartesian philosophy are heavy. Christian theologians passed this nonsense to ministers, who taught ordinary worshippers. For a long time scientists excused animal pain in experiments under this dark belief. It still goes on. The results have been a license to those who chose to be cruel on the one hand, and a guilt trip for animal lovers on the other. It's past time to turn these tables, don't you agree?

It may not be easy. If one cannot face judgment for his or her unpaid debts to God and man, one certainly won't want to bear account for injury to animals! Those who follow the Cartesian model, must be tempted to bury their heads in the proverbial sand of "reason," while reality bites them in the rear! If you have been caught in that philosophy, please reconsider!

Why would anyone believe the heartless Cartesian philosophy? One might ask, "Why do people become abusers or neglect their children?" In all societies where the life of man or beast is not valued, insane cruelty reigns.

Throughout history, animals have been treated badly. There are exceptions, but this has been the general rule. Ignorance of animals, and their needs, as well as blatant cruelty, results in animals being ill-fed, poorly doctored, cruelly worked, tortured or beaten — as though they were disposable machines. Wild animals also suffer.

But then human history shows we are no less unkind to our fellow man. Experts today know, from studies of violent criminals, there is a link between animal cruelty and deranged, vicious crimes.[53] Beware the child who enjoys hurting little animals!

HANDLING BIBLE ERRORS

As you read this brief assessment of Christian history and the Bible, I hope you see where, if not why, we went astray. For those deeply troubled that "the Bible has errors in translation," the Almighty is able to handle all kinds of human error. He has done so since Adam's fall, and he has a plan to help.

The Bible is still divinely inspired — even most translations can't escape God's anointing. The Bible cautions that no one should to add to and take away from God's Word. [Deut. 4:2; 12:32; Rev. 22:18-19] We humans have a tendency to continue to do so, however. Eve added to and took away from the first commandment to not eat the forbidden fruit. [Compare Gen. 1:16-17 with Gen. 3:2-3] Bad translations which imply animals don't have souls and spirits violated this command.

Because of preconceived ideas and cultural bias, translators may not have realized their errors. I hope that their errors were unintentional. We must all bear account to the Lord for how we handle His Truth. There is abundant mercy for unintentional transgressions.

You don't have to learn ancient Hebrew and Greek to read the Bible. Modern translations get the major points very well. Just because some translators did not get everything right, we can believe that they tried. They had a very difficult task. Translation is not easy.

Anyone who has learned more than one language, knows the difficulty in accurately translating anything. Words with multiple meanings are very difficult to translate. Additionally, since the Lord confused men's words and language at the Tower of Babel [Gen. 11], we've all had trouble communicating clearly. We daily need the Lord's help to understand each other. Sometimes only He can un-confuse us. (Maybe He intended it that way.)

Allow the Holy Spirit to be your teacher, as I have striven to do here. The Lord has promised that His disciples will know the truth. Even if God has to move heaven and earth, He will show us His way. He certainly has done that to give me these answers — the details of which would fill another book!

IT'S IRREFUTABLE!

The Bible is clear. Animals have souls and spirits, just as man does. In that regard, we are no different. We can celebrate our similarities! We humans are all part of the animal kingdom. God intends for all His creation to be part of His kingdom, it appears.

Now you know what the Bible says. It is irrefutable. The difference between man and beast is not that man has a soul or spirit (Gen. 1:20; 7:15; Eccl. 3:21). We are both tripartite beings: Spirit, soul and body.

> *The difference between man and beast is not that man has a soul or spirit (Gen. 1:20; 7:15; Eccl. 3:21), but that man is created in the image of God, whereas the beast is not.*[54]

While I am not sure what being "created in the image of God" truly means, I am not ashamed to be compared to animals. Most are of the highest character and very good company. We have much to learn about and from animals. Now we will have a groundwork laid to explore more about animals in eternity. Let's see what else the Bible has to say!

CHAPTER 5

IN AWESOME WONDER OR ANIMALS AT CREATION

All things bright and beautiful, All creatures great and small, All things wise and wonderful, The Lord God made them all.[55]

Fair songsters, come; beneath the sacred grove
We'll sit and teach the woods our Maker's name.
Men have forgot His works, His power, His love,
Forgot the mighty arm that reared their wondrous frame.[56]

O Lord my God, when I in awesome wonder, consider all the worlds Thy hands have made, I see the stars, I hear the rolling thunder, Thy power throughout the universe displayed, Then sings my soul, . . . How great Thou art![57]

An ancient fable tells about a mouse born in a chest who lived all her days on food the woman of the house stored in the chest. One day the mouse dropped out the side. As she was searching to find her way back in, she stumbled on a very delicious morsel. As soon as it was in her mouth, she exclaimed what a fool she had been to persuade herself that there was no happiness in the world but in that box.[58] When I study Scripture and this vast world around us, and am confronted with new things, I feel a bit like that mouse. There's a lot "delicious morsels" outside our boxes. It's overwhelming at times to think how much!

If true genius means making complex things simple, then Genesis is a record of astonishing genius. In a few hundred words, the first chapter reports the creation of stars, planets, moon, earth, plants, birds, fish, insects and mammals.[59] A few years ago, a microbiologist friend, specializing in phage genetics, particularly viruses, told me she could not keep up in her own "small" field. The information collected to date on the origins of life is gargantuan. Yet, there's a lot more to discover, and scientists cannot agree how to interpret what they already have.

Consider how the Bible begins:

"*In the beginning, God created . . .* " Gen. 1:1a [KJ]

This simple statement tells profound things. Before there was a beginning, God was there. This Creator is un-created. This earth, conceived by an Infinite Mind and Heart, was made by divine plan! Its complex beauty testifies that a consummate Artist created this universe. And that was only the beginning. The Artist still works. The picture is not complete. This leaves me awestruck. How about you?

The Bible begins and ends with animals in an important role. In the first book, first chapter, we find God and His creation of animals. God made animals before humans. This could be a foretaste of heaven, a piece of the answer to Mom's question.

GOD CREATES

Let's be honest. It's a journey of faith to "look" before recorded history. We have no human witnesses. There's no way to reproduce it in a laboratory. Only God Himself knows the truth. Whatever you believe is on faith — whether you take the creation story literally, figuratively, or not at all. As a lawyer I deal with legal proof. No one has proven conclusively that this world, and all that is in it, was not created just as the Bible states. How would we know if someone did prove it? The Bible gives only a skeletal sketch of most things. Sometimes in clear simple terms; sometimes in illustrations and parables. The Creation story is like that. It's very difficult to know what really occurred without direct proof. The only One there was God Himself and many don't believe in Him. Only by faith, can anyone know.

Because the Lord Jesus Christ is real to me, and I have chosen to obey Him, the Bible is my primary authority — my constitution and law. If I cannot find Scriptures — and that is plural — to back up my beliefs, they are mere theories and not a basis for faith. Debates among scientists about our origins will continue as long as this earth remains. The Bible settles the matter for people of faith. The Bible needs no defense. Its Author is alive and well able to defend it.[60] Every time I ask my Lord for wisdom and understanding, He gives it to me, as James 1:5 promises. Sometimes it has taken years, because I have a habit of asking "Ph.D." questions when my grasp is kindergarten level. The answers to Mom's question took years to collect and comprehend.

MY BELIEFS

When the God of the Bible made Himself known to me, and I first made a total commitment to serve Him, I realized that my intellectual and spiritual heritage conflicted with the Bible a great deal. Yet God is not the author of confusion. [1 Cor. 14:33] "My thoughts are not your thoughts, Nor are your ways My ways," says the Lord. [Isa. 55:8] I determined to let Him be my source of knowledge, wisdom, and understanding. [See Prov. chps. 1-3; Isa. 11:1-2; 1 Cor. 1:18-31] As a result, my thinking became clearer. I have no problem believing Almighty God *could* make everything in six literal days if He desired.

It is logical that the Lord would make a mature world.[61] Eggs need chickens. Babies need mothers. Change in fragile ecosystems kills. A quick creation is very practical. Such a world might appear much older than it is.[62] Whether the creation account is literal or metaphorical is not a stumbling block to my faith. I pray it is not to yours. God can do anything He pleases. [Eccl. 8:3] I'm thankful that He is a good God!

THEORY OR FACT

The purpose of this book is not to debate evolution and creation science. I'm a lawyer, not a scientist. However, even a non-scientist can observe and read. Many things cannot be explained by evolutionary theory. Physical evidence, like fossil records with human and dinosaur footprints together, as well as biological complexities and anomalies, belie evolutionary specie development.

For example, the woodpecker's long tongue is attached and stored uniquely in its brain cavity; this tongue is too unique to have evolved. Complex human-like eyes are found only in squids, octopuses, and humans; yet these species are believed to have evolved from different roots.[63] I learned as a veterinarian's daughter that mutants seldom live or are healthy; those that are, like mules and jennies, are sterile.

Too often the theories are taught as proven fact, when many evidentiary and logical holes are found in it. This is why there *is* a debate about evolution. On the other hand, creation science advocates don't have it altogether either.[64] The debates rage about evidence and methodology on all sides. (Egos appear to be involved, as well.)

No science can reconstruct the Beginning. It can only guess. An "educated guess" is still a guess. Sorting through the name-calling and rancor is difficult. It is not easy to separate theory from fact. We all bring biases into our formulae, biases which we hang onto like bulldogs. In this writer's observation, the jury is still out. No theory of earth's origin appears to have earned the right to be elevated to the status of "proven fact."

It is very unsettling to learn what we believed to be truth, is in fact, not truth at all. My college professor, Dr. Wik, told us: "New ideas are very difficult and disturbing, especially when they uproot old ones. Change is painful." I know he was right, but to be alive is to be forever changing.

The following quote by Bosworth regarding faith in God puts things in clearer perspective:

> *Because of God, His faithfulness, and His promises, faith is the surest ground that it is possible to stand on. To the man who is not enlightened or who does not see the promise of God, it is stepping out into space; but to those who have faith is God's Word, it is walking on the foundations of the universe.*[65]

BIBLE EVIDENCE

Let's go walking on the foundations of the universe. With childlike faith, let's examine the Bible. Science can help us, but this is not a science debate. Whether your faith is in science or other methods, we can look at the Bible together. It doesn't matter whether we believe the Bible creation account literally or metaphorically to discuss the issues in Mom's question. Mom's question doesn't hang on whether God made the world in six days. Like that proverbial mouse-in-a-box, let us find the pleasant goodies awaiting outside our comfort zone.

A useful method of Bible study is to collect everything about a topic, and then prayerfully analyze it. Also, I believe God plans each lesson, each topic-encounter with care. I pay attention to the first mention of a topic in the Bible, for in it are clues to God's thinking on the matter. To the observant person, first impressions are usually reliable. Succeeding images should confirm and expand on the first interpretation.

ORDER FROM CHAOS

The Bible begins with a description of God creating this universe, this green earth, and all life upon it — and doing so by design. From this we gain our first impression of the Father's attitude about His animals. It is done in an orderly fashion demonstrating careful planning and skilled craftsmanship.

Consider the miraculous construction of this blue-green jewel, our home, the earth. Christian astronomer, Hugh Ross, identified more than forty different criteria which are essential in order for life to exist.[66] Some seem to be at variance with "natural laws," but without these variations life would not be possible. For example, consider the unique way water behaves among liquids, the way H_2O behaves among gases, and the way our Sun behaves.[67] Many scientists today say current evidence points irrefutably to an "anthropic principle," i.e., this earth did not happen by chance.

The mathematical probability of this creation, with all its life forms, happening by chance is so low as to be essentially impossible. Life on earth seems designed especially and uniquely for humans and other living things; it is "an exquisite harmony of critical factors."[68]

ORDERLY PROGRESSION

Read the first two chapters of Genesis and note the progression. Only after making the heavens and earth, the waters, the sun, moon and stars, and plant life, did our Creator make the animal kingdom. First, the "stage" (Earth) was constructed. The "sets" were placed (the sun, moon, stars, planets and plant life). Then He filled it with "actors" in this drama of life.

The number and variety of the actors is incredible. Depending on who's counting, there are millions of species which have been identified, some extinct. Science has not yet identified all the species and sub species of animal life. Consider, too, the variations within each species. The dog family alone consists of a large variety — from African wild dogs and Australian dingos to domestic Great Danes and Chihuahuas. God started with huge varieties and numbers. That's awesome!

HE FILLED THE SEAS AND AIR WITH LIFE

In making animal life, first God filled the seas and air:

> *Then God said, "Let the waters abound with an abundance of living creatures, and let* ***birds*** *fly above the earth across the face of the firmament of the heavens." And God created the great* ***sea creatures*** *and every living thing that moves, with which the waters abounded, according to their kind, and every winged bird according to*

its kind; and God saw that it was good. And God blessed them, saying, "Be fruitful and multiply, and fill the waters in the seas, and let birds multiply on the earth." So the evening and the morning were the fifth day.

Gen. 1:21-23 [NASV]

BIRDS IN THE AIR

The Lord must love birds. He made such a variety and endowed them with so many talents! They range from tiny hummingbirds to great condors. Coloration goes from drab sparrows to brilliant-hued parrots and peacocks. From the screech of the owl to the song of the nightingale, bird sounds fill the earth. Watch a swallow's graceful whirl through the air, or the soaring eagle riding the wind as though it were a horse! Birds scatter seeds, fertilize the fields, eat insects, and do other useful things. They have served us as companions and couriers.

As we learned in a previous chapter, birds are not as dumb as we once thought. They communicate, use tools, take care of each other, and exhibit complex social structure. Consider the monogamy among species of geese and ducks. Henry Thoreau, in *Walden*, described the intelligence of a partridge hen and her chicks avoiding being discovered.[69] In their migratory flights, geese fly in "V" formation to conserve the energy of those which ride the wake of the lead birds.

God's feathered friends are fascinating. Helicopters are but a poor imitation of the mobility of a miniature hummingbird. Airplanes have nothing on the swooping agility of hawks, falcons, and eagles. On the jet stream, eagles have been observed asleep, wings locked, coasting on the wind current. This makes even more meaningful God's promise that a man who trusts Him shall "mount up with wings as eagles." [Isa. 40:31] Birds, the first of the animal kingdom to be created, are wondrous!

LIFE IN THE WATER

Consider the animal life in the waters, both fresh and ocean waters. In the Amazon River alone, are numbered more than one thousand varieties of catfish! Mom and I watched a television nature program that told this fact. One type of catfish after another was shown. Some were humorously strange; all were distinctly "catfish," whiskers and all. More types of catfish could yet be discovered.

This was only one species of fish in one river! Mom and I were awed. We talked about what fun God had making those catfish. That's proof of a Divine sense of humor. A thousand kinds of catfish? Why? Why not!

We weren't alone in thinking the Lord had fun:

> *In any case, God has done unusual things. I think He did much of creation just for fun, while His sense of design humor gives the materialist and skeptics some sleepless nights.*[70]

It boggles the mind to consider all varieties of fish, fowl and furry friends the Lord made — not to mention the insect world. Counting the balanced life in each ecosystem, "awesome" seems a very weak term to describe our Creator.

This could not be accidental. The beauty and harmony in the seas, ponds, creeks and rivers are a wonder indeed. From the phosphorescent waves lapping a shore at night, to the colorful tropical fish, to the songs of whales, the sea is a wondrous place. The way species help each other and need each other is also mute testimony to the genius of their Creator

Man is just beginning to explore secrets of the waters. The ocean and outer space are the last great frontiers. We've been gaining knowledge of depths formerly unknown. Mapping the ocean floors by satellite has opened a view that man has never before seen. Studies of porpoises and whales are revealing that these large-brained mammals have great intelligence and complex languages. They have sonar abilities beyond our present mechanical ability, and a social structure showing a high degree of cooperation. Whales even "midwife" the birth of each other's babies. Watch whales or porpoises sporting in the ocean or a sea horse caring for its young. Be prepared to stand in awe.

Those that go down to the sea in ships,
Who do business on the great waters;
They have seen the works of the Lord,
And His wonders in the deep.

Psalm 107:23-24 [NASV]

The way things work together demonstrates a presence behind it of a caring, patient, infinitely creative Person of unlimited intelligence, wit, and wisdom. It leaves me almost speechless. (As woman *and* a lawyer, I am rarely at a loss for words.)

LIFE ON THE LAND

Coming to the land, the Bible succinctly describes God's sixth day of the Creation, when the Lord made the land animals and mankind:

Then God said, "Let the earth bring forth the living creature according to its kind: cattle and creeping things and beasts of the earth, each according to their kind"; and it was so. And God made the beast of the earth according to its kind, cattle according to its kind, and everything that creeps on the earth according to its kind. And God saw that it was good.

Gen. 1:24-25 [NKJV]

God made myriads of tiny animals. Insects are the most varied and interesting. For example, I recall hearing that engineers studied the bumblebee and said it was impossible for the bumblebee to fly. Its large yellow and black body was too large for its small fly-like wings to lift and sustain its flight. Nobody told the bee. If you know the Lord, you know He loves do to the impossible.

Where I lived in Kentucky, the timbers of my old garage had deep holes about a third of an inch wide. They were made by a wood-boring bee which looks like a bumblebee. My garage was made of oak. Oak gets harder with age. You could not hammer a nail into the timbers! Yet this bee could drill a hole!

The Lord thoroughly enjoys making wonders. The insect world is full of marvels. The bumblebee and the wood borer give lessons in faith. The impossible is possible for our Lord, and to those who believe! [Jer. 29:17, 27; Luke 1:37].

ANIMALS AS TEACHERS

As Proverbs 6:6 and 30:25 says, we can learn from the ants. Humans make careers of studying plant and animal life. Our universities and libraries are full of books, videos and other collections. But we still have much to learn, don't we? Our earth-home is a marvelous ecosystem. From ants to zebras, there are complex communities of animals. Animals communicate and interact in ways which aid all concerned.

Go study the animals. Even in this fallen world, they can teach us much about our Creator. Ponder what He has made. If not in person, then perhaps through videos and books about animal intelligence, animal wonders, animal antics. Meditate on nature's harmony and interrelated diversity. The reading and observation I've done have been eye-opening, instructive and fun.

Consider the evidence of cosmic humor and playfulness. God is the God of Isaac ("Isaac" means "laughter" in Hebrew). Possums play dead. Certain caterpillars defend themselves by looking like vomit or bird droppings. Birds fake broken wings to draw predators from their nests. Some fresh water mussels have a body part which fools fish, so the fish unwittingly carry off mussel larvae. In my research I learned that mice can sing, and bears and birds get intoxicated (intentionally by all appearances) by imbibing fermented berries. God made this world to be fun as well as interesting.

ANIMAL BEHAVIOR

Consider personalities of different animals. Behaviorists have discerned affection and emotion in the interaction among and between species. Terms such as loyalty, kindness, honesty, and unselfishness (as well as negative terms) are used to describe animal behavior in their natural habitats.

Animals show attributes which humans share, such as intelligence, language, problem-solving, social structure, play, food-storage, tools-usage, and artistic ability. They display emotions ranging from fear, anger, love, grief, and depression, to compassion to their species and other species. Animal also share human traits of cruelty. This includes eating their prey live, slavery and warlike behavior.[71]

If animals are "beast-machines," then the U.S. Federal Drug Administration should be notified, as should pharmaceutical companies. On January 5, 1999, the Wall Street Journal reported that the FDA approved the first antidepressant for dogs who suffer from "separation anxiety"! It's one of a number of drugs being developed to "treat behavioral problems" in pets. The drug is the old human antidepressant, Anafranil.[72] There are now therapists for animal's emotional disorders. Animals *are* emotional beings. It is incontrovertible.

GOD'S ATTENTION TO ANIMALS

In an incredible two days, the fifth and sixth days, God created the sea and land animals, including birds and insects. If you take those "days" at face value, what percent of the time was spent creating living things versus creating inanimate creation? One third of those "six days" was put into making the animal kingdom. If time is valuable, then the animals are surely important. The Personality of the Universe loves His personable animals.

ICING ON THE CAKE

At the end of the sixth day, God took a few minutes and made the human race:

> *Then God said, "Let us make man in Our image, according to Our likeness; let them have dominion over the fish of the sea, over the birds of the air, and over the cattle, over all the earth and over every creeping thing that creeps on the earth." So God created man in His own image; in the image of God He created him; male and female He created them. Then God blessed them, and God said to them, "Be fruitful and multiply; fill the earth and subdue it; have dominion over the fish of the sea, over the*

birds of the air, and over every living thing that moves on the earth." . . .Then God saw that everything He had made, and indeed it was very good. So the evening and the morning were the sixth day.

Gen. 1:26-8, 31 [NKJV]

We humans may be a five-minute special. Special we are, but let us not get an inflated idea of our value. Time, as well as size, are not the sole arbiters of value, but if God charged by the hour, what would be the relative value of fish, birds, beasts compared to man? An humbling thought! We are more like animals than some philosophers and theologians will admit! Humans share characteristics of insects, fish, birds, and mammals. Spending time observing the animals can be life-changing. They each tell us something about the Artist who made us all.

God took obvious care in making His animals. The proof is in creation itself: the huge variety of species totally suited to and integrated into their habitats, living in incredible harmony in delightful diversity. Because this earth is marred by sin, trying to picture it when God first made it is like trying to picture an exquisite banquet after it is half-eaten. Yet, the evidence is there of consummate artistry. The signs point to a caring, witty, intelligent Creator.

As the grand finale, He made us — the human race. Humans may be the icing on the cake of creation. But what is icing without a cake? We need the cake more than the cake needs the icing.

CHAPTER 6

THE NAMING OF THE ANIMALS

And the Lord God said, "It is not good that man should be alone; I will make him a helper comparable to him." Out of the ground the ***Lord God*** *formed every beast of the field and every bird of the air, and* ***brought them to Adam to see what he would call them****. And* ***whatever Adam called each living creature, that was its name. So Adam gave names to all cattle, to the birds of the air, and to every beast of the field.*** *But for Adam there was not found a helper comparable to him.*

Genesis 2:18-20 [NKJ] (Emphasis supplied)

"Naming something gives it worth," my priest, Vic, once said in a sermon.

This concept is not new. Naming something establishes character and importance as well as worth.[73] When I applied this concept to animals, "a light came on" with respect to Mom's question. While Adam was not around when God made the animals, he became acquainted with every animal by naming them. Did God have Adam name the animals so each animal would have worth to Adam?

NAMING PETS

Children often made a big deal out of naming pets. I did. The names we give our pets often reflect our own values, as well as the value we place on the animal. Most breeders do not name kittens or puppies in order to give that privilege to the new owner.

When Gretchen, our 90-pound, 9-month old German shepherd, came to our home, she was "T-Bone." That name was on her AKC registration. Mom and I immediately renamed her. Mom's apricot-white toy poodle came to us as "Chico." That was the nickname of our recently deceased cousin whom we loved. We renamed the poodle as well. We had Gretchen, so we decided the six-pound poodle needed a *big* name. Killer and Goliath were quickly eliminated. We finally agreed on Samson — a Biblical strong man and lion-killer. I later discovered the meaning fit perfectly. Samson means "sunlight" in Hebrew. Mom's happy poodle was always a ray of sunlight. The proverb, "A good name is more to be desired than riches," works for dogs too. [Proverbs 22:1]

UNINHIBITED NAMES

Why people pick certain names for animals is another question! In *St. John In Exile* (a favorite video/movie of mine), the Apostle John (played by Dean Jones) is an old man living on the Isle of Patmos. John's cell is a cave. John names the rats in the cave — Caiaphas, Annas, and Pontius Pilate — after Jewish and Roman leaders who hung Jesus on the wooden cross to die. It added splendid humor to the script.

Our pets have included Tabuk, Ruckus and Hey-U. My champion lilac-point Siamese is JaSiDa, meaning "yes, yes, yes" in German, Spanish and Russian. Creativity in naming animals is not uncommon. Consider Edgar Allen Poo for a dog and Zorro for, I assume, a black cat. Anyone remember the 1960s song that went: "Walking my cat named Dog"?

If we develop a relationship with an animal we tend to name it. In her book, *Naming the Animals,* Adrian Room says,

> *So because animals play such an important role in our lives, we give them names, just as we give names to the*

children who are born into our families. Well, not in quite the same way, since we are often less inhibited, more adventurous, when it comes to the naming of animals.[74]

The only animals we avoid naming are those we intend to eat. It's difficult to kill anything or person you've come to know by name. (Military trainers know that killing an enemy is difficult when that enemy ceases to be a nameless, faceless entity.) Farmers may name their milk cows, but not steers meant for the butcher. Few people have "the stomach" to eat an animal they have raised and named. "Boy, doesn't Sweetpea taste good," just isn't palatable to people with any conscience! Isn't that interesting? We are all descendants of Adam.

HUMANS AND ANIMALS RESPOND TO NAMES

To be nameless and ignored is to be a non-person or valueless. Animals, like people, react to this. They know when they are not valued and behave accordingly. Animals who are called by name, who are spoken to and listened to, behave differently.

This is demonstrated in humans as well. Some homeless people go for years without being touched or called by name — with attendant depression. According to letters to Ann Landers, women whose husbands never use their given names feel neglected and unimportant. Lovers enjoy speaking the name of their beloved. A teenager grows giddy when the "first love" calls him or her by name. Yet is crushed if the object of his or her affection doesn't even know his or her name.

When someone remembers our name, we usually feel special. Politicians, salespersons, and teachers know this. We are all called names — given names, nicknames, bad names, good names. "Names" can include titles, like lawyer, mother, friend. (It's better than being ignored.) Our self-worth and identity are often tied up in our name.

Animals learn the names we give them. My Gretchen knew Samson's name and would go find him on command. This tells me animals perceive themselves as persons. "Naming" cements a relationship with the animal. Naming becomes the vital communication which connects you with the animal. Animal trainers and experts agree, the more you "call an animal by name," the more you discover the animal's intelligence and worth. Here we find more keys to the answer to Mom's question.

The first task God gave Adam, after the glorious creation, was to keep God's garden. [Genesis 2:15] The second task, closely related to the first, was to name the animals. In this slim verse, much is said. In her book, *Adam's Task; Calling the Animals by Name*, animal trainer Vicki Hearne discusses what it means philosophically to name an animal. I found her statements profound:

> *...when God first created the Earth He gave Adam and Eve "dominion over the fish of the sea, ... the fowl of the air, and over every living thing ..." Adam gave names to the creatures, and they all responded ... without objection, since in this dominion to command and to recognize were one action. There was no gap between the ability to command and the full of knowledge of the personhood of the being so commanded. Nature came when called, and came the first time, too, without coaxing, nagging or tugging.*[75]

The Lord had Adam call His animals by name. Adam was cemented in relationship with those first animals, don't you think?

THAT FIRST "NAMING PARTY" IN EDEN

Imagine, if you will, the scene in the Garden of Eden as Adam named the animals. Creation sparkled with freshness and newness. The very air felt charged with God's fragrant presence. The energy of creation must have hung in the atmosphere like the aftermath of a lightning storm. Imagine the intoxicating perfumes of the flowers and fruit. The beauty of the new earth and sky must have been incredible.

Adam had a veritable feast for all his senses. No discord, evil, or death existed in the Garden of Eden. Harmony reigned in all the diversity of pristine creation. Life was green and strong! Perfect creation reflected the pure unadulterated image of the Creator — God who is love, light, peace, wisdom, joy, and life! This is the setting in which the Lord brought the first animals for Adam to name. It was party time!

Young animals are full of curiosity and play. Having watched my own animals lovingly groom each other and then tease one another into play activities, makes me think this naming party was joyous. I imagine it filled with the melodious sounds. The calls, cries, and music of every creature from the crickets to the mastodons trying out their new voices, was surely glorious. It must have been a huge romp of animals frolicking in the sheer joy of living, accompanied by birds, bats, and insects cavorting in the air on new wings. Animals have good noses, so each had their own pleasant aroma. Each one explored the whole new Garden, enjoying new smells, tastes, sights and sounds for themselves. Fun sport — a party!

A puppy, kitten, pony or other young animal is so full of trust, curiosity, and play. We can imagine Adam being both amazed and entertained by those first animals. What an adventure of discovery. Remember the first time you touched the velvet soft nose of a horse or looked in the beautiful brown eyes of a deer? Touching the lizard's strangely cool and smooth skin is very different from burying your hands in the lanolin-rich wool of a sheep. Adam's eyes must have "popped" at the splendid colors of the tiny hummingbird in contrast to the huge dark condor. The grass-sweet smell of a cow's breath is not unpleasant, but I wonder what the skunk smelled like before the Fall?

As humans and animals became acquainted with their new selves, with one another, and with Eden, their sense of discovery, coupled with good will, must have been wondrous to see. Wouldn't you love to go back in time to join them? I would! God found it very good indeed. (Gen. 1:31) And so did Adam.

What a brilliant way to introduce newly-created Adam to the whole animal creation. What a clever way to begin the relationship between man and animals.

NAMING ESTABLISHES RELATIONSHIP

Did God wish Adam to develop a relationship with each animal?

In Bible times, naming a person or thing was an important event. Look in any Bible dictionary or history of the Hebrew people and the Near East; there you will find a section on names. Much thought and prayer went into the naming of Hebrew babies.[76] The belief was that names revealed the character and nature of the one being named. Names were often picked by a person in authority.

Names usually had meaning. Many times the name signified position, function, or relationships. Sometimes it was chosen prophetically, such as Jesus or Yeshua which means "The Lord Saves." [Matt. 1:21; Luke 1:31] Or the name may have related to a circumstance of birth. For example, Jacob means "heel catcher" or "supplanter," since he came out of his mother's womb holding the heel of his twin, Esau. [Gen. 25:26]

Naming is still important in most cultures. Americans tend to pick names for sound or association, more than for meaning. Most parents everywhere carefully choose their child's name. A person's name may influence his or her character, calling, and destiny because of the power of words. ("Jean" means "gift of God" — which I strive to be.) After all, being called names, like "stupid" or "smart" influences children strongly.

In the Bible, the Lord sometimes gives a person a new name when that person enters a covenant relationship with Him. A covenant signals a major life change or a change in the character of that person. Abram (exalted father) became Abraham (father of a multitude). His wife, Sarai (contentious) became Sarah (princess). Jacob was renamed Israel (he who strives with God). Jesus gave Simon (hearing) the additional name of Peter (rock). A friend of mine told me about a cabdriver, who after becoming a Christian legally changed his name from "Sin" to "Christianson."

Walking my dogs some years ago, I was approached by a boy who wanted to pet them. Mike (not his real name) was poor and lived in a rundown house nearby. (I added the boy to my prayer list.) He joined me on my daily walks with the dogs and he and I became friends. During one of our walks, Mike informed me that their family dog's name was Satan. It shocked me anyone would name their animal for the Devil. Such an evil name! I don't know who named the dog, but the name disturbed me. The name chosen for their dog demeaned the dog, and revealed their self-image. Satan lived with them and their lives were hell. The dog's name symbolized how they believed.

Mike told me his father was an abusive alcoholic. (Mike admitted he was afraid of the brutal man.) That belief translated into action in the father. Thank God, Mike was making an effort to escape the poverty of mind and body. He attended a good church and sought out good friends like Mom and me. Not long after we met, Mike's father shot himself in front of his family. While his father's suicide was a horrible thing, within a few months, Mike and his family were free of the terrible abuse and their lives quickly improved.

We lost track of Mike. His family moved and so did we. I've often wondered what became of Mike (and his dog). What a contrast Mike's life was to the peace and love that Mom and I knew with our animals. Samson brought sunlight into our home and hearts. JaSiDa daily reminds me the promises of God are "yes!" There's something significant about names we bear and choose.

There is some God-given inclination within us that prompts us to name our animals. We are all sons and daughters of Adam. God wished the animals to be named, and His wishes are programmed into our consciousness. Like Adam, the names we choose reflect the value we place on each animal. It also reflects the value we place on ourselves and things around us.

What sort of meanings did those first names hold? How and why did Adam picks the names. Did he name them to identify species and families of animals, or did he give them individual names? Or both? In picking a name, did Adam focus on a character quality or other trait, or a circumstance reminding him of the animal? I wish we knew. The Lord knew that naming something gives it worth. It's a piece of the puzzle to answer Mom's question.

ADAM AND THE FIRST ANIMALS

What were those first animals like? What relationship did Adam form with the animals? What happened at that "naming party?" Lacking eyewitnesses, we rely on other evidence. All we have is the Bible and traditions. We can glean enough to reconstruct a bit of the scene. (This is where my legal training becomes useful.) Bear with me as we make a case.

The few things we glean include: all were vegetarian; communication between species, including man, was uninhibited; love was the golden rule, as God walked among them daily.

EAT YOUR VEGETABLES!

"Eat your vegetables," was the admonition from the beginning — even broccoli. From Scripture, we learn that man and beast began as vegetarians. God told Adam that plants were for food for man and animals. [Gen. 1:29-30] From tiny plankton to trees which provide fruit, nuts, leaves, bark and wood, plants still provide the "staff of life" for the animal kingdom. Flesh-eating may not have occurred until after the Great Flood of Noah. [Gen. 9] There is a promise that carnivorous behavior will end in the new creation, or Heaven. [Isaiah 11]

Science may look at prehistoric bones but they can only guess what early animals were like physically. Without the ability to time-travel, it remains a guess. Also, bones cannot tell us about intelligence, character traits, or social structures of the first animals. Studying living animals may or may not give an accurate portrait of how their ancestors were in Eden. Reconstructing the past is as risky as predicting the future. Otherwise different juries hearing the same case after an appeal would reach the same verdict. But they rarely do.

LEFTOVERS

It is difficult to imagine what the pre-Fall earth was like. Eden, the Garden of God, must have been heaven on earth. In Hebrew, Eden means *delight* or *pleasure*. What most of us have known in this life as delight or pleasure would fall far short of Eden. The image that comes to me is arriving very late for a lavish banquet. The master chef's artistry is demolished. Only leftovers are strewn about the table in disarray. The freshness and beauty are gone. Decay has entered the banquet room. It doesn't even smell as good. That's what the earth is like now. Our view of Eden is skewed.

Patterned after heaven, the first Eden knew no decay, pain or death. [Rev. 21:4] No cruelty or corruption of character marred that place. Man and animal were perfect in beauty and health, as well as temperament. Total peace and harmony ruled.

Even now in its fallen state, some of earth's wilderness areas reveal harmony and incredible peace. The premise of "survival of the fittest" is a lie. I have experienced that peace and harmony in wilderness areas where humans had not been in years. Entering a deep forest or gazing upon glaciated mountains garlanded with ice and dancing streams, I have felt the same quiet awe that I feel in worship services with believers. A calm peace exists there seldom felt in areas filled with humans. Such harmony is not available anywhere among men, except where the Lord God is worshipped. Perhaps it is because creation — except humans — willingly worships our Creator.

Untouched by human cruelty, wilderness animals are usually unafraid and often exhibit sensibilities unlike those dulled by cruelty and other vices of man. Consider Charles Darwin's words:

> *No man can stand in the tropic forests without feeling that they are temples filled with the various productions of the God of nature, and that there is more in man than the breath of his body.*[77]

The Bible says in the beginning, the new earth was watered in the morning by a mist. A cool breeze blew in the evenings. God and man walked together. [Gen. 2:6 & 8] Don't you know the animals trailed along? Dogs, cats, horses, birds, elephants, kangaroos, monkeys and meerkats joined God and man in fellowship. Mine treat me that way.

What beauty they shared. Eden provided a feast for the eyes, a symphony for the ears, a delight to the nose and palette, and a sensory tapestry to touch. But the king and queen of pleasures must have been the sweet fellowship between God and Adam, and between Adam and the animals.

TALKING ANIMALS?

From ancient times, people have believed the first animals could talk, think, feel and make moral choices. Have you ever spoken to an animal and swore it understood you? Or had it understand without a word from you! Most animal lovers have.

That's not crazy. Why would books, movies and television programs featuring talking animals, from *Babe* and *The Horse Whisperer* to the old "Francis the talking mule" movies, and *Mr. Ed* on TV be so popular? Whether Adam spoke the language of the animals, or the animals could speak like men, there is something to this legend.

Parables, myths, and fables dating back thousands of years have animals talking among themselves and to humans. All animals evidence communication skills, even if primarily nonverbal. Given the differences in how we are made, it is a challenge to know if and when they are communicating, let alone what.

From the growl of bears to the dance of the honeybees, all living creatures appear to communicate. In fact, animal behaviorists are discovering they not only communicate, but have complex social structures.[78] Wouldn't you think that "complex social structures" require communication skills? The "language" may be primarily body language with a mix of sounds, but that can be very effective.

This is no surprise to most animal owners. All of my animals, from cats to dogs to horses to cows to geese, have understood me when I spoke to them. They clearly read body language — both mine and that of other animals. That is the common experience of all animal observers. The fact is, animals are remarkably good at understanding humans.

Brad and Sherrie Steiger instigated an experiment using human language with their Labrador Retriever, Moses. Moses developed a remarkable understanding of human language.[79]

The Steigers learned that silent-movie producer, J. Allen Boone, read daily to the famed German shepherd, Strongheart (first major dog movie star). Thus the Steigers daily read the Bible to Moses and said a prayer with him. They spoke to Moses as though he were a child rather than a "dumb animal." Soon Moses did exactly as he was told even when there was no voice inflection or physical motion from the owners. The Steigers kept records. They concluded the dog understood English conversations and could problem-solve.

Perhaps Moses inspired the Steigers' collection of animal intelligence and communication stories. A favorite of mine is the account of a small girl who climbed into the pen of a supposedly dangerous rhino. The child achieved instant communication — something no other human had ever done — causing the huge rhino to become "a love rag" in her hands.[80]

HORSE TALK

From his youth, Monty Roberts studied wild horses in Nevada, and from them learned the language of horses.[81] A master at it, he has used these techniques to effectively and gently train roping, gaming, and race horses, as well as other animals. He calls himself a horse *gentler*, not a horse *breaker*.

Roberts' philosophy and life experience in "joining up" with horses, deer, and other animals excites me. It matches my own amateur experience. Through gentleness, humans can become a productive team with animals. If asked to do so, such animals will injure or kill themselves to please their human masters. Cruelty breaks an animal's spirit, resulting in a poor slave rather than a working companion. Man working in partnership with an animal is one of the most beautiful things in the world.

Monty Roberts and those like him, have proven beyond a doubt that animals have a language and will work willingly with humans when humans understand and treat them properly. Monty Roberts (who is endorsed by the Queen of England) and Buck Brannaman have both influenced modern horse training for the better. Brannaman, another "horse gentler,"[82] became a consultant for the movie, *The Horse Whisperer.* Their work provides insights into how professional trainers view horses. Roberts holds seminars to instruct in the language of horses.

LOVE IN THE GARDEN OF EDEN

I can see Adam developing a personal relationship with each animal — learning their likes and dislikes, character traits, strengths and talents, with each personality becoming dear to him. The first animals, fresh from the Creator's hand, would have been full of love. Can't you see Adam, caretaker of the earth, spending time with each animal? How they must have loved one another, this first man and these first animals.

This is not so strange. Besides forming bonds with domestic animals, we hear stories of trainers and naturalists bonding with lions, gorillas, and other animals they train or study. There are well publicized accounts, like Elsie the lion, Koko the gorilla, Dian Fossey's wild gorillas, as well as Namu the killer whale. Those who observed these animals, knew them as sentient beings — as *personalities* who gave and received affection. The shadows of Adam and the Garden fall long!

ST. FRANCIS OF ASSISI

In the person of St. Francis of Assisi, church history perhaps provides the closest example to what Adam had with animals. Born in Italy in 1182 A.D., Francis converted to Christianity as a young man. He was faithful in his spiritual journey until his passing in 1226. Founder of the Franciscan order in the Roman Catholic church, St. Francis is one of the most loved and pivotal figures in Christian history. His prayer which begins "Make me an instrument of Thy peace," is frequently repeated today in word and song.

Of importance here, was Francis' relationship with animals. St. Francis developed his relationship with animals when he spent time in woods and fields, sleeping on the ground. To him, both animals and man belonged to God and were loved by their Creator. His was a democratic faith, which treated man and beast alike. He called animals "brother" and "sister."

Legend has it that Francis' first congregation consisted of a flock of birds. Seeing a gathering of a large number of birds of different varieties, Francis began to preach. More birds came. The birds remained motionless, even as he moved among them and touched them. Francis told the birds that they owed much to God since they had the freedom to fly, wonderful and colorful clothing, food without work, and the ability to sing. He discussed their preservation in Noah's ark and the environment which was theirs to enjoy. His sermon allegedly ended:

> *So the Creator loves you very much, since He gives you so many good things. Therefore, my little bird sisters, be careful not to be ungrateful, but strive always to praise God." [The birds began to] spread their wings, and reverently bow their heads to the ground, showing by their movements and their songs that the words St. Francis was saying gave them great pleasure. ... Finally, when he had finished preaching to them and urging them to praise God, St. Francis . . . gave them permission to leave. Then all the birds rose up into the air simultaneously, and in the air they sang a wonderful song.*[83]

While there is no way to confirm or deny this story, there is some evidence of similar experiences today. Entertainer Pat Boone wrote in one of his books that crickets joined him one evening as he sang praises on his parents' porch in Tennessee. As a professional musician, Mr. Boone would know when the random cricket "songs" changed to harmonize with his vocalization.

I have seen my own pets respond to the Gospel. During prayer meetings, my late Siamese "Kitty," acted as though she were in catnip when we sang praises to God. She did the same thing when I sang in the spirit alone. She also came to me for prayer when injured or ill. "Let everything that has breath praise the Lord!" is a Scripture which says more than most folks realize. [Ps. 150:6]

Another favorite story of St. Francis concerns a large wolf which was terrorizing an Italian town, eating both humans and animals. Unafraid, Francis went to find the wolf.[84] Upon finding the animal, Francis admonished the wolf about terrorizing this town, whereupon the wolf cowed at his feet in sorrow. After they reached an agreement, the wolf walked back into town with Francis. The frightened townspeople were introduced to the wolf by St. Francis. The people agreed to feed the wolf and the wolf never hurt anyone again. Due to St. Francis' intervention, the wolf lived as friend to the townsmen until it died several years later. To this day, there are images of a wolf connected to the town of Gubbio, Italy. The Scripture, "Blessed are the peacemakers for they shall be called sons of God" [Matt. 5:9] takes on a new meaning, doesn't it?

Another report involves St. Anthony of Padua (ca. 1195-1231), an associate of St. Francis.[85] Unsuccessful in trying to convince persons in the town of Rimini of the true faith, Anthony went to the mouth of the nearby river. There he called to the fishes in God's name since the faithless Rimini heretics refused to listen to the word of God.

> *And as soon as he said that, all of a sudden such a great throng of large and small fishes gathered before him as had never before been seen in that sea or river.* [86]

The idea of these fish with their heads out of the water looking at Anthony — big fish beside the small fish, without any disturbance — seems unreal. Once they were gathered, Anthony preached to them in a fashion similar to Francis with his birds. He reminded them of the greatness of their freedom, provision, and privileges from God their creator. He referred to the Bible, which states that a great fish rescued Jonah the prophet. Another fish offered tribute money for our Lord Jesus. Still others became food for Jesus, the Eternal King. At these words, the fish opened their mouths and nodded their heads, giving signs of their reverence. When the townspeople of Rimini came and saw the fish, they listened to Anthony and repented. Anthony dismissed the fishes, which all swam away, "expressing their joy and applause in amazing games and gambols."[87]

REAL AND COUNTERFEIT COMMUNICATION

Some claim to have the ability to communicate with animals

nonverbally or telepathically today.[88] In reading various accounts — knowing the gifts of the Holy Spirit [1 Cor. 14] — I know God could give people the ability to know an animal's mind or memory. He does that in gifts of healing for people. I am not alone in "knowing" things about animals which appear to be beyond normal observation.

At the same time, I am skeptical when such abilities appear to be based in occult or ESP practices. These are counterfeits of the Lord's spiritual gifts and are prohibited by Scripture. It can be challenging to verify which are godly and which are not.

I have no doubt that we could have some like St. Francis and St. Anthony among us today — gifted in understanding animals' own languages. Not all of that "gifting" is supernatural. Most animal-human communication just requires intelligent observation to learn how the animals communicate, and to teach the animals what we are saying, too.

Was Adam able to commune with the animals more than St. Francis, St. Anthony or Monty Roberts? His God-given job was to care for them. God surely gave Adam natural and supernatural abilities to understand and care for each different species.

JOHN WESLEY'S THEOLOGY

John Wesley was an Anglican priest and forefather of Methodism. Wesley believed God endued animals with innate principles of self-motion, understanding, will, and liberty (freedom of choice) just the same as man, although perhaps in different degrees. Wesley believed animals possess moral goodness and are beautiful, and that animals were created immortal.[89]

Wesley further believed that only man is "capable of God," that is, of knowing, loving and obeying God. Animals, on the other hand know, obey and love God through knowing, obeying and loving man. That was his explanation of why, when Adam sinned, all creation was subject to the penalty.[90]

Scripture and human experience do *not* bear out the idea that God and animals communicate only through man.[91] The ravens who fed Elijah surely got their orders directly from the Lord. [1 Kings 17]

Nonetheless, many of Wesley's ideas appear sound. Men and animals communicated in the Garden, as Adam and Eve conversed with a serpent. [Gen. 3]. Man was made steward over all creation, therefore, his garden and the animals will only thrive if he is a good steward. Man is the primary channel of blessing to the whole creation, as well as a major channel of neglect and destruction. Man's fall from grace affected the whole earth. Wesley is not alone in his beliefs. That is pretty much universally believed.

PURPOSE ACCOMPLISHED

Adam came into a vital relationship with every animal at the first naming party. The Lord wisely accomplished His purpose. Man was established as a steward over all living things, plants and animals.

To communicate is to establish a relationship. The more you communicate with someone, the more intimately you know them and they you. The same is true of animals. That is why when you have a pet for many years, its death is a very painful loss. Relationship is the foundation for love.

God saw to it that man and animals could have relationships. Adam's relationship with those first animals must have been awesome. Since sin had not yet entered the world, nothing was "wild" in the sense of being an enemy to humans or to other animals. There was no disorder, no confusion. Nothing killed nor ate each other. The lion lay down with the lamb, and the ox and bear ate grass together. When God walked the earth in the cool of the evening, I'll bet Adam was not the only one who sought out the company of the Creator. Those loving animals would likely not be left out! Mine sure get pushy to be with me. What a frolic! What a delightful pleasure!

Everything that had breath praised the Lord and rejoiced in God's goodness and His gifts. Wonderful peace and harmony existed in all creation. It was the Garden of Eden — the Paradise we lost.

CHAPTER 7

THE FALL OF MAN AND THE ANIMALS

And the Lord God took the man and put him in the garden of Eden to tend and keep it. And the Lord God commanded the man, saying, "Of every tree of the garden you may freely eat; but of the tree of the knowledge of good and evil you shall not eat, for in the day that you eat of it you shall surely die."

Gen. 2:15-17 [NKJ]

So when the woman saw that the tree was good for food, that is was pleasant to the eyes, and a tree desirable to make one wise, she took of its fruit and ate. She also gave to her husband with her, and he ate.

Gen. 3:6 [NKJ]

"Cursed is the ground for your sake; In toil you shall eat of it all the days of your life. ... In the sweat of your face you shall eat bread till you return to the ground, For out of the ground you were taken; for dust you are, and to dust you shall return." ... Also for Adam and his wife [Eve] the Lord God made tunics of skin, and clothed them. ... the Lord God sent him out of the garden of Eden to till the ground from which he was taken.

Gen. 3:17, 19, 21, 22[NKJ]

THE BIBLE IS BLOODY

Some people avoid the Bible because of the bloodshed. From cover to cover it is a book bloody with slain animals. It starts immediately after the fall when God Himself clothes Adam and Eve with animal skins. Blood flows freely through the pages of the Bible. The Bible clearly records events, such as the dedication of Solomon's temple, when hundreds and even thousands, of animals were ritually killed. [1 Kings 8:62-63; 2 Chronicles 7:4-5, for example.] Thousands of bulls, goats, and sheep were sacrificed and their blood poured on the altar. The priests and Levites, no doubt, stood ankle-deep in blood and gore within the Lord's temple complex. It must have been a nauseous experience to anyone not hardened to blood and death.

Why would a loving God require the lives of innocent, sweet-natured animals? Animal sacrifice — and the Bible has a lot of that — seems very cruel. To answer Mom's question, we must address this seemingly impossible question. In the next two chapters, we will do so.

A LICENSE FOR CRUELTY?

God's command for animal sacrifices has been misconstrued as a license for cruelty to animals. Too often such cruelty is justified by using Scripture. This, in turn, has offended many animal lovers, and caused them to turn away from the Bible and its God.

What sort of God requires the lives of countless innocent animals? What kind of God allows human cruelties to animals? As I prayed about this, this thought occurred to me. If a person who knew nothing of modern medicine watched a surgeon performing open heart surgery, wouldn't that uninformed person think the doctor brutally cruel?

Our ignorance of God and His ways clouds our judgment in the same way. Some people never get beyond the slaughter to know the truth. What good reason would the God who is Love, have to require the bloodshed of innocent animals? Keeping an open mind, let's explore what the Bible says.

ADAM'S DISOBEDIENCE

What does this have to do with Mom's question, you may ask? "How relevant is this to whether my dog or cat will be in heaven?" In the seeds of Genesis are the hidden images of the heaven and earth to come. Key pieces of the puzzle which answers Mom's question are in these first short chapters of the Bible.

To understand God and the role of animals, we must examine Adam's disobedience. Everything on earth changed with Adam's disobedience. We need to understand what was lost to know what may be regained in heaven. Read this in Genesis Chapters 2 and 3.

We must know where we came from to understand where we are heading. We don't get to heaven by accident. We must learn *how* to get to heaven. Besides, we appreciate most those things we had to take action to obtain.

DON'T EAT – DON'T DIE

Let's look closely at this first drama. God had given Adam — male and female — one job: care for this garden earth. God gave one command, the first law: don't eat from one tree or you will die that very day.

A simple command. Adam could eat anything they wanted from any tree except one — the tree of the knowledge of good and evil. Would you find that hard to obey? (I'm not sure about me. I like to think I'm a good, basically obedient type person, but I've done too many ornery or stupid things.) We already know the variety offered was endless. Why is the one forbidden thing so attractive?

THE WILY SERPENT

> *Now the serpent was more subtle* and *crafty than any living creature of the field which the Lord God had made. And he [Satan] said to the woman, Can it really be that God has said, You shall not eat of every tree of the garden?*
>
> Gen. 3:1[Amplified]

Among the animals there lived a certain snake — a very wise and crafty beast. We will talk more about him later on. He's mentioned in Revelation 12:9-13, 15-17; Isa. 27:1; Ps. 74:14; 104:26; & Job 41. He was created to be "king over all the sons of pride." [Job 41:34] Legend has it that this Serpent had legs on which he walked about and he was very beautiful. Legend also has it that this Serpent was a real fast talker.

This con artist snake questioned Eve about the forbidden fruit. She listened. There was no reason not to trust this intelligent animal — unless "crafty" is a clue. Newly created, this woman had no experience of deceit. Because of the snake's subtle questions, the woman's understanding of God's simple command became twisted. It still happens today.

> *And the woman said to the serpent, "... from the fruit of the tree which is in the middle of the garden, God has said, 'You shall not eat from it or touch it, lest you die.'"*
>
> Gen. 3:2-3 [NASV]

Eve made a fatal mistake. She added to and took away from God's command. She added "touch it" and took away the "surely," the certainty of death. [Compare Gen. 2:17 with Gen. 3:3.] That paved the way for what followed. The woman began to examine the forbidden fruit. (There's a difference between healthy curiosity and unhealthy curiosity.) Eve found the forbidden fruit attractive. It was gourmet food, delightful to look at and desirable to make one wise. Can't you hear her brain work: "What could it hurt to take one little bite?"

That lying serpent persuaded the First Couple that the forbidden Tree of the Knowledge of Good and Evil was a good thing. It would make them like God! [Gen. 3:1-5]

Neither human did anything about the snake's distortion of the truth. The man knew God's command. He stood by and did nothing. Rather than dealing with the snake and confronting the woman, he joined his woman in eating the fruit. Perhaps it seemed easier. Perhaps both were seduced by the promise of power.

Knowledge is power. Our ancestor rejected his Creator to attempt being his own god. How foolish to think we can become "like God." We are created; God is the un-created Creator. God has all power, all wisdom, all understanding; he is the source of all knowledge. My chair cannot become me, and I cannot become God. Adam and Eve fell for it. They disobeyed the first law. They choose to eat the forbidden fruit.

FALL OF MAN

Theologians refer to Adam's disobedience, his sin, as the "Fall of Man." This Fall resulted in immediate changes. First, Adam and his wife became ashamed and confused. Anyone who covers their private parts with tree leaves is clearly shamed and confused.

Second, major fear flooded Adam and Eve. They hid from God, the only Being Who both loved them and could help them.

Third, Adam lied to God. God knows everything we think, do, and say, even before we do or say it — and loves us anyway.

Fourth, Adam, man and woman, rationalized their mistakes by passing the blame. The man blamed God for giving him the woman, then blamed the woman for giving him the fruit. Blaming God takes either a lot of guts or little sense. (I vote for the "little sense.") The woman had no one else to blame but the snake. Neither confessed their own complicity.

A CHANGED WORLD

The day Adam and Eve took a bite of the forbidden fruit, the world changed. We still live with the consequences. Because God assigned Adam (male and female) dominion over all the earth, everything under Adam's authority went down with him in a sense. When man sinned, all of creation was subjected to "futility." (Rom. 8:20) Theologians agree a proverbial Pandora's box of good and evil was opened.

All creation is connected — ask any biologist. Adam's fall set off a chain reaction felt to this day. Adam's sin affected the land and all living creatures under man's dominion. Kill the trees, insects die; kill the insects, birds die; kill the birds, carnivores die. Everything we do affects others. It's the ripple effect — just as a stone thrown in a pond sends ripples to the shore. Good deeds help others. Evil deeds produce grief and pain.

For instance, when someone commits a crime, or when married couples break their marriage vows and abuse each other and/or divorce, they affect all around them. Their families (adults, children, and animals), finances, and employment suffer; they are all altered, even shattered. Consequently their community, state, and nation are affected. Studies have proven this, if you need studies. Adam and Eve's sin infected all human offspring and the whole earth, in a tidal wave that only the Creator could stop.

DEATH CAME THROUGH ADAM'S DISOBEDIENCE

In the day Adam ate the forbidden fruit, death came. God saw it arrive, riding Adam's disobedience. Like a parent watching his child fall into a fire, it was a terrible thing to behold. Like a fire in a wind storm, it spread to all creation — to all the things God referred to as "very good." Death's effect would impact all under Adam's authority. [Romans 8:20-21.] This sin entered Adam's essence; all Adam's offspring have this fatal tendency to sin. [Romans 6]

Imagine what happened to the Garden. The darkness of disobedience and death flooded the Garden. It permeated everything. Like an evil fog it continues to cover this earth. Because we were born into that fog we cannot know what was lost. We truly see through darkened glass only a shadow of what was. And what will be. [1 Cor. 13:12]

While the animals were innocent — except for that crafty serpent — the Fall brought death to them, too. They were affected by Adam's sin, yet not by their own choice or will. But we all experience the effects of sins of others, don't we?

GOD'S LAW AND ORDER

Adam's disobedience to God's commandment, or law, brought forewarned consequences — *death*. God is holy and just. He is the source of all law, of all that is good. Law is holy and good. [Rom. 7:12, 16; 1 Tim. 1:8] Without it, there are anarchy, chaos, and death. This principle is illustrated in history and science. God's Word is His law.

To understand the Fall we need a look at the nature of God's laws. I see two types of laws operating in nature. The first type is immutable or unchangeable. The second is variable. I believe both operate from God's being.

UNCHANGEABLE LAWS

The Bible says God does not change. [Malachi 3:6] The immutable or unchangeable laws originate in God's very substance or being, and His nature or character. These laws cannot change.

The Bible describes His substance. For example: (1) God is the Rock. [Deut. 32:15; Isa. 26:4; 1 Pet. 2:8]. (2) He is breath, and Spirit, and the Divine Wind (same word — different meanings). [Gen. 1:2; Job 33:4; John 3:5-8 & 4:24] (3) God is light. [Ps. 27:1; John 1:9 & 8:12; James 1:17] We see these as the laws of science or nature. Rocks, wind, and light all involve physical laws which are constants.

Looking at just one physical attribute is a lesson: God "dwells in unapproachable light" and God *is* light with no darkness in Him at all. [Ex. 33:20; 1 Tim. 6:16; James 1:17; 1 John 1:5.] He is also a consuming fire. [Heb. 12:29] This explains why the Bible warns that no mortal flesh can see God and live. No travel agent books vacations to the sun. Fire consumes flesh — a painful experience at best. Obviously, if you and I are to fellowship closely with God, we must be changed.

All immutable laws, like those of light, emanate from God's being, nature, or substance. These are the foundations of physical laws of energy, matter, and velocity — as well as spiritual laws governing character and behavior.

God's nature or character is also unchangeable. For example: (1) He cannot lie. [Num. 23:19] (2) He cannot be unfaithful. [1 Tim. 2:13) (3) Since God is love, it follows that He cannot be unloving. [1 John 4: 8 & 16] (4) God's Spirit is Wisdom, so God cannot be unwise or foolish. [Isa. 11:1 & Prov. 8:12]

Just as the leopard cannot change his spots, God cannot change — or He wouldn't be God. The Living God is the source of all immutable laws.

CHANGEABLE LAWS

The second kind of law may be changed. This type of law comes from God's will, His mind, or heart. For examples consider these: (1) When God was going to destroy the whole earth and one man, Noah, caused Him to change His plan. [Gen. 6] (2) Abraham almost talked God out of destroying Sodom and Gommorah, where his nephew Lot lived. [Gen. 19:16-33] (3) When Moses was leading the Hebrew people from Egyptian slavery to freedom in Canaan, Moses was alone with God on the mountain receiving God's Law, the Commandments. The Lord interrupted their meeting and told Moses the people made and were worshiping a gold calf. Like a husband finding his wife in bed with another, God was furious. He decided to destroy them and start over. Moses talked God out of this plan. God changed his mind. [Ex. 32.1-14] God can change His mind or will. Intercessors — what some call "prayer warriors" — know that. So did Balaam's donkey. It's a heart thing.

COMPARING THE TWO LAWS

To illustrate, consider a parent disciplining a child about fire's dangers. Dad says, "Child, fire is hot. If you touch the fire, it will burn you." If the child disobeys, he or she is burned. Dad may add: "Play with that fire, and I will punish you." It's easy to see the difference.

The second kind of rules or laws train and protect. "Love" without limits is not love at all. Every child will test a parent, teacher, or other person in authority, to see where the limits are. Security lies within those limits. Most children and animals sense that.

Smart parents don't easily change such rules. Compromise sends the wrong message — the message that laws and rules may be disobeyed. Good parents do not compromise the law. Most criminals believe they will succeed in crime. They probably became destructive lawbreakers because they got away with wrongdoing as children. God is a smart parent. He knows and disciplines those He loves. [Heb. 12]

WHICH LAW FITS THE FIRST COMMANDMENT?

The Bible is not clear whether the commandment about the

tree of knowledge was based on an immutable law or God's will. Personally, I think it was a mix: Like the kid playing with fire, Adam got burned, so the punishment was built in. But there were elements of God's will in this first commandment which permitted God to act mercifully, out of His will or mind.

The Commandment was: In "the day" Adam ate the forbidden fruit, he would "die." (Adam had no "temporary insanity" defense.) Genesis 3:22 says God has the knowledge of good and evil. Evidently that knowledge can be as lethal as fire. When Adam ate the fruit, he took a destructive fire into his flesh. (This fiery knowledge also acts as a preprogrammed conscience.) Adam was not ready to handle such knowledge, any more than an infant can handle fire. Fire and knowledge can be killers as well as forces of good.

Sin mastered man. Like a disease, it entered his vital parts. It attached itself to Adam's genetic essence, and began working death in all it touches. A war started. Inside Adam. It spread to all creation. A war of the good and holy against sinful, evil, destructive forces; a battle between of the image of God in us against the serpent's lie.

Many have attempted to describe Eden and the Fall. For example, John Milton, in the 1600s, wrote the epic poem "Paradise Lost." Yet, words are inadequate to describe what living humans have never known. How a rainbow or a rose be described to one born blind? Can you describe the melodies of birds to the deaf? Can you teach numb fingers what a baby's skin or silky feel of llama's wool is like? Can you describe to a man born in a desert what a rain forest smells like? Adam's Fall makes us all blind, deaf, and senseless dead men — lost without the Lord of Life.

WHO OR WHAT WAS THAT SNAKE?

How did that crafty serpent react? I suspect that the first sounds of mocking, devilish laughter were heard in the earth. Like shattering glass, it broke the tranquility of pristine creation. It was a sound heralding disaster. All creation must have given its first long collective groan. [Rom. 8:22; Jer. 12:4 & 11] Who or what was this serpent?

The Bible identifies it as Satan. "*Satan*" is a Hebrew word. It means *adversary*. *Devil* is a Greek word for *slanderer*. These terms have become the crafty reptile's names as he continues to deceive and torment humans. This Devil nearly destroyed Job. [Job, Chapters 1& 2] Jesus called him a liar and the "father of lies." [John 8:44] Satan appears as an angel of light, and his servants appear as righteous. [2 Cor. 11:13-15] Temptation, as Eve and Adam learned, is Satan's key to gain power over humans. [John 8:44; Matt. 4:3; 1 John 2:16] What an animal!

The physical description of this ancient serpent is riveting. We don't know his size in Eden, but the devil is no little, humanoid, red imp with horns and a spear. John, in Revelation 12, saw Satan as a terrifying being of immense size and power. A huge red dragon with seven heads, whose tail could sweep one-third of the stars from heaven. John said Satan has his own angels or messengers, and is "the accuser of the brethren" before God.

Isaiah described him as "leviathan," "the fleeing" and "twisted" serpent and prophesied its final destruction. [Isa. 27:1] The Psalmist said leviathan is many-headed and that it "sports" in the sea. [Psalm 74:14 & Psalm 104:26] God described leviathan to Job as a fierce, mocking beast which men cannot subdue or vanquish; a being which Lord made without fear, like nothing else on earth. This terrible beast is "king over all the sons of pride." [Job 3:8; & 41, especially 41:29 & 33-34]

This describes a being which modern man has no record of seeing in the flesh. Whether fact or metaphor, the description means Satan is a serpent no mere human can control nor defeat.[92]

Only its Creator has more power. (Why the Lord God Almighty, the One who is Love and Truth, would create such a creature is another issue. It is not necessary to Mom's question to address that question here.) The Bible says the devil's role as the deceiver of man will stop only at the end of this age, when Satan will be thrown to doom. [Rev. 20:10] Meanwhile, we must deal with this dangerous animal God's way, or be destroyed — just as Adam and Eve were.

THE EFFECT OF THE FALL ON ANIMALS

What was the reaction of other animals to the deceit of the Serpent, Satan? They were innocent witnesses to the Fall of Adam (including Eve). Satan surely laughed at man's foolishness to believe eating fruit could make man like God. A created thing can never become the un-created Creator. Man cannot **be** God. Did Adam's animal friends hear Satan's mocking laughter? Raucous laughter must have grated in their ears!

Were they ashamed that a fellow animal deceived their human friends? The animals who loved Adam would be bewildered. Man, their master and caretaker had fallen out with God, the Master and Caretaker of all.

I think the animals smelled or felt the terror which overcame Adam as the forbidden knowledge was ingested. Didn't confusion beset the animals, too? Don't you know the same darkness fell over their souls and spirits? Some went wild — never again to trust humans and refusing to submit to man's tarnished authority. Perhaps a few desired to help Adam.

When Adam and Eve turned from each other's nakedness and began the terrible game of hiding, how did it affect the animals? Harmony was replaced with discord. When the man and woman ripped leaves off branches to fashion crude coverings, did the birds in the trees twitter in dismay? When animals are confused or frightened, they tend to fight or flee. In the cool of that fateful day, how terrible it must have been for the animals! What disaster the Lord found when He came to walk with Adam and Eve that evening. [Gen. 3:8]

Surely, pandemonium broke out in the animal kingdom that day. John Wesley said the very foundations of animals' nature were put out of course, turned upside down. We still reap the fruit.

It was horrible, the blackness which descended on hearts of man and beast. Adam hid from and blamed God and Eve for his sin. Eve passed the blame to the serpent. It was the darkest day of history. Sin destroyed the Garden of God.

Animal trainer, Vicki Hearne, surmises a loss of man's authority, an incoherence, which made most animals wild:

> *Then Adam and Eve themselves failed in obedience, and in this story to fail in obedience is to fail in authority.* ***Most of animate creation, responding to this failure, turned pretty irrevocably from human command.*** *The tiger, the wolf and the field mouse as well as, of course, the grasshopper refuse to come when called to recognize our naming. One may say that before the Fall, all animals were domestic, that nature was domestic.* ***After the Fall, wildness was possible, and most creatures chose it, but a few did not.*** *The dog, the horse, the burro, the elephant, the ox and a few others agreed to go along with humanity anyway, thus giving us a kind of second chance to repair our damaged authority, to do something about our incoherence.*[93] (Emphasis supplied)

One act changed the world. A peaceful paradise became a savage jungle — if not instantly, then certainly over time. I recall hearing Ed Cole, a Christian teacher, say that obedience is better than sacrifice, because we can never regain by sacrifice, what we lost by disobedience. A mirror, once broken, is never the same. Virgin creation was raped by man's Fall. Innocence lost is gone forever.

Look around. How lost the Garden of God still is. Man continues to disobey his Creator, still believing he can be his own god. Animals reflect the same wildness and confusion at man's incoherent instability. Full of lies and inconsistent behavior, we are untrustworthy and therefore unloving. The miracle is that dogs still choose to love and be faithful to us.

WHAT COULD BE DONE?

If Adam's Fall took all creation down, what could be done? It looks to me like God was in a fix. While the Fall appears to be catastrophic, the Bible's God was not wringing his hands in despair. Disappointed, yes. Without alternative plans, no.

God plans ahead. He did have a plan B (and maybe plans C through Z). God's attitude toward His creation never changed. He still loves us all.

So, why didn't God let Adam physically die on the day he ate that fruit of forbidden knowledge? If Adam, both male and female, had suffered a physical death on that fateful day, the Lord's plans would have been thwarted. He made a masterpiece in creating this earth, and man was a lead actor in this work. Adam and Eve had no children yet. Adam was created to become God's kids, His loving family.

The Almighty needed time — time to redeem fallen creation. Man needed time and opportunity to grow up into the kind of lover God made Adam to become. Mature love, like fruit, is produced only by mature persons. The Bible doesn't say love is a "gift" which God gives and suddenly we are lovers. (Except in the sense when you believe in Jesus, and ask Him into your heart to be Lord and Savior He gives you His nature — which is love.) Biblical love is a living thing, like a seed which must be planted and cultivated to produce God's character in us. Keeping love growing is like gardening in a desert; if you don't take care of it consistently, it will wither and die. Study the Bible if you want to check this out.

God's plan was to keep Adam and Eve physically alive for more than a literal, 24-hour day. Being a good Judge, Lawgiver, and King [Isa. 33:22], the Lord provided two kinds of death, spiritual and physical. That both fulfilled the requirements of justice, and gave God's wayward creation time to learn and make better choices. Our gracious God stayed the execution of His lawless humans, until redemption could be accomplished. This stay of execution, however, was not without a price.

DEATH: WHAT DID IT MEAN?

God told Adam that on the day he ate the forbidden fruit he would surely die. Adam had to "burn" in sin's fire. What did "death" mean? When did the first death occur? What was it like?

If you have tried to explain death to a child, you know it's neither easy nor pleasant. Did Adam ask the Lord what the word *die* meant? Sounds like a smart thing to do — before eating what you shouldn't. Did Adam ask such questions? There is no record he or she did.

Adam had no experience of death of any kind before they ate the forbidden fruit. Nothing had died. (Some theologians and scientists argue death must have occurred prior to the fall. To my knowledge, there is no basis for that.) The Bible teaches that death entered the world through sin. [Rom. 5:12 & 1 Cor. 15:20-22] Without sin, there was no death. Until he sinned, Adam could not have had a clue what "die" meant. The earth was fully alive.

How does the Bible define "death," anyway? Scripture teaches it has two meanings: (1) In physical death, the breath or spirit and soul leaves the physical body. [Phil. 1:20-24; Rev. 14:13; also John 5:25 & 1 Tim. 4:1] (2) In spiritual death, you are separated from God, who is Life. Spiritual death comes in two subcategories: the "this life" and "eternal" kinds. Disobedience kills our relationship to God. Some deeds kill like cancer, by degrees; others kill quickly, like massive head injuries. [Eph. 2:1 & 5; also Luke 1:79; 1 John 3:14; Rom. 6:23; John 3:36; & Rev. 2:11]

Since the Fall, all humans suffer both kinds of death. In this life, we are born dead to God, i.e., in relationship. [Eph. 2:1] After this life, the righteous who have physically died will be resurrected to live eternally [Isa. 25:6-8; 26:19; Dan. 12:2; Rev. 20:13], and the wicked to eternal punishment. [Matt. 5:22, 30; 10:28; Mark 9:43-48; Jude 12-16; Rev. 20 & 21] The Bible defines "righteousness" and "wickedness," if you wish to study it.

WHY TWO DEATHS?

Why does "death" have two meanings? I think the Lord is a great lawyer He gave Himself legal options in giving the first commandment. Here is my case for that.

That day of disobedience, Adam had to die or God would be a liar. Some kind of death had to occur when the man and woman bit into the forbidden fruit. God ordained and chose the spiritual death to occur first, for a reason.

Evidences of this spiritual death are that Adam saw his own nakedness; he feared, hid and lied to God. Spiritual death entered Adam as surely as a child who falls into a fire is burned. Most theologians agree. The Apostle Paul understood when he wrote we are all "dead in our transgressions and sins." [Eph. 2:1] Adam and Eve's behavior, described in Genesis Chapter 3, proves they were suddenly separated from God. The relationship between God and Adam was broken. Man withdrew from God. The man renamed the woman, Eve, treating her also as separate from himself, when God still calls us, both male and female, "Adam." [Gen. 5:1-2]

Christians who have a regeneration experience through Jesus Christ, uniformly describe the reversal of spiritual death as coming from darkness to light, from despair to hope, from loneliness to love, from being orphaned to adopted. A sign of this regeneration is an overwhelming love for God and others, even those difficult to love. Many new Christians also usually treat animals better (until they learn some Cartesian theology).

These are but glimpses of what it was like before the Fall. It is impossible, unless God gives supernatural understanding, to imagine the changes sin and death brought to Adam and Eve — and to all creation. To be separated from God is to be separated from all that is good: love, life, light, wisdom, truth, joy, peace, truth — for God *is* the embodiment of these and their source for all His creation.

ON THAT DAY, SOMEONE HAD TO DIE

God's law required a physical death that day. Another law was instituted: the right of substitution. If God was to spare Adam, it would require a substitute to die. While dead spiritually, Adam's physical death could be delayed by a stand-in. Ah! A brilliant solution.

It was the first of many substitutes for man's sin. God provided the substitute sacrifices to spare His children. Is this not a reasonable explanation for what writer of Genesis succinctly recorded:

> *For Adam also and for his wife the Lord God made long coats (tunics) of skins, and clothed them.*
>
> Genesis 3:21. [Amplified]

"Skins" became their clothes. Skins are much different from leaves. God replaced Adam's leaves. Think about it. The word is "skins" — not "wool" or "hair." You do not get "skin" without killing an animal. Notice the word is plural.

More than one animal died. These were Adam's substitutes. The first animal sacrifices. Animals would die in place of Adam and Eve.

Skins are taken off dead animals and tanned into leather. The skin is both the largest organ and, in all warm-blooded animals, the organ with the most nerve endings. The skin is where sense of touch is exhibited. Lovers love to touch and be touched. Hugging, stroking, and kissing are skin activities. To be burned, whipped or skinned alive are cruelest of tortures. To lose your skin, by fire or other means, results in death. Therefore, the merciful always humanely kill an animal before skinning it.

ONE DAY IS AS A THOUSAND YEARS

Adam had to die spiritually *and* physically. One death was immediate, and the other took longer. Adam did die physically on the "day" he and she disobeyed. How? God controls time. The Bible tells us, one day is as a thousand years to the Lord. [Psalm 90:4] The Lord used His time and not earth's to calculate the "day" of Adam's physical death. It was a long day. God planned that option.

Adam would have time to procreate. God could work on man's education and training on how to handle the knowledge of good and evil. The Lord could start to make lovers out of His selfish man-child. Scripture bears this out. Adam and Eve had many children.

But, for two thousand years, those first humans, from Adam to Noah, lived long lives — hundreds of years. Adam died physically at age 930 years. That was within God's "one day." None, not even Methuselah, lived longer than a thousand human years. [Gen. 5]

The effects of Adam's deaths are the subject of numerous sermons and theological works. For example, their spiritual death was also shown in their first sons: Cain murdered Abel. [Gen. 4] We touch on them only as relevant to the answer to Mom's question.

After the Great Flood and Noah, our life span became like today. At age 130, Jacob told Pharaoh his years "were few and unpleasant" and he had not "attained the years that my fathers lived." This apparently surprised that Pharaoh. [Gen. 47:9] Today, it has become more common for people to live beyond one hundred years. However, I find the thought of living hundreds of years almost inconceivable. We don't think eternally, but thank God He does. His plan allowed man to survive. God has hope for the human race.

GOD'S JUSTICE

Why didn't the Lord just forgive and forget? That would mean Adam would never realize the price of unrighteousness, or the price of how our actions affects others. That would not be kind. If the Bible makes anything clear, it is that God is just, holy and righteous. [Jer. 9:24; Ps. 89:14]

In an age where "love" is too often defined as a license to do what we want, and at a time where ethical behavior is thought foolish or irrelevant by too many, it seems necessary to speak a word about justice. As a lawyer, I hope I have gained some understanding of justice, although that is not the key. Proverbs 28:4-5 are clues to the key.

Only evil people hate God's good laws. Love is the foundational law of God, a royal law. [Lev. 19:18; Deut. 6:5; Mark 12:30-31; James 2:8] Justice and righteousness are critical elements which preserve a free society. Without law and order, there is anarchy. In lawlessness, people live in fear and doubt. Neighbors or strangers steal, maim, or kill each other. You keep life, limb and property only as long as you can protect them. "Survival of the fittest" describes anarchy. Law-abiding citizens and good government are essential requisites for a prosperous, secure society. Safety and peace have always had a price in this fallen world.

Real love is just and treats others right. Criminal justice requires the innocent's swift acquittal and the guilty's quick punishment. Civil justice rewards righteous deeds and penalizes unrighteous ones. The apostle Paul recorded: "The wages of sin is death, but the free gift of God is eternal life in Christ Jesus our Lord." [Romans 6:23] Justice is balanced and instructive.

All creation watched to see what God would do with His disobedient humans. If God let man get by with his first offense, what would happen? Wouldn't God be sending a message for all creation "to do your own thing, baby!"? He had to make Adam and Eve an example. Justice required it. Love demanded it on behalf of all Adam's future offspring — and all creation. Mercy tempers justice, so Adam got to live and fulfill his days.

If God meant to redeem man and have redemption "stick," He had to teach the man and woman the cost of sin. They must know and remember it forever. It would be very *unloving* to leave humankind as they were — deceived, ashamed, afraid, liars, and cowardly "buck-passers." God had to address Adam's sin, a killer-cancer to him and all God's creation. The judgment of death had to happen on the very day Adam and Eve took that first bite.

And death did.

ADAM'S SUBSTITUTE

The Bible says in that first 24-hour day, God provided substitutes to bear physical death for Adam. They are called "sacrifices" because it was costly. These were priceless.

This first sacrifice set a precedent. Each sin has required a substitute to stand in for the sinner's life. God has provided many substitute sacrifices since those first ones. Abraham discovered this when God told him to sacrifice his son, Isaac. [Gen.22] Jews offered lambs, kids and bulls to God until the destruction of the temple in Jerusalem about 65 A.D. These were a foretaste of the sacrifice of God's own Son, Jesus of Nazareth, some 2000 years ago.

Which precious animals — ones God made and Adam named — died because of Adam's sin? Imagine the Lord having to choose the sacrifices as Adam and Eve watched. Other animals must have been there. Animals love to be with us, and I'm sure they loved to be with the Lord. As the Lord God stroked the animals, tears of grief must have run down His face. How terrible a grief to know —as only He could know — what was to come on both man and all creation.

The Lord surely must have taught them, man and animal, explaining the need for a sacrifice to stay the full penalty of sin. (Good parents instruct as part of discipline.) God may have explained the life or soul of the flesh was in the blood, which is why it could atone for or cover sin. "...For it is the blood by reason of the life/soul that makes atonement." [Lev. 17:11] Without shedding of blood there is no forgiveness. [Heb. 9:22] God probably told them this was a temporary fix. The blood of bulls and goats could not cleanse the human conscience or make man alive spiritually. Another sacrifice, a perfect, obedient, innocent human, was required. God would become man and come in the fullness of time — when the human race was truly ready. [Hebrews 9 & 10]

Curiosity, blended with an unfamiliar dread, must have filled the animals' hearts and souls as they gathered around God and Adam. Did they want to comfort God? My animals always want to comfort me.

Adam and his wife must see their substitutes die. The animals Adam and Eve had once stroked, petted, and loved would now become their clothing. They would wear those skins as a constant reminder of the cost of sin.

WHAT ABOUT FAIRNESS?

"No fair!" That's right. Adam was unfair to disobey and bring death into Eden. Life has never been fair since Adam ate the forbidden fruit. Was God unfair in treating His animals this way? Don't they have rights, too? Sin and war are never fair. Innocents often are injured or die in war. Adam's sin brought on war between good and evil. Couldn't God do something?

Wait until the puzzle is put together. We don't yet really see God's love and His marvelous relationship with His creation. Looking at the pieces alone can be confusing. God's masterpiece, even if some scenes are unpleasant, is wondrous in its whole. God had a plan for the animals, too — even the serpent Satan and his kind.

ACCUSTOMED TO DEATH

Through history run rivers of blood, shed because of human disobedience. Even our entertainment reflects a love of bloodshed. Yet, daily, humans and animals give their lives for others. The altars of sacrifice are often outside of temples. Homes, streets and battlefields can be counted as "altars," I believe. Yet, many are so accustomed to it we don't think it terrible.

Also, road-kill (animals killed on the highway by speeding vehicles) is the closest many of us get to real death. We speed by it on our way to somewhere else. Most Americans are sheltered from the death of both humans and animals. We have no time for death. We die in hospitals and nursing homes, if possible. We buy meat killed and cut up. Pets are "disposed of" by veterinarians or humane societies. We try to keep death from dirtying our homes and hearts. While we often view death in movies, we are emotionally removed from it.

I'm being harsh only to illustrate my point, not to condemn. I pray the Lord will give us each grace to face death for what it is — and what His sacrifices mean.

Go with me, with prayerful imagination, back to the Garden on that fateful day. Let me warn you — the descriptions are graphic.

THE FIRST DEATH, THE FIRST SACRIFICE

The time for the killing came. You know the animals were gathered, too. All creation must have watched, listened, and smelled, tasting the air.

There were at least two animals — maybe more. There had to be enough skin to make two human-size garments. The Bible and many traditions hold that the earth was filled with giants before the Genesis 6-9 Flood. If Adam and Eve were giants, a number of skins would be required, unless those first animals were also oversized. Two garments can take many skins.

Adam and Eve probably laid their hands on the sacrificial animals. Imagine how you would feel. As they felt the animal's life in their hands, Adam and Eve's thoughts must have been full of sorrow and remorse, even fear. These animals were their companions. Did Adam call them by the names he had given them? Did they speak to the animals as their hands touched them? Did they apologize? Or did they harden their hearts and ignore the animals because of guilt?

These animals trusted Adam. The human and animal knew each other better than you or I can imagine. There would be no struggle. The animals surely came willingly to the people they loved. Was the animal silent? I think so. How like the Lamb of God [John 1:29; Acts 8:32-35; Matt. 27:11-14], these first sacrifices must have been:

> *Yet He did not open His mouth; Like a lamb that is led to slaughter,*
>
> *And, like a sheep that is silent before its shearers, So He did not open His mouth.*
>
> Isaiah 53:7 [NASV]

Did the first man and woman then try to get out of this terrible task? Did they ask to die as they deserved? Wouldn't you? God is a good parent. In His infinite wisdom, He knows the right discipline necessary to teach the consequences of our actions.

Have you ever killed an animal by hand? Have you ever watched it done? The first time makes most people sick. Only mentally ill people enjoy killing animals, and they usually end up killing people too. While people can become callous to butchering animals, it wasn't meant to be pleasant.

I believe God required Adam and Eve to participate in this first slaughter. This is based on His commandment that the sinner must choose and offer animal sacrifice himself. [Lev. 4:2-4, 13-15, 22-24, 27-29 & 32-33] The sinner had to bring a live animal before God's altar. The animal had to be the man or woman's best — a choice animal, a favorite. Then the sinner had to lay his or her hand on the animal's head and kill it. This was in the presence of the priest. Note that the sinner, not the priest, killed the sacrificial animal. The priest's role was to pray and put the blood on the altar to atone for the sins.

Do you think the priests told the sinner to look into the animal's eyes? Have you ever looked into the eyes of a lamb or goat kid, or a calf? They are beautiful — soft and brown, so innocent and trusting. Touching and looking at the animal who is about to die for your sin must be very difficult! Putting my hands on that sacrificial head and praying that God transfer my sin to an innocent animal would break my heart. How would you feel?

To refuse is only to make matters worse. Sin affects the human, and all under his or her stewardship. Refusal means sin continues to reign in the sinner. To refuse is further disobedience. It makes the heart callous to God and to others. God's protection and provision cannot operate. Death, and its handmaiden disease, has an immediate claim. Only the substituted blood can stop that. If the sinner wants to live, he must kill his sacrifice as God prescribes. God accepts an innocent animal in his place. This is what the Biblical sacrifices meant.

Imagine Adam's experience. No human had ever seen death. None had ever killed before.

When Adam took the knife, did his hands tremble? Was Eve able to follow God's instruction to make the killing stroke quick? (To be "kosher," sacrificial animals must be killed quickly and cleanly, and bled immediately to ensure death.)

Did Adam find himself weeping, blurring his eyes as he cut his animal friend's throat? Did man and animal exchange one long last look, as the killing blow fell? Was it very quick or it take more than one knifing? As that first life ebbed out, what was it like? Horrible, I'm sure.

BLOODY SACRIFICIAL DEATH

Blood spurted everywhere. Sacrificial death is not a pleasant, clean affair. Cutting the throat, severing major arteries, kills in seconds. But blood can shoot out as the heart pumps its last.

Did Adam and Eve keep a hand on the animal friend's body? Did the animal go limp under their bloody hand? Did they feel its life leave, taken by death? Did they watch or turn away as the animal crumpled to the ground, its life shattered? Were their ears troubled by the gurgling noise they made as they died? When its body crashed to the ground did Adam's heart break, too?

As the warm red life spattered and stained Adam and Eve, dripping down their leaf-covered nakedness, what did they feel and think? Knowing the animal's soul was in that blood, did the terrible cost of sin impact them? Did they see the animal's eyes, full of life, darken and glaze over, as its breath, its spirit, left that perfect, beautiful body. Adam had to know the paradox of God's grace, the blood covering his sin.

The eerie feeling, as death swallows life, is unforgettable. Probably these sin-stricken humans saw — and smelled — the bodily functions of the animal fail. The animal's clean coat would be soiled by its own blood and by the involuntary discharge of bowels and bladder. Some few have smelled Death itself, as a sickeningly sweet aroma. The soul-life has fled. Only an empty shell remained.

Did they see the strange jerking dance of death in those bodies? Did Adam feel the body heat leave as the corpse grew cold? The muscles freeze into rigor mortis after a while. Could they easily forget those sacrifices? Adam's offspring should not.

I think the good Lord designed physical death to look, smell and sound like a hellish nightmare. The Bible makes it abundantly clear, the living God wants His creation to have life, abundant life, eternal life. Because of Adam's disobedience, there is now a terrible price for such life. Death, the absence of life, is a horrible thing. There is nothing good about death and its companions, decay and disease.

NOT FAIR! HOW CRUEL!

"NOT FAIR!" "CRUEL!" you may cry. I agree. Adam was not fair when they ate the fruit that brought death to all creation. Genesis 3:12-13 indicates Adam showed no real remorse for disobeying God. The animal sacrifices were surely meant to be a cure of that lack.

God's unchangeable laws had to be fulfilled. Justice is

consistent because it's founded on love. God is love, therefore He is just. [1 John 4:8 & 16; Ps. 89:14] Understanding justice is key to knowing God, I believe. [Prov. 28:4-5] Justice always rewards the right behavior and punishes the lawbreaker. Mercy tempers justice, but never foolishly. Wisdom gives leniency only to the lawbreaker who chooses, or is likely to choose, not to break the law again. It is foolish to be merciful to a hardened criminal. That endangers good citizens. God is never foolish.

"It's God's fault! Couldn't God do something?" God *did* do something. Adam was falling into the fire of death, and God extended His hand of mercy like leather gloves — in the form of those animals — between that fire and Adam. God stayed Adam's execution to prevent Adam's physical death. It was costly, but necessary.

Holy justice requires a life for a life. It is the law of the universe. God's law is perfect and good [Ps. 19:7; 1 Tim. 1:8] Don't blame the God or His law. That is "passing the buck" — blaming someone else for human faults. It only makes things worse. Facing the truth makes life a lot easier and more pleasant in the long run. Adam, not God, killed those animals. Adam wrote their death sentence when he disobeyed God.

NOT MEANT TO BE EASY

The first sacrifice was meant to be difficult for Adam and Eve. As a veterinarian's daughter I saw many sick and dead animals. The times I have had to kill an animal, it was extremely difficult for me. I never got used to it. I only accepted its reality. If I thought an animal died for my mistakes, I would be devastated. And that's how it should be. If you enjoy the killing, something is terribly wrong.

I hope Adam and Eve killed their substitutes with absolute horror and great remorse. I hope they begged God for help, for another way, even to die themselves instead. This was not an animal they did not know. Adam named these animals. These were friends and companions. They cared for them, talked with them, and saw each other daily. Don't you think the first humans lost their breakfast, lunch and dinner? I wish they'd vomited up that forbidden fruit.

But it was too late. Sin and death had arrived on planet earth.

GOD CLOTHED THEM

Can you see God tenderly picking up the fallen forms, and beginning the unpleasant task of skinning them? The Bible says, God clothed Adam in skins. The Lord may have done the skinning. He may have supervised Adam, making man do the unpleasant task.

Whoever tanned the skins had a nasty task. Tanning is a smelly, messy business. First, you must skin the animal. Then you have to scrap the skins until they are "fat-free," before you stretch them to dry. In warm weather, the odors become very unpleasant. The Garden would have been warm.

Have you ever seen an animal skinned? Beneath the skin are naked wonders put together in awesome complexity — raw muscle, nerves, tendons, bone, interconnected organs. God's creation is fearfully and wonderfully made! Did Adam notice? Were they further shamed and nauseous at seeing the bare remains of animals which gave life and skin to cover Adam's nakedness?

Did God require Adam to burn the animals' bodies? This would be in line with the Mosaic law of animal sacrifice for sin. Did He require that Adam and his Eve eat the sacrificial meat before Him? In every bite was a reminder of the beloved animal, its life and name.

How costly those first long leather clothes were! I believe the Lord wept as He fashioned Adam's twin set of clothes from these precious leathers. How did this "fashion" feel to Adam and his wife when they put it on? I've lived where animal fur seems like the only way to keep warm in winter. Did Adam and Eve experience that? Did they feel warm furs cover their cold naked souls? Did the remorse nearly kill them, too? Did they feel God's grace as their sins were covered by their friends' blood?

What a cost — to wear the skin of one of their animal friends! Did the name of this animal shout within Eve, and roll like an echo through the ages? Every time they touched that soft leather or woolly coat, it was a reminder. Precious companions died so Adam could live. Adam's clothes were to be continual reminders that the wages of sin are death. [Rom. 6:23] That is what animal sacrifices were all about. Animals gave their lives to satisfy holy justice, to spare humans for a few years from death so God could begin to work His redemptive plan.

Did they ever speak the animals' names in gratitude, in the years they wore those skins? Or did they suppress the memory?

FORGETFUL HUMAN RACE

Adam's race has proven forgetful. Gratitude is not a normal handmaiden of a sinful heart. Mom told me about desperate young women she helped during the Great Depression. Without jobs, only prostitution or suicide was left. Mom arranged for them to have food, shelter, clothing, and to find jobs. Later, if she'd see them on the street, they usually ignored her. Mom said she understood. I never have.

We humans have "forgotten" what Adam learned about animal sacrifice. We suppress painful memories — especially our own failings. As Adam's offspring, we blame others or blame circumstances. Unfortunately, we also forget the good things, such as God and His promises.

EVICTED FROM THE GARDEN

Adam had to be removed from the Garden of Eden. The Lord sealed its entrance. The Lord had a good reason for that, too. The way was blocked by human disobedience to the Tree of Life:

> *Then God said, "Behold, the man has become like one of Us, knowing good and evil; and now, lest he stretch out his hand, and take also from the tree of life, and eat, and live forever," therefore the Lord God sent him out from the garden of Eden, to cultivate the ground from which he was taken. So He drove the man out; and at the east of the garden of Eden, He stationed the cherubim, and the flaming sword which turned every direction, to guard the way to the tree of life.*
>
> Gen. 3:22-24 [NASV]

The Tree of Life had never been forbidden to Adam. Now the way to it is barred. Life and sin are incompatible. God would not let man live forever in his sin, his disobedience, which affects all creation. He had a plan, although humans have usually been blind, or have ignored His way.

Adam now faced life as a struggle. If living a hundred years seems long to us, how about the prospect of nine hundred years? Was that long enough for Adam to learn anything?

While they could not return to the Garden, Adam and Eve surely retained indelible memories of Eden's beauty and wonders, of that naming party and what those animals were all like before. Memories of betrayal, disobedience and the unspeakable horror of death. Of sacrificial love which cannot be repaid. The knowledge of good and evil came with a high price. The forbidden fruit proved a poor counterfeit for what they lost. Did all seem lost forever?

THE FALLOUT; THE PAIN OF ALL LIVING THINGS

The Fall's fallout brought pain. Beloved masters "died," and death, disease, and disharmony entered the world. Adam's spiritual death affected man's relationship with animals, as well as with God. Fellow animals died as sacrifices. Death creates a terrible loss for those left behind.

Don't you know that the good animals — those offended by the Serpent's betrayal — felt unspeakable sorrow? Animals grieve when a loved companion dies.[95] Elephants,[96] primates like gorillas and chimpanzees,[97] as well as other animals, such as dogs and cats, clearly experience grief and loss when a member of their community or family dies. Owls have been observed grieving over the loss of mates, very angry because humans appear at fault for the death.[98] Many species are either too different or the evidence is not gathered, as to whether they grieve. We simply don't know much about the inner lives of hedgehogs and crickets.

Mom knew that dogs grieve. A puppy sold to a lady with a terminal disease, was returned when the woman died. The woman lived years longer than predicted — reportedly because of that dog. The dog was pregnant when her mistress died and came to us a nervous wreck. (I'm sure being pregnant didn't help!) I didn't understand or like the dog. Mom told me the dog was grieving and in about a year would recover. Mom was right. After a year, she became one of the best dogs we ever had. Mom knew dogs. Many of you reading this book have also witnessed such behavior.

I believe those first animals grieved the Fall of man, with his spiritual death, and the death of the substitute animals.

How can we even begin to imagine what the Fall meant to the animals? The Hebrew people have an interesting phrase, *za'ar ba'alei hayyim*. It means "pain of living things."[99] Rabbinical tradition tells that Rabbi Judah ha-Nasi was punished by the Lord because he did not show mercy to animals; when he changed his attitude the punishment was removed. The rabbis note that Moses and David became leaders only after being shepherds. God's mercy to animals is given prominence in rabbinic literature, and along with it, man's duty to not cause animals pain. Even inflicting of necessary pain is frowned upon.[100] How wise!

> "...the rabbis based a great deal of their legislation and interpretation on the principle of *za'ar ba'alei hayyim ["the pain of living things"]. ....***(Shab.128b)."**
>
> [Id.] (Emphasis supplied)

The Jewish Torah, the first five books of the Bible, shows God's view on animals. Jews, who wrote almost all the books of the Bible, teach that man is responsible to God for animals:

> *"Moral and legal rules concerning the treatment of animals are based on the principle that* ***animals are part of God's creation toward which man bears responsibility****. Laws and other indications in the Pentateuch and the rest of the Bible make it clear not only that* ***cruelty to animals is forbidden*** *but also that* ***compassion and mercy to them are demanded of man by God****."*[102] (Emphasis supplied)

Genesis teaches that disobedience has a high price. It costs the lawbreaker, and all around him or her — especially those who love him or her. Sin is the cause of the "pain of all living things." God feels that pain, too. What affects His loved creation, hurts the Creator.

Oh, for us to be His healer and comforter! To help heal His loved creation would be a joy! What Adam lost, cannot be regained. But the Lord had a plan which includes heaven. There is hope!

WHY? WHY? WHY?

Why did the Lord God require the death of those first animals? Love. God loved Adam and Eve. Made in His image, they were His children. His love compelled Him to do something to spare their lives — no matter the cost to Himself. Parents are like that. Yet, Adam had to learn to cost of sin. It was a hard, but necessary lesson.

And it did cost an unspeakable amount. That is the true meaning of "sacrifice." It cost God much to spare Adam's life. It meant subjecting all creation to futility for thousands of years. It cost precious lives of magnificent living creatures, God's beloved animals.

Ultimately, it cost the life of God's Son, "the Lamb of God who takes away the sin of the world." [John 1:29] The Lord, Father God, loves us enough to sacrifice all it takes to make us His very own. He is not alone in that endeavor.

To let death take what He loved, had to bring immeasurable pain and grief to God. Adam's Fall and his redemption caused unspeakable suffering to the Lord. But love doesn't let children grow up rebels. The Lord couldn't leave Adam dead in his sin. So He gave a substitute, a costly sacrifice. He gave the lives of His favored pets.

God loves you and me the same way. He won't spare the lives of others He loves to gain your safety, to spare your life. The Lord wants you to walk with Him, and us, and His animals in the new Eden, in heaven itself. He continues to use animals to assist Him in achieving that goal. Have you ever experienced that kind of love? Animals freely demonstrate it, don't they?

CHAPTER 8

WHO WERE THE FIRST ANIMAL SACRIFICES?

How far the little candle throws his beams!
So shines a good deed in a naughty world.[103]

"I see the lives for which I lay down my life, peaceful, useful, prosperous and happy, ... I see that I hold a sanctuary in their hearts, and in the hearts of their descendants, generations hence. ... It is a far, far better thing that I do, than I have ever done; ..."[104]

Heroes, those who live and die sacrificially, come in all shapes and sizes — not just human. A stray dog gave its life for my grandmother, Nella. Mom told me about it. I suspect the dog came to Nella half-starved and mangy. Nella took the dog in. It became her companion. One day, Nella went into a field, possibly to pick poke or dandelion greens for dinner. There was a bull in that field, but Nella either did not know or forgot about it. (I have been chased by a bull. It is terrifying when a ton of hoofed and horned aggression charges you.) As the bull charged Nella, the dog went for the bull. Nella got over the fence safely. Unfortunately, the bull killed the dog. That is sacrificial love.

History is replete with similar stories of dogs and other animals giving their lives for humans — or even other species. Some risk life and limb for strangers, others for loved friends.[105] In the excavation of Pompeii, after Mount Vesuvius erupted and destroyed the city about 70 A.D., evidence was found of a dog lying across a child, apparently trying to protect the child.[106] More contemporary is the case where firemen found a dead German shepherd which died covering a toddler with its body during a house fire.[107] The child was alive with only minor injuries. Susan McElroy, reporting this, makes a profound statement:

> *What has always struck me most about these kinds of stories is not how they occurred, but that they occurred. There is enormous importance in the notion of another species voluntarily defending us, sometimes with its very life. We treasure these heroic animals and their uncompromising devotion. . . . Yet, ironically, humans who are willing to return the favor . . . are frequently perceived . . . as lunatics or fanatics.*[108]

Such animal heroism is remarkably common.[109] I have encountered numerous reports about all kinds of animals acting in compassion, even giving life or limb. The art of self-sacrifice seems to be a common trait in the best of God's creation.

It was surprising to me how many wild animals are heroes or rescuers of humans and other animals. For example, a wild eagle helped rescue a lost woman hiker. The woman had taken a wrong turn and hiked about two miles out of the way. (That is a long way in the mountains.) A gray eagle squawked, scolded and swooped at her, until she asked the bird if she were going the wrong way. At that question, the eagle grew silent and flew closer, holding himself still. The woman turned around and hiked back, finding she had taken the wrong trail. She got back just as they were ready to send out search parties![110]

This is similar to a fable Russian author, Leo Tolstoy recorded. A Tsar, hunting with his favorite falcon, sought some water to quench his thirst. Finding a dribble coming down a hillside, he put his cup under until the dripping water filled his cup. As he put the cup to his mouth, the falcon flapped its wings, bumping the Tsar's hand so he spilled the water. A second time the same thing happened. On the third occasion, in anger the Tsar killed the falcon. Meanwhile, the Tsar's servants had gone up the hill to the water's source, and came back empty-handed. They explained a serpent was in the spring, and the water was poisoned. It would have killed the Tsar. "Foully have I recompensed the Falcon; he saved my life, and I killed him for it."[111] How like Adam we all are!

A badger took care of a lost boy in Canada in the 19th century for several weeks, sharing its den and bringing the boy food. The origins of Rome, Italy, according to legend, involves two boys (one by the name of Romulus) who were raised by wolves. Numerous accounts of wolves and other wild animals adopting children dot human history. The sea animals also are heroes. Through the ages, accounts of dolphins rescuing humans from sharks and from drowning are fairly common.

There are abundant records of heroism by dogs, cats, mules, horses, pigs, birds and other animals for the benefit of man.[112] *Guideposts* and other publishers have books of such anecdotes. Awards to heroic pets have been given by various groups.[113]

The first animals must have been the same. Why not, when our awesome God gave His only Son in total sacrifice to redeem humans from our sins?

Viktor Frankl wrote that in the German concentration camps some would give away their last piece of bread, proving that the freedom to choose one's attitude, one's own way, is the last freedom man has.[114] "The greatest power that a person possesses is the power to choose."[115] Animals clearly have the power of choice also. Some choose to be mean, senseless killers — like the devil, the Serpent. Some choose to be heroes — to live and die sacrificially.

OLD SOUP, THE ELEPHANT

An awesome example is found in the story of Old Soup, an Indian elephant. Old Soup was estimated to be about a hundred years old in the summer of 1937. Owned by a Major Daly, this elephant and others were loading cargo, bags of rice, near Cawnpore, India. As he had in the past, Old Soup delighted at the sight of the Major's young son and daughter. The children waved to Old Soup as they stood by their nanny.

Suddenly an angry sound tore the air. A young elephant went mad, crushed his handler, smashed against the barge, broke rice sacks on his back, slinging them like confetti. Trumpeting wildly, he took off. The children were in his path.

The nanny started to pull the children to safety, but froze. The mad pachyderm spied them and charged. Old Soup suddenly pulled from his handler, trumpeted a challenge, lowered his tusks and headed for the rogue elephant. The Major and his soldiers were too far away to help. Only Old Soup could save them.

Shaking the earth, the elephants collided. The rogue turned again to the children, but Old Soup slammed him a second time. Again the rogue started for the children, again Old Soup trumpeted and lunged. The two "gray mountains" locked tusks and jabbed each other, blasting and pushing. Old Soup, his ears in tatters and his body battered, managed to catch the crazy bull off-guard. His tusks gored the young rogue's soft underside several times. The wounded youngster then attacked Old Soup with a vengeance.

Elephants rarely fight to the death, but this proved the exception. The battle raged on for more than an hour, as children and nanny huddled nearby. Plunging tusks repeatedly into each other, one finally hit a vital organ. The defeated giant went to its knees and died. The victor raised his trunk and gave a long eerie blast. His right tusk was shattered. He was bloody from stab wounds. His ears hung in tatters.

The grateful children ran to the elephant. Old Soup was their savior. The weary bleeding giant extended his trunk gently and nuzzled them. The elephant recovered and was retired by the Major to his home as a pet.[116]

TWO KINDS OF ANIMALS

Old Soup and the rogue are evidence of two kinds of animals: (1) those who intelligently serve God and man; and (2) those who insanely rebel. What a contrast between the serpent which deceived Adam and other animals, like Old Soup, who come to man's rescue, even against their own kind! What a price love will pay!

Who knows why some love and serve humans, while others turn mean and violent. Sometimes this happens without human cruelty, as in the case of that rogue elephant — although abuse is a probable primary cause. The fact is, sometimes animals "go bad" just like humans do.

Given that animals clearly make choices, as I have seen mine do, it may lie there. God gave humans and animals a choice. Adam and some angels sinned against God. [2 Peter 2:4] Clearly animals can rebel also.

WHEN GOD CHOSE ADAM'S CLOTHES

That brings us back to the Garden when God called on certain animals to die for Adam and Eve. Like Old Soup and Nella's dog, don't you think the animals willingly gave themselves to God for man?

I do. I believe they willingly laid down their lives. Imagine different animals stepping up before God, volunteering to die in Adam's place. Perhaps this was the scene:

Lamb:

Excuse me, Lord God, Your Excellency. May I please have a word with you? I love Adam and I'm young so let me die for him. Please, please, Lord? He's made a dreadful mistake, I know. It's simply awful. But, if Adam must die, would You accept a substitute? Please accept me as a sacrifice for him and her. My skin, with its soft wool, would protect and warm them.

Goat:

You are so wise, just, and kind in all your ways, Lord God. This must be difficult for you since You love Adam and Eve with all Your wonderful heart. We love them, too. I've really enjoyed Adam. We've had some great times together, kidding around and stuff. My hide is tough, Lord. I think Adam will need such toughness now. Let us help. Please, Lord, let me die for them — Whatever death is anyway.

Pigeon:

Father of all living things, how we praise you for giving us life! The joy of flying free above the clouds is akin to the wonder of knowing You. Adam is so like You that we would do anything for him. Adam has been very good to me. I'd like to ask you to let me die in Adam's place. Please, please, let me be the one. While I'm small, my feathered skin would keep Adam dry in the rain and dress him or her in soft beauty.

Bull or Cow:

Lord, Master of the Universe, I am the one who should die for Adam and Eve. The others are good to offer, Lord, but my skin would be the largest and make a suitable suit. Adam takes such good care of me and my fellow cattle and all other animal friends. He is a good man, Lord. I know he made a bad mistake but You are forgiving. I would do anything for Adam and Eve. It would be a privilege to die in their place. Please, I must be the one.

Just fantasy? I think not. What do you think?

BIBLE ANIMAL HEROES

We will see that there is precedent for the idea in the Bible. The Bible has its animal rescue stories. We have previously discussed the story of Balaam's donkey who interceded for the foolish prophet. [Numbers 22] Another example is the whale who obeyed God in swallowing Jonah (without chewing him up or digesting him). [Jonah 2] Think about the ravens which fed Elijah. [1 Kings 17]

We might also add the fish which managed to get a large coin of the right denomination in its mouth and hold it there until Peter caught the fish and opened its mouth so he could pay the tax for Jesus and himself. [Matt. 17:27] Somehow I don't think Peter (a professional fisherman) threw the fish back in gratitude.

Balaam's donkey, as we discussed earlier, served her master sacrificially. Taking numerous beatings to save her master's life is love in any language! The donkey was smarter and more loving than the man. The man never figured out what was going on until his eyes were opened! But greed and anger have always dulled human wits, blinded our eyes, and stopped our ears.

I myself fluctuate between wondering what my animals see that I do not and being glad I don't know! Now I strive more than ever not to cause them pain because of my sin.

A STUMBLING BLOCK

Animal lovers stumble over the sacrifices that God requires — while theologians struggle with the problem of animal suffering. In writing this book, new insights or ideas have occurred to me — among them are animals volunteering to die for Adam, for us. I believe the Lord inspired these insights. Like a good lawyer, I also believe hard evidence supports these theories. Your responsibility is to check it out; to consider all the evidence before rendering a verdict, and then to render a verdict as true as you are able to give.

So why would an animal sacrifice itself for you or me? It has to be love — at least as much as we can understand that term. Only lovers throw themselves into risk, enduring pain, for the sake of something higher. The fearful avoid such and run away. The best animal trainers throughout the ages, understand. Animals, like humans, perform best when they love what they are doing, or when they are motivated out of love of the person asking them to take such risks. Heroes lay down their lives for the greater good because they love God, country, family, and friends.

I think this is what Vicki Hearne was talking about when she wrote about horses who will endure pain to work for us:

The horses...embrace heroic precisions when they can.

* * *

What matters is an understanding of the horse's capacity for caring about beauty, precision, perfection of performance. This gives his or her pain meaning and context, ... ***To say that pain is meaningful is simply to say that for the creature experiencing the pain there is something that matters more than comfort, for the moment at least; something that is the ground of a certain creature's being, what it cares about, toward which it is oriented, in relationship to which pain isn't quite pain anymore, not anything that matters.*** *This is probably not something anyone can make a judgment about for anyone else. My pain, like my death, belongs to me uniquely most of the time.*[117]

Did God act cruelly in requiring the animals' lives? That question can have several answers. First, I cannot believe that God forced any animal against its will to die for Adam. I think they went willingly. Why? One of the most telling things about animals, which shouts of the attitude of their Creator toward them, is that cruelty doesn't work. The neglected, beaten, or broken-spirited animal, neither performs beautifully nor looks beautiful. The best trained, the champions of performance are treated very well.[118]

Mom's adage — God is love, and if it isn't love it isn't God — works. The fact that animals both give and respond extraordinarily well to love, is mute testimony that a loving God created them, and that He inspires them and cares for them. Although, admittedly, sacrifice does not involve "training" or "art" for the animal, the principle is relevant.

Secondly, like Old Soup, when someone is in danger, many instantly risk life and limb to try to save her or him. Self-sacrificing acts are not uncommon among humans or animals. Whether it is against a robber or a rapist, or on a battleground, people think it good and brave to fight for family, friends, and country. Where did the idea originate that such behavior is good? It began in the Bible, in Genesis Chapter 3.

In Ephesians 1, Paul stated that before the foundation (literally "casting down") of this world, the Lord chose us and preplanned our adoption as His children through Jesus Christ. In Jesus Christ, God became man, and laid down His life as a sacrifice for our sin, our mistakes, so we might live, and live eternally. He became the Lamb of God [John 1:29]. God is the ultimate risk-taker for those He loves.

I believe the Lord explained His plan to become a human and to take on Adam's sin, and all the disobedience which Adam's offspring, you and I included, have done. I believe the animals listened and understood God's self-sacrificing nature, the very core of real love. He made them to be like Himself. They would understand.

It is little wonder some of God's creatures choose to act like Him. For humans who see with eyes of faith, creation still reflects the nature of God, even in its corrupted state.

GOD'S MERCY TO THE ANIMALS

The quality of mercy is not strain'd,
It droppeth as the gentle rain from heaven
Upon the place beneath: it is twice blest;
It blesseth him that gives and him that takes:
"Tis the mightiest in the mightiest: it becomes
The throned monarch better than his crown...
But mercy above this sceptred sway; ...
It is an attribute to God himself;
And earthly power doth then show likest God's
When mercy seasons justice.[119]

I believe God Himself took the pain of death for those sacrificial animals. While Adam's Fall brought death's associates (pain, disease and sorrow), God's grace and mercy were present in power. Adam and Eve did not know it, but those animals felt no pain in dying. There is much less suffering in violent animal death than humans imagine. God gave animals a gift: to be killed without pain.[120] He gave them "shock." Isn't that just like a loving God?

In trauma, a natural, powerful anesthetic literally floods the body. Mortally wounded people report feeling no pain. Animals appear to be similarly pain-free. People may see their own blood before they know they are injured. Only if they survive, when the "shock" wears off, is pain felt.

No matter how horrible the killing appeared to be, God's mercy covered the animals that Adam killed. God cared. I believe He cared enough to share or bear the pain of all living things. He still does. This is another piece of evidence that God loves animals — and man.

WHICH SPECIES WAS THE FIRST SACRIFICE?

Which animals did God permit to be the first sacrifices to clothe the Adam? The Bible does not say. However, given God's appointment of the domestic lamb, goat, bull, turtledove or pigeon as acceptable sacrifices for sin in Leviticus 4 and 5, these are the likely candidates. Knowing the nature of dogs, cats, horses and other animals to act heroically, God probably had a lot of volunteers. For me, it would have been hard to choose.

I think the lamb is most likely because it is so cute and innocent. Its wool is pleasant to touch, its face is sweet, and its eyes are like liquid trust and peace. They are a delight to watch and their helplessness evokes a desire to protect them.

Abel was a keeper of sheep and he sacrificed a lamb in the first recorded animal sacrifice by man. [Gen. 4:4] The lamb was God's choice for the Passover sacrifice, celebrating the freedom of Israel from slavery some 400 years B.C. [Exodus 12:21] Most important, the lamb is a symbol of the Messiah, Jesus of Nazareth, who is repeatedly called "the Lamb of God," our Passover sacrifice. [John 1:29, 36; 1 Corinthians 5:7; 1 Peter 1:18-19] The lamb must have been at least one of those which gave its life and skin for Adam and Eve.

PUTTING THE PUZZLE TOGETHER

When you put the pieces of Scripture and experience together, there is plenty of evidence that God loves both man and beast. The sacrificial love-nature of the Creator is reflected in many animals who give their lives for others. The love of God is reflected all around us in our animal friends both wild and tame. So is the nature of Satan, and the cruel effects of disobedience to the One Who is Love.

Now we see the answers to these questions: Why did God subject the animals to the consequences of Adam's Fall? Why did God call for the sacrifice of animals for man's sin? Why is the Bible such a bloody book? There may be more the Lord wants us to understand, but this is a good start.

Writing about Adam's Fall and the animal's roles has not been an easy task. I have wept as I have studied, written, and rewritten these words. I don't believe I could have done this without the sustaining grace of the Lord. I've seen too clearly my own neglect, my blindness, my insensitivity to God and His creation and my animal friends. How little I really know about them and God's plans for them!

Just as God volunteered to give his Son, Jesus, I believe these animal friends volunteered to die for Adam and Eve, for you and me. It was motivated by their love for Adam. Adam was made in the image of God, but has no exclusive contract on God's attributes. Animals reflect God's nature and character, also. All creation reflects its Creator.

Animals are still saviors and preachers, demonstrating the Good News of God's love to us. The "wild" animals teach by example. The domestic animals show us God's nature in their patient service and forgiving affection toward their human masters. Just as the animals responded to St. Francis of Assisi, these first animals rejoiced at the goodness of God. They keep telling us about His goodness, too.

Adam knew God's attitude about His animal creation. God always gives His very best. His volunteers do, too.

While I have never had an animal give its life for me, I certainly have known those who, I believe, would have. Noble animals they were, full of the love of their Creator. Why should we not wish such companionship in heaven? Wouldn't a just and loving God provide the same?

What is God's attitude about His animals? I think Isaiah was told something about God's attitude about animal sacrifice and the value of each animal to Himself. [See Isaiah 66:1-3]

Animal sacrifice was instituted until God's plans were fulfilled, so that sacrifice was no longer necessary. Historically, animal sacrifice ended with the destruction of the Jewish temple in Jerusalem in the first century after Christ's death. Christians believe that God's plans are fulfilled in Jesus Christ. If you don't believe that, will you risk the alternative?

Looking at Scripture as a pattern, in the next chapters we will begin to see more evidence of God's future plans for his creation. The God of Love, the God of life, is ultimately the God of resurrection. If anything shouts from the pages of the Bible, it is that Jesus Christ is the Resurrection and the Life. We shall see that He is so — for *all* His Creation.

CHAPTER 9

COVENANTS: BEGINNING WITH NOAH AND THE ARK

Now the earth was corrupt in the sight of God, and the earth was filled with violence. ... Then God said to Noah, "The end of all flesh has come before Me;... Make for yourself an ark of gopher wood; ... with rooms, ... I, even I am bringing a flood of water upon the earth, to destroy all flesh in which is the breath of life, from under heaven; and everything that is on the earth shall perish. But I will establish My covenant with you; and you shall enter the ark — you and your sons and your wife, and your sons' wives with you. And of every living thing of all flesh, you shall bring two of every kind into the ark, to keep them alive with you; they shall be male and female. Of the birds after their kind, and of the animals after their kind, of every creeping thing of the ground after its kind.

Gen. 6:11,13-14, 17-20 [NASV]

"And as for Me, behold, I establish My covenant with you and with your descendants after you, and with ***every living creature*** *that is with you: the birds, the cattle, and*

> ***every beast*** *of the earth with you, of all that go out of the ark, every beast of the earth. Thus, I establish My covenant with you:* ***Never again*** *shall* ***all flesh*** *be cut off by the waters of the flood;* ***never again*** *shall there be a flood to destroy the earth.*
>
> *And God said: "This is the sign of the* ***covenant*** *which I make between Me and you, and* ***every living creature*** *that is with you, for perpetual generations...*
>
> Gen. 9:9-17 [NKJ] (Emphasis supplied)

Did you realize that all animals have a covenant with God? That's "animals" as in cows, and lizards, and sparrows, and insects. The excerpts from Genesis quoted above about Noah and the Ark, are relevant passages for Mom's question. What other promises do you think the Lord made to animals? What do these promises mean? Do they relate to the questions about animals in eternity?

WHAT IS A COVENANT?

Many people don't realize what "covenant" really means. Covenants are vows for life. At one time, they involved speaking curses and blessing on each other; breaking your covenant vows brings the curses and keeping them brings the blessings. The dictionary defines "covenant" as a binding agreement between two or more persons; a compact; a contract. The concept of a covenant may mean little to one without knowledge of the ancient understanding of covenant — especially a blood covenant.

Americans no longer have covenants which resemble an ancient covenant. Adoption is the closest thing to a covenant we have in our Western society. It is almost impossible to cancel an adoption decree. Marriage used to be an irrevocable covenant. It has become a mere non-binding agreement, even with most Christians. Becoming blood brothers (or sisters) is another example of a covenant. "Testament" in the phrase "last Will and Testament," is a synonym for "covenant." The Christian "Old Testament" and "New Testament"[121] divisions of the Bible are divisions between the old and new covenants, which the Lord made; first with the Jews or Hebrew people, and second with all men who become disciples of Jesus Christ.

In theology, "covenant" represents the promises God makes with man. It also relates to man's vows to God. A Biblical covenant is a promise or set of promises which last for life or eternity. Breaking covenant brings dire curses on the breaker.[122] When the Lord promises something, it is a sure thing. He never breaks covenant. He cannot lie - or He wouldn't be Who He says He is!

The Hebrew word for "covenant" is *b^{e}riyth*. It means "a cutting" from the ancient practice of passing between the divided portions of a sacrificial victim — as Abraham did in Genesis 15. (I believe the sacrifices to clothe Adam involved a covenant of redemption for all flesh.) If blood is shed, the makers are taking a holy vow which must not be broken. One never entered into a covenant lightly, since it bound that person to the other for life or eternity.

The Bible records over a dozen covenants which the Lord God made. Some include animals. The Noahic covenant is the first of several. Animals are important to the Creator or He would not have made an everlasting covenant with them! It may shock a few people to learn that the Almighty entered covenant with "dumb" beasts. It's in the Book.

NOAH AND THE GREAT FLOOD

I opened this chapter with a long quote about the Great Flood or Noahic covenant — God's promise to Noah and all animals not to destroy this world with another flood. Note that this is a perpetual covenant. The Lord repeated "never again" thrice for emphasis. [Gen. 9:11-17]

While many have heard the story of Noah and the Ark as children, most have not studied it as an adult. I gained a new perspective when I did. Genesis Chapters 6 through 9, cover the Noahic Flood. The term "all flesh," which includes animals, is a key phrase throughout the Scripture to understand God's plan for animals. Previously, I thought the phrase applied solely to humans. In some contexts that is correct; however, often "flesh" is an inclusive term for all creation. In Genesis 6 the Lord said "all flesh" had become corrupt and then sent the Flood to cleanse the earth.

The Great Flood and Noahic covenant involve important points and a pattern. These are keys to Mom's question. The Bible shows that the Lord used earthly things to give man patterns, types and shadows of heaven and the world to come. [Hebrews 8:5] Moses was given the patterns of things for the tabernacle of God. [Exodus 25:9 and 40, and Numbers 8:4] Solomon was given the pattern of things for the temple in Jerusalem. [1 Chron. 28, 11-19]

Believing in a literal Biblical Creation or Great Flood may not be essential to answering Mom's question. But then, it may be. Faith is a requirement in the Biblical plan. Ask yourself: "Do I believe the Bible is mostly myth? Do I believe we originated out of chaos, descending from apes? Or do I believe we are created in the image of the Un-created Creator, a Being of absolute power and goodness?"

Do not confuse the ability to "believe" (or think) as you wish, with the right to do so. We each have the capacity to do murder. No civilized society gives its citizens the right to do murder.[123] If I understand the Bible, the final judgment of the Lord will involve what we believe, as well as what we have done.

God is interested in both man's beliefs and his actions. The Lord is a just lawgiver, defining what is right and wrong to believe and to worship. Beliefs govern actions. Love is the royal law, so whatever is not loving is wrong. God is also judge and king or governor over all this earth. (Isa. 33:22) He is withholding judgment, for His own good reasons. It pays to understand His laws, justice, and mercy. Scripture was given by God to guide us into all truth. The "types and shadows" help us understand what we've never seen: the reality of God's heaven and eternity. Like blind men need the seeing, we need the Lord.

Many believe that Noah's Ark is a type and shadow of God's salvation. This type is fulfilled in God's Messiah, whom

Christians know to be Jesus of Nazareth. Let's look closer at this type and shadow.

A CORRUPT WORLD

Only ten generations after Adam fell, humans went totally bad. [Gen. 5 & 6.] (I use the word "bad" in the pejorative sense of evil, wicked, corrupt, murdering and cruel, not a slang compliment.) The first Adam and Eve's first two sons got into it and Cain killed Abel in a fit of jealousy. Abel's blood still cries "murder" from the earth. [Gen. 4 & Heb. 11:4 & 12:24] Only one and one-half of God's days, i.e., 1500 years, and man was very corrupt and wicked: "every intent of the thoughts of his heart was only evil continually." [Gen. 6:5]

The Lord was sorry He created us and was grieved. The Lord said:

> *I will blot out man whom I have created from the face of the land, from man to animals to creeping things to birds of the sky; for I am sorry that I have made them.*
>
> Gen. 6:7[NASV]

Animals were included in His indictment. Why? Remember animals have choices, too. The old serpent fomented Adam's Fall. Satan must have led other animals into insanity. It goes without saying that wild animals, especially carnivores, are "wild" because they are unpredictably dangerous to humans. "The survival of the fittest" is a sign of anarchy — of disharmony, of the loss of Eden for animals, too.

Some domestic animals are "rogues," — irreconcilably dangerous. You might say they are like Satan, the evil serpent who is the arch-enemy of man. Animal trainers agree that rogues are few. These are animals with the equivalent of a criminal personality. Both Monty Roberts, in *The Man Who Talks to Horses* and Vicki Hearne, in *Adam's Task*, speak of rare horses who are man- killers. When a half-ton or more of horse is pure meanness, it is indeed dangerous. "Wild" animals are not rogues in this sense, although some may be.

This is **<u>not</u>** to say all animals who injure humans are rogues.

Animal experts agree that most animal injuries are because the animal is acting naturally. For example, most dogs bite or harm humans for reasons perfectly understandable to a dog. We should examine our behavior to find out if we are doing something to make the animal bite, kick, or otherwise do harm.[124] Even though animal rogues are rare, just as with human homicidal maniacs, they do exist. Imagine the earth *filled* with such humans and animals!

The Bible says that the "earth was filled with violence." [Gen. 6:11-12] "It was corrupt – depraved and putrid" [Amplified Bible]:

> *...for* ***all flesh*** *had corrupted their way upon the earth. Then God said to Noah, "The end of* ***all flesh*** *has come before Me; for the* ***earth is filled with violence because of them****; and behold, I am about to destroy them with the earth."* Gen. 6:12-13 [NASV]

I'm glad I missed that era of history!

GOD'S JUST JUDGMENT

Man, the leader and instigator, was not the only "flesh" which the Lord said was corrupt and violent. "All flesh" in this passage included both man and animal, because both were destroyed.

In some cases it is not clear if "all flesh" describes only humans, or includes both humans and animals. (See for example, Gen. 7:15, 16 & 21; Lev. 7:15-21; 17:11-16; Num. 16:22; 18:15; Job 34:15; Ps. 56:4, 65:2; 136:25; 145:2; Isa. 40:5-6; Jer. 32:27, for a partial list.[125]) The prophets, Isaiah, Jeremiah, and Ezekiel, used "all flesh" when speaking of God's judgment and destruction on sinful nations, tribes or peoples. We know from Joshua, and from Jonah, that such judgments included animals, as well as people.

Why would God, a loving and good God, order the destruction of children and animals? Are they not innocents? Christians need to realize that passing from this life can mean a release. See Isaiah 57:1-2. As a lawyer, I have learned something about the effects of severe abuse. For example, adoptions which fail, frequently involve children who were severely abused prior to the adoption. Abuse has long-term effects. The younger the abuse occurs, the less likely there will be recovery.

For example, I know of a faith-filled Christian woman and her adopted son. The adoption occurred when this son was an infant. Prior to the adoption, he'd been burned repeatedly by cigarettes, among other abuses. In spite of a loving and nurturing home, and prayers of his adoptive mother and her believing friends, this child grew up a criminal. He repeatedly broke the law and endangered his adoptive mother and other family members. Violence ended his life. He died a relatively young man. Imagine the pain and fear his family must have endured. In one sense, his death was merciful.

A television program reviewed the deprivation of orphaned and fatherless children in post World War I Germany. These children were discontented and dysfunctional. They became the men and women who brought Hitler to power. They formed the cruel SS troops which enjoyed torturing and killing for the Reich.

Psychologists, sociologists and criminologists find that young children who are abused repeatedly, physically and/or sexually, can be difficult, if not impossible, to rehabilitate. This is not to say that we should not try. Nor to say that there are no success stories. It is merely to acknowledge that the ability and resources to help them are limited, and the failure rate is dismally low. Such children can be dead inside — to love, trust, relationships and everything good. Tragically, they are very dangerous to themselves and others.

The same holds for animals who have been terribly misused or abused. Some go crazy and are dangerous to have around. The movie, *The Horse Whisperer,* deals with a horse crazy with fear — due to severe injuries. If cowboy and horse-gentler (Robert Redford) had not been able to get through to the horse, it was scheduled for destruction. Death can be merciful to those animals who cannot recover from abuse. It can be the only way to safeguard their potential victims. They are dangerous to themselves and others.

GOD'S "HOUSECLEANING"

Because of one man, Noah, the Bible says the Lord decided to only "clean house" rather than demolish the earth. If there had not been one righteous human, God would have trashed everything. The Lord God chose instead to keep on working to save, to redeem, all flesh from Adam's Fall.

THE BIG RAIN

> *In the six hundredth year of Noah's life,... all the fountains of the great deep burst open, and the floodgates of the sky were opened. and the rain fell upon the earth for forty days and forty nights. .. and the water increased and lifted up the ark, so that it rose above the earth ... and all flesh that moved on the earth perished, birds and cattle and beasts and every swarming thing that swarms upon the earth, and all mankind; of all that was on the dry land, all in whose nostrils was the breath of the spirit of life, died. ... Only Noah was left, together with those that were with him in the ark.*
>
> Gen. 7:11 [NASV]

In the Great Flood, the Lord flooded, then soaked and scrubbed the earth really good — with lots of water. This was more than a great rain, as I had always thought. Waters burst from above and below the earth. It was cataclysmic.

Interestingly, it had never rained before. Pre-Flood, the earth was watered every morning by a mist. [Genesis 2:4-6] This Flood is not just a myth. Both archeological evidence and sociological evidence support this. There is evidence showing a great flood happened an estimated 4,500 years ago in the Black Sea area. Most cultures have a Great Flood story, i.e., that there was a great flood which covered the earth and killed almost all human and animal life, including a race of giants.[See Gen. 6:4 re: giants.] Some scientists agree there is geological evidence of this flood in rock strata around the world.[126]

The Great Flood brought about major changes, just as the dividing of the earth during Peleg's time must have done. [Gen. 10:25] The earth prior to the fall and Noah's Flood was a different place. Some scientists say there is evidence that the Earth, prior to the Great Flood, was like a huge greenhouse. Earth's land may have been one mass, with the current continents joined together — as their puzzle-like pieces fit well together. This land mass really may have been sandwiched, as Genesis 1 describes, between two bodies of water: the firmament or heavens above, heavy with cloud cover; and waters trapped under the earth like a massive artesian well spring. The resulting greenhouse effect could have provided an environment for life forms to grow huge in size and to live longer than we can. (Apparently, archaeological evidence shows dinosaurs and giant human footprints together.) It also would provide enough moisture to cover the earth in a Great Flood — probably before the huge mountain ranges, on land and in the sea, were made or re-arranged by cataclysmic events.

There is nothing in science which can provide us with information about the Pre-Flood relationships between humans, nor the relationships between animals, nor the relationships between man and animals.[127] At this point, the Bible stands pretty much alone as a source to explore those relationships. It is very succinct, so even then, much of what we think is speculation.

THE LORD'S GREAT PLAN

The Lord planned well for this saving of Noah and the animals. A hundred years before the Flood, God told Noah to build an ark, to gather male and female of "every living thing of all flesh." [Genesis 6:13-22 & 7:1-5] Everything was included: birds animals, and "creeping things." Creeping things appears to describe insects and reptiles. Of the domestic animals and the birds, Noah was to take "seven sevens" of each kind, both male and female. The rest were by pairs. Noah was to take food for himself, his family and all the living things. What a huge task!

God's interest and concern for each and every living creature is demonstrated in these detailed provisions. Every species was preserved, from aardvarks to zebras. All came from elephants to swallows to cockroaches.

GOD'S ARK OF SAFETY

The ark was a large structure: 300 cubits long, 50 cubits wide and 30 cubits high. [Gen. 6:15]. A "cubit" is the length between a man's finger-tips and elbow. The average size arm on a man today is about eighteen inches. The Ark was at least 150 yards long, 25 wide and 15 yards high. (About the same number in meters.) Think of it! One-and one-half football fields long! If Noah was a big fellow, a giant, it would be much larger.

It needed to be a large structure. There had to be room and food for 75 people, plus all the land animals and birds.

LOADING THE ARK

> *And Noah did according to all that the Lord had commanded him. ... Of clean animals and* ***animals*** *that are not clean and birds and everything that creeps on the ground,* ***there went into the ark to Noah*** *by twos, male and female, as God had commanded Noah.*
>
> Gen. 7:5, 8-10 [NASV]

How did Noah gather and load all those animals and birds? The Bible says **the animals came to Noah**; and that they went into the Ark with Noah. [Gen. 6:20; 7:8-9, 14-16.] The whole operation was a volunteer thing. The Lord undoubtedly called the animals; and the chosen ones heard and obeyed. They came to Noah.

There is precedent for this calling of animals and their obedience. Ravens obeyed the Lord in bringing food to the prophet Elijah in the desert. [1 Kings 17:1-7] Lions obeyed the Lord in several different instances. [1 Kings 13 & Daniel 6]

There are numerous present-day accounts of wild animals coming to people as apparent answers to prayer. The February 1999 issue of *Guideposts* tells of a young man who was grieving over his mother's untimely death. Daily he took his grief to the Lord, as he sought solace at her grave. In the lonely cemetery, a hawk approached him. The man fed it, trying to entice it to his hand. Finally, the hawk alighted on his arm, without hurting him. At that moment the man's grief left him. The hawk then disappeared, as though its mission was accomplished. The Lord sent those animals to Noah, to fulfill His purpose. (I think Noah may have prayed for his animal friends.)

WHO WAS THIS MAN, NOAH?

My friend, Jan, taught adult Sunday School lessons on "Bible Stories You Thought You Knew." The one on Noah was insightful and I'm incorporating some of her ideas here.

First, let's set the scene. Noah marked the tenth generation from Adam, which ancients believed was the number of "completion." Lamech was Noah's father. He named his first son "Noah" because it means "rest." [Gen. 5:29] Lamech prophesied Noah would bring rest to the earth in his time. Noah, as tenth, was expected to give them rest from the curse on the ground. Every time Noah heard his name, he was reminded of his destiny.

A reading of Genesis chapter 5, reveals these first generations measured their lives in centuries, not decades. Noah was born 1056 years after Adam was created, and 126 years before Adam died. Noah would have known six of his nine male ancestors for years. Only Adam, Seth and Enoch were gone. Noah's grandfather Methuselah lived until the year of the Great Flood — about 600 years of Noah's life.

Before television and public schools, sitting around telling stories was probably how children were trained and entertained. Like most grandfathers, Noah's forebears must have loved to tell about the early days. All knew Adam. Adam and Eve must have shared about the beginning and the Fall. Uncles, cousins, and female relatives may have joined in. What do you think Noah learned?

LEARNING ABOUT HIS PAST

Noah must have heard details of the pre-Fall world — how Adam walked with God every day in that special Garden. What the cool of the evening was like in the Garden of God. The sound of the Lord's voice. The incredible beauty of God as they talked face to face. The fragrant perfume of God's own being, mixed with the aromas of perfect and pure plants and animals which had no decay, no death. What peace and joy perfect obedience to the will of God, brings. Oh, what insights into intimacy with God and God's creation, Noah's grandfathers must have given him.

Most youngsters enjoy learning about animals. Noah must have asked about the animals. Adam surely spoke of the pre-Fall animals: what they were each like, how he named them, his intimate acquaintance with each one, as well as each one's unique qualities and abilities. The peace, the rest, the wonderful relationship existing between man and animals. The language of the animals and what it was like to understand and talk with them. How they all ate plants and not each other. How, prior to the thorns and thistles, neither man nor beast struggled with hunger or want. How things changed when man was cursed. What the Lord meant in giving man authority over all the animals and how to exercise that authority well. How to handle or treat each one.

In order to bring rest to the ground, Noah had to learn to walk with God as Adam did before the Fall. Like Adam, Noah needed to know the animals by name, which really means knowing their ways. Just as Enoch (the grandfather who never died) [Gen. 5:24], walked with the Lord, Noah had to walk with God, so he could do this.

"He must have been like a super-duper St. Francis of Assisi," Jan told us. "Noah must have had God's grace to talk to animals, to understand them, and command them."

THE HARMONY OF ARK AND NOAH'S REST

"Rest" includes peace from the striving for food. When the carnivores and prey animals were together on the ark, there had to be truce and a rest from striving for food.

There is no record that Noah kept any animals as food on the Ark. According to Jewish rabbis of old, humans were not allowed to eat meat until after the Great Flood. (Only the sacrifice of animals to God had been allowed. [Gen. 1:29; 9:3])

The animals probably also were vegetarian. If they *were* already carnivorous, then the Lord must have given grace to the carnivores to become as pre-Fall vegetarians — at least for the year they spent together on the Ark. The atmosphere of the Ark must have returned to that of the Garden of God for the confinement: Man loving animals; animals loving man; and all caring for each other. That's the way it ought to be!

This would be a type, a foretaste, of heaven. Heaven is the ultimate place of rest — not from healthy, fulfilling work, but from the curse and toil of it. In order to experience heaven on earth, peace must exist for all God's creatures, great and small. This fits with the late Agnes Sanford's theology about praying for the earth and its creatures so that we may live in harmony and peace.[128]

Noah needed the faith and skills to manage those animals and require peaceful co-existence on that ark. Even the preparation for the voyage must have required such skill and grace. The best foodstuffs were needed to keep the animals healthy on the long voyage. The best of the species would have volunteered for the new beginning. Given the number of animals on earth, the size of the Ark and the length of time they would spend on it, it is understandable it took a hundred years. It was a huge undertaking.

Don't you think the animals helped prepare the ark and gather food? Beasts of burden, such as oxen, llamas and elephants, have hauled stuff for humans since ancient times. Elephants are "pre-machine cranes" for heavy lifting. Wild animals may also have helped.

It is not hard to believe that beavers cut down gopher trees and helped strip and shape the logs, oxen hauled the wood, and elephants lifted up the wood and pitch to the human and simian carpenters. All could help gather foodstuffs and bedding materials for themselves and others. Birds, rodents and ants are good at gathering. Parrots may have directed traffic. Bees could make honey in abundance. Humans and bears like honey! Sweet energy for work and play in their year-long confinement.

AFTER THE FLOOD

God used the ark to preserve a remnant of people and

animals to replenish the earth after its bath. It is like Him. [Ps. 91 & 1 Cor. 10:13 support this.)

When the waters receded, Noah and the animals came out of the Ark onto dry land. Noah offered an animal sacrifice, then, before everyone disbursed, the Lord God Himself made the following covenant:

> *Now behold, I Myself do establish* ***My covenant*** *with you, and with your descendants after you;* ***and with every living creature that is with you, the birds, the cattle, and every beast of the earth with you; of all that comes out of the ark, even every beast of the earth.*** *And I establish My covenant with you; and* ***all flesh*** *shall* ***never again*** *be cut off by the water of the flood, neither shall there again be a flood to destroy the earth. And God said, This is the sign of the* ***covenant*** *which I am making between Me and you and* ***every living creature*** *that is with you,* ***for all successive generations****: I set My bow in the cloud, and it shall be for a sign of a covenant between Me and the earth.*
>
> Gen. 9:9-13 [NASV] (Emphasis supplied)

Every time we see a rainbow, it is God's sign that He is keeping His promise. It is a promise that is good forever. It serves as a "type and shadow" of the promised redemption of the Messiah. The promise was not just to humans — even though it has been taught that way. The promise reflects God's attitude toward His animals. What did this promise mean?

The Ark is a picture of the Lord's salvation or redemption of the world. Most of the time, ministers include mankind alone in this redemption. A fair reading must include *both* man and animal. The Lord's covenant includes both. The Noahic covenant is eternal for man and animals. There is nothing in Scripture which supports excluding the animals.

ALL FLESH

God said "all flesh," not just "human flesh." The word "flesh" is not limited to human beings in the Bible, just as it is not so limited in modern English. The same original Hebrew word for "flesh" is used for human flesh [Gen. 2:21,23], and for the flesh of animals. [Exodus 12:8; 16:3; Lev. 7:15 & 8:17; Num. 11:4 & 13]. Paul wrote:

> *All flesh is not the same flesh, but there is one flesh of men, and another of flesh of beasts, and another flesh of birds and another of fish.*
>
> 1 Corinthians 15:39 [NASV]

This phrase, used throughout the Bible, has several meanings. One is literal, i.e., muscle, sinew and skin — the mortal flesh. Another is the "soulish desires," i.e., behavior that focuses on selfish satisfaction, rather than pleasing God. God's permissive will — if there is such a thing — sometimes allows man and animals to do "fleshly" things without immediate consequences. (There are still consequences, including a loss of harmony.)

Following the Flood, God's permissive will or law changed. Man and animals were permitted to eat flesh. If they had done so previously or not, meat eating was now "legalized." Obviously many choose to do so, even whole species, *homo sapiens* (man) included.

After the Flood, the eating of meat remained surrounded with many restrictions.[129] Rabbis were entirely against wanton killing, just as they were against causing pain to animals. One of the seven Noahian laws prohibits eating a living animal's flesh. (How cruel!) This rabbinical teaching applies to all people, including non-Jews. Also, blood was never to be eaten and meat was to be eaten in moderation. The Biblical basis is recorded here:

> *So God blessed Noah and his sons, and said to them: "Be fruitful and multiply, and fill the earth. And the fear of you and the dread of you shall be on every beast of the earth, on every bird of the air, on all that move on the earth, and on all the fish of the sea. They are given into your hand.* ***Every moving thing that lives shall be food for you. I have given you all things, even as the green herbs. But you shall not eat flesh with its life***

[nephesh], that is, its blood. Surely for your lifeblood I will demand a reckoning; from the hand of every beast I will require it, and from the hand of man. *In from the hand of every man's brother I will require the life of man.*

Whoever sheds man's blood, By man his blood shall be shed; for in the image of God he made man. And as for you, be fruitful and multiply; bring forth abundantly in the earth and multiply in it.

Gen. 9:3-6 [NKJ] (Emphasis supplied)

God forbade humans to partake of the blood, because the soul-life is in the blood. Religions and cults which partake of blood violate this command of God. Blood pudding for example, a European dish is strictly taboo for Jews and Christians. [Acts 15:19-20] Why does God prohibit eating blood? If there is anything to the old saying that we become what we eat, perhaps that explains it. We are not to be vampires. He has different plans for us.

As we discussed earlier, God graced both carnivores and their prey. Equipped with sharp teeth or beaks, and claws, usually carnivores kill their prey swiftly — long before the shock wears off. Shock and the lack of fear of death is a gift of God to animals which prevents pain while becoming dinner.[130]

Eating flesh is not the condition of man nor beast in heaven — as we shall see. Heaven's feasts must be indescribably delicious. I like meat. But I doubt the most avid steak-lover will miss his or her meat! Our God could make eggplant taste as good as the best meat on earth, if that makes you happy. In heaven the citizens are all happy! Mom's knows, I'm sure!

ANOTHER COVENANT — THE FARMER'S BLESSING!

Noah's covenant is perhaps the most important for Mom's question, but the next covenant is astonishing to me:

In that day I will make a covenant for them with the beasts of the field, with birds of the air, and with the creeping things of the ground.

Hosea 2:18 [NKJ]

Hosea recorded that God made a covenant with insects and wild beasts so they would not destroy crops grown by God's chosen people. It's a blessing to faithful farmers. While the covenant existed for the benefit of God's people, it was made **with** the animals and insects!

Farmers would love that covenant operating in their fields! Rabbits, rodents and deer can be very destructive. Insects can destroy entire fields of crops.

Don't you wonder what the Lord promised to those creatures? Hosea didn't say. It could have been good things to eat, or nice weather, or cozy dens or nests. Perhaps it was Heaven.

IMPLIED COVENANTS — OTHER PROMISES TO ANIMALS

There are other scriptures which imply covenants even though the word is not used. For example, ravens fed the prophet Elijah while he hid by the brook from King Ahab and Queen Jezebel. [1 Kings 17:1-6] God may have made a covenant with those ravens. Scripture says ravens are fed by God. [Job 38:41] They also have the unpleasant task of "picking" out the eye of the mocker. [Prov. 30:17] We had a pet crow, Pete. Crows are cousins to ravens. Crows and ravens are intelligent, clever birds. God is a most fair employer and would compensate the raven well for its services.

Another possible example of the Lord's care of and covenant with animals is Jesus' statement that not a sparrow falls to the ground without God seeing, and that he feeds the birds of the air. [Luke 12:24; Matt. 10:29-31; and Luke 12:6-7; see also Job 38:41; Ps. 147:9] Philosophers have noted that God cares for the beasts of the wilderness in areas where human population is scarce — if I recall my college philosophy classes. It is God and not man who cares for the wild animals and supplies them the necessities of life. His love and compassion extend far beyond just those "made in His image." When you covenant with someone, you pledge to care for them. Our *evidence* is building.

In truth, there is much in scripture which indicates that animals love and obey their Creator, normally without question. Consider the unbroken donkey's colt which willingly let Jesus ride him through noisy crowds into Jerusalem. [Matt. 21: 1-7; Mark 11: 1-10; Luke 19: 29-38] The lions shut their mouths in the presence of Daniel, yet they quickly killed his accusers. [Daniel 6: 16-24] An awesome example is the lion which killed only the prophet who disobeyed the Lord; yet did not kill the prophet's donkey, and stood with the donkey until the prophet's body was taken away. [I Kings 13]. Birds brought back the olive branch to the ark. [Genesis 8] The Lord must reward such obedience!

Loving humans echo this in their care of animals. We spend hard-earned money on food, toys, vet bills, and even burial arrangements for our animals. It's not hard, because animals love us so well. There are many who know the love of God through dogs, cats, horses, pigs and other intelligent pets. Some pet owners consider their animals' love, company and loyalty superior to humans they know — and that's a sad commentary on human love.

Some have experienced the love or compassion of wild animals, as we discussed previously. From dolphins saving the shipwrecked, to eagles guiding lost hikers, to badgers and wolves sheltering and feeding lost children, the accounts prove a God-like caring at the heart of many of the wild, as well as domestic, animals.

Possibly it explains why many of us enjoy the Disney fantasies and movies like *Mouse Hunt* and *101 Dalmatians* where animals act intelligently — even with compassion. Somewhere inside us we recognize there is a degree of truth in these tales.

ANIMALS FASTING TO ESCAPE JUDGMENT

In the book of Jonah, we learn God forgives animals. When Jonah pronounced judgment on the city of Nineveh, the animals were included:

> *And Jonah began to enter the city . .. Then he cried out and said, "Yet forty days and Nineveh shall be overthrown."*

* * *

> *Then word came to the King of Nineveh; ... the King [decreed], "Let* ***neither man nor beast, herd nor flock****, taste anything; do not let them eat, or drink water. But let* ***man and beast*** *be covered with sackcloth, and cry mightily to God; yes, let everyone turn from his evil way and from the violence that is in his hands. Who can tell if God will turn and relent, and turn away from his fierce anger, so that we may not perish?" Then God saw ... and God related from the disaster that he said he would bring upon them.*
>
> *[Later the Lord said to Jonah, who was angry that God had mercy on the Ninevehites]: "and should I do not pity Nineveh, that great city, in which are more than one hundred and twenty thousand persons cannot discern between their right hand and their left, and* ***much livestock****?"*
>
> Jonah 3:4, 6-10; 4:11 [NKJV] (Emphasis supplied)

Have you ever heard of animals fasting? The "livestock" of Nineveh did. That term included horses, donkeys, camels, cattle, goats, sheep and other domestic animals. Why would livestock need to repent? Maybe these livestock were mean and dangerous, like their human companions. Perhaps it was beastiality, that depravity where humans and animals have sex. Whatever it was, the sins of Nineveh threatened both man and beast. God had had a "belly-full" and pronounced judgment on every living thing in Nineveh. Is it surprising that the animals had to repent and did so? I've watched my animals show guilt, act sorry they did something that injured or irritated me or another animal, and modify their behavior. It is not unusual.

GOD'S CARE FOR ANIMALS

God recognized and honored that fast. Here's proof God's mercy is not only toward people. He forgives and has mercy on animals. It makes me wonder, if an animal "goes off its feed," is that animal perhaps fasting with a purpose? I read of a cat which quit eating when its dying master did, and died days after the man did. People have told me that they felt that their dog or other animal joined them in prayer. It makes sense that animals can fast with a purpose.

GOD, THE COVENANT KEEPER

The Biblical God is a covenant maker. The Jewish people have enjoyed the longest covenants with the Lord. The fundamental proposition upon which Judiasm rests, is that Israel and God are eternally joined through covenant.[131] In defining the nature of a covenant people, Arthur Hertzberg said that when the people God has chosen, obey His divine commandments, they experience His nearness greater than any other peoples; that He is not a divine despot, so obedience to God's law is not slavery, but the way to a recurrent encounter with Him.[132]

Christians also are covenant people, although too few of us really understand what that means. Real faith is based and grows in informed obedience to the Lord's truth. The more we know, the more we can believe and obey. The more we trust and obey, the more God can entrust to us. The more the Lord entrusts to us, the more benefits we can enjoy. With our freedom, we will affect all around us, including our animals. We can be like Noah, a bearer of rest and a buffer between sinful actors and the Lord's just judgment. In other words, we can be a blessing to all creation — as the Lord intended Adam and Adam's offspring to be.

To the people who know God's covenant, there are paradoxes. Consider that it takes slavish obedience to the laws of music or art to achieve the freedom which mastery brings. Obedience to the Lord, the Creator, brings wholeness, beauty and freedom unknown to the rebel. One cannot but wonder what those animals will experience who, because of their obedience, enjoy the Lord's covenant.

This study is proof that God does not think of the animals as existing solely for man's use and pleasure. God uses them, blesses them, judges them and rewards them. It was exciting to learn that the Lord established irrevocable covenants with animals. Words cannot describe my feelings. All flesh, all creatures — the Lord God loves them all.

These covenants are a major piece of the puzzle. Mom's question has quite an interesting answer. Keep in mind, we are building a case, precept by precept, to see whether the Bible teaches that animals will go to heaven. Mom's question does have an answer.

I only wish the animals could tell us more about the Lord's relationship with them. Aren't you glad we can be joined in covenant to God, along with the animals? Noah's covenant is a wonderful promise for eternity. This may have been what Solomon was thinking when he wrote:

> *But for him who is joined to all the living there is hope, for a living dog is better than a dead lion.*
>
> Eccles. 9:4 [NKJV]

CHAPTER 10

JOB AND OTHER OLD TESTAMENT NUGGETS

"Listen to this, O Job, stand and consider the wonders of God. Do you know how God establishes them? ...The wonders of One perfect in knowledge...? ...The Almighty — we cannot find Him; He is exalted in power; and He will not do violence to justice and abundant righteousness. Therefore, men will fear Him; He does not regard any who are wise in heart."

Job 37:14, 16, 23-24 [NASV]

Are you as amazed as I am at how much the Bible says about animals? When we speak often about a subject, it usually means it is valuable to us. Animals are a vital part of God's plan. It was not until I studied to answer Mom's question, that I saw the Biblical importance of animals. But there's more!

In the Book of Job are significant passages about animals. Since it can be considered an early source, this emphasizes its consequence. Job dates back to the early Biblical patriarchs. References have been found placing Job as early as 2000 B.C.[133] In my opinion, it's a key book to understand the Lord God. Yet Job, like Revelation, can be an extremely difficult book to comprehend. Why?

JOB AND HIS FRIENDS KNEW GOD.

Job walked with God. The first chapter describes Job as "blameless and upright." Yet after Satan walked into God's throne room one day and got permission to test Job, all that Job had was wiped out in a series of disasters — children, wealth, and health. His wife even suggested Job curse God and die. Job's three friends, Eliphaz, Bildad, and Zophar, likewise knew the Lord. You can tell this by studying their speeches in Job chapters 4 through 31. Each knew God well.

In these chapters, Job's complaints are debated by Job's friends in turn. Each tries to reason why disaster has struck and what Job must do to be back in God's graces — all assume Job has sinned. Job complains the Lord is not treating him right. Job's complaints against God are filled with truths about the Creator and His character. So are the discourses of Job's three friends. Even though they condemn Job without answers [Job 32:3], these men clearly knew a lot about God. (The term "Job's comforters" was well earned. Family and friends are most likely to be "Job's comforters" to us.)

Some of their wisdom is rather pithy humor. For example, Zophar tells Job:

> *An idiot will become intelligent when the foal of a wild donkey is born a man.*
>
> Job 11:12 [NASV]

The reason Job is difficult to understand is because these men were a mix of truth and error. The dialog between Job and his three friends switches between truths and fallacies. They are like a tangled skein of yarn which is difficult to unravel. In this respect they are like Christians today. We, too, have truth and error about the Lord and His Word tangled up together, as this study demonstrates.

Sorting the good from the bad takes the Lord's help. Unless you understand God better than these men, you can't do it. That's a challenge! Even as a Spirit-filled Christian, with the advantage of Jesus and Holy Spirit dwelling *in* me, not just *with* me, and having the whole Bible as a source of insight, I'm not positive I know the Lord as well as Job and his friends. [Col. 1:27; John 14:16-21; 17:12, 16-24] However, I've found God loves to reveal Himself and His truths to those who trust Him. [James 1:5] He's given me great insights into His kingdom, and for that I am very grateful. My constant prayer is Exodus 33:13: to please Him more, that I may know Him more. It's a great adventure.

ELIHU: A KEY TO JOB

In Job 32, we meet a fourth man, Elihu. Most Bible commentators either ignore Elihu or count him with Job's three friends. That's a pity. I've found Elihu the key to unraveling truths in this Book of the Bible.

Chapter 32 starts with Elihu, a young man, waiting until his elders have their say. Then Elihu angrily castigates all four:

> *Then the wrath of Elihu, the son of Barachel the Buzite, of the family of Ram, was aroused against Job; his wrath was aroused because he justified himself rather than God. Also against his three friends his wrath was aroused, because they had found no answer, and yet had condemned Job.* Job 32:2-3 [NKJ]

Who was Elihu? Was his anger justified?

His name and genealogy are clues. Elihu means, "God Himself" or "God who Is." By translating the names of his fathers, a picture of Jesus the Christ emerges: Ram means "one who came from on high." Buzite means "one despised and shamed by men." Barachel means "one blessed and anointed by God." Add them together and a picture of the Christ emerges. Jesus was and is God Himself, the *I Am* of the Bible. [John 1:1-5, 14; 8:55-59] Jesus came from on high. [John 3:16; Eph. 4:8] He was despised and shamed by men. [Luke 22:63-65; Isa. 53:3-4] Yet Jesus was (and is) the blessed Anointed One. [Ps. 2:2; Acts 2:36] ("Christ" means "anointed one" in Greek.) [Heb. 9:11]

When you study Job 32 and 33, there are other things which point to Elihu being a type or shadow of the Messiah, the Christ, as Savior and Judge of all. [Acts 17:22-31; Matt 25; James

4:12] Every time I read Elihu's discourse, I get new insights. Elihu is a prophet and judge (like Samuel [1 Sam. 7]and Deborah [Judges 4-5]) who brings Job and his friends face to face with the Almighty. Elihu's discourse runs from Chapter 32 through 37.

There are interesting statements about animals in Elihu's discourse, too, such as:

> *For by these He judges peoples; He gives food in abundance. He covers His hands with the lightning and commands it to strike the mark. Its noise declares His presence.* ***The cattle also, concerning what is coming up.*** Job 36:31-33 [NASV]

This snippet seems to say the Lord lets animals know things before they happen. He does that for people. [John 16:13] Those who observe animals are not surprised. Animals don't get hit by lightning very often. Certainly, it appears some animals are prepared for future events.

In England during WWII, people observed that their cats seemed to know exactly when and where German bombs were going to land.[134] Pets have gotten upset hours before earthquakes. Dogs have shown awareness their master or mistress was going to have heart attacks, seizures or accidents. Some know when their owner will return, going to the door shortly beforehand.

A coal miner in West Virginia fed a rat down in the mine; one day the rat ran around in a frenzied manner until the miner followed him; behind him the ceiling collapsed where he'd stood.[135] It's not clear how they know. Why wouldn't the Lord let animals know future things?

OUT OF THE WHIRLWIND

Eli's speech brought Job face to face with the Lord God. After Elihu's speech, the Bible's next words are:

> ***Then*** *the Lord answered Job out of the whirlwind and said, . . .*
>
> Job 38:1 [NASV]

"**Then**." followed Elihu's discourse. It was neither Job's words nor his three friends which brought the Lord's answer. Isn't that telling?

What did the Lord say to Job? Read Job 38 through 42. It is a beautiful paean. The Lord exults in the Creation. Through a series of questions, the Lord describes the measurements of the earth and its universe. "Have you ever in your life commanded the morning and caused the dawn to know its place...?" The Lord goes into a series of questions about animals: "Can you hunt the prey for the lion?" "Will the wild ox consent to serve you?" "Do you give the horse his might?"

The Lord continues through a long list including lions, ravens, mountain goats, wild donkeys, wild ox, ostriches, horse, behemoth (some believe this is the hippopotamus or elephant) and finally leviathan. God describes mostly wild animals — those who usually do not submit to human governance.

Most of His recorded speech is about these living creatures. Why? Because our Lord delights in His creation. Like the consummate Artist that He is, He has bragging rights. How interesting that when God instructs us, he keeps pointing to the animals. "Go the ant and learn her ways." [Prov. 6:6]

How like Him most of us are! Who has not been fascinated by animals? We love nature stories and films featuring animals — real or fictional. In learning *about* animals, we learn a lot *from* animals. When we actually *care* for an animal, we learn the most. They are good teachers about God.

It is as though God is instructing about man's relative importance in the grand scheme of things. Creation is much greater than man. Animals have a huge part. Job got an earful. It made him realize that justifying himself, rather than crediting God, was not too smart. [Job 32:2] Sometimes after we've walked in intimacy with the Almighty a while, we tend to grow cocky.

Modern Christianity has brought an intimacy with God as father, brother, husband and friend. However, too often we get too casual and disrespectful. A fearful respect and reverence are also due the Almighty. When trouble hits us, like Job, we complain and blame God. We "make ourselves out better than God" as the Amplified version of Job 32:2 says. When trouble comes our way, we believe we are right and God is wrong — as the Jerusalem Bible puts it. The Lord God is still infinite, all-knowing, and all-caring. He deserves our total respect, trust, and love. We should be defending Him, rather than complaining. We should remember His speech to Job, that song of creation which demonstrates His power and love.

THE MAJESTIC HORSE

The Bible has good things to say about horses. The Lord Himself brags about the horse:

> *Do you give the horse his might? Do you clothe his neck with a mane? Do you make him leap like the locust? His majestic snorting is terrible. He paws in the valley, and rejoices in his strength; He goes out to meet the weapons. He laughs at fear and is not dismayed; And he does not turn back from the sword. The quiver rattles against him, The flashing spear and javelin. With shaking and rage he races over the ground; And he does not stand still at the voice of the trumpet. As often as the trumpet sounds he says, "Ha!" And he scents the battle from afar, And thunder of the captains, and the war cry.*
>
> Job 39:19-25 [NASV]

This passage is, in Hebrew, a poetic description of a horse — I believe a war horse. It presages the second coming of the Messiah. [Revelation 19:11-14] The King of Kings returns to earth as a mighty warrior on a white horse. His armies follow on white horses. There are horses in heaven. Like the horses I experienced in my youth, they are fine, good animals, capable of protecting those whom they love!

Many city dwellers have little personal contact with horses. While we can watch movies and read books, it's not the same as actually touching them and getting to know them. As related earlier, I had the advantage of being the daughter of the town veterinarian; therefore, I grew up riding horses. I still love to be around horses when I have the opportunity.

When I was a child, I discovered a book about "haute ecole," French for "high schooling" horses. The book was filled with wonderful photos of muscular white horses doing things I did not know horses could do. Called "dressage" and "airs above the ground," these horses performed movements that looked like dancing, controlled leaps into the air, precise rearing on their hind legs. I loved it! These Lippizaner stallions have the strength and training to do these highly stylized movements. The elaborate maneuvers are an art form as much as gymnastics or figure skating. Beautiful to watch, it's called the "ballet" of the equine performances. When I read in Job the description of the horse, I think of these stallions.

For thousands of years, horses have served man in war and for other useful purposes. Xenophon, an ancient Greek military genius, wrote the first known manual on training war horses. Some of his wisdom is still passed on to the best horse trainers. I wonder if he ever read Job?

Alexander the Great, (356-323 BC) King of Macedonia, had the most famous war-horse. Legend has it that as a twelve-year-old boy, Alexander chose and mastered the great stallion, Bucephalus. Alexander was reputedly the only man able to ride Bucephalus. Fearless in battle, the horse was quite protective of his master. The stallion became indispensable in helping Alexander conquer most of his known world. Alexander and his armies conquered Greece, the Persian Empire and Egypt — all before he died at age 33. A monument of the great horse was erected in Macedonia to honor the stallion.

War is certainly not the only or most important role horses play. Being mounts for Jesus and His armies in that last battle is a brief event if taken with a historical, even eternal, perspective. Look at the role horses play now. In industrialized societies they are primarily pleasure animals, used for trail riding, shows, and racing.

Horses are fun companions. Mine have given me hours of joy. They tease and make me laugh. They enjoy exploring the land. They are compassionate when I am sad or hurting. To this day, I find that a pleasure ride on a good horse is both enjoyable and restorative. As a child, I boasted I would live to be 127 and would ride horses the day before I died!

Horses are serving today as recognized therapy animals. Case studies of schizophrenic and psychotic persons[136], as well as those ill with multiple sclerosis,[137] have shown remarkable healing from riding on, and interacting with, horses. Given the sensitivity of a horse to touch, and the fact that riding is a most relaxing, yet invigorating exercise, it is little wonder that our Lord designed the horse as a healer.

LEVIATHAN, THE GREAT SERPENT

> *Am I the sea, or the sea monster, that Thou hast set a guard over me?*
>
> Job 7:12[NASV]

The leviathan is the last creature the Lord God described to Job, and with this He closes Job's instruction. Most teachers sum up and emphasize key points at the end of their discourse. Why did the Lord end His discourse with this creature? What was He saying to Job and to us?

The leviathan is an unknown creature. Scholars disagree as to what it is or was. Some vote for the crocodile of the Nile. Crocs, however, are not taken with fish hooks, to my knowledge. The description of the leviathan doesn't wholly fit a crocodile. Others think the leviathan is a sperm whale. Others think it's an unknown sea serpent, like the Loch Ness monster.

As we discussed in Chapter 7, I argue the leviathan is the Great Serpent, Satan. This matches the description in Revelation 12 and in Genesis 3. If so, God's closing words to Job describing Leviathan, was in fact a description of Satan or the devil.

God was warning Job against pride. Leviathan is the "king over the sons of pride." This serpent then is the deceiver and accuser of man [Rev. 12:9-10] and the father of lies [John 8:44]. Satan loves to tempt man into the prideful belief that we can be like God. When the devil succeeds, we are under his dominion. God made him king over "sons of pride."

This makes sense. The book of Job opens with Satan gaining permission to destroy everything but Job's life. [Job 1] When the Lord ends His talk with Job by describing Satan as an animal God created, an animal of immense power and cunning against which man is no match, it is a message. A message to Job and to us to avoid pride, especially spiritual pride in what a righteous person we are and how "in" with God we are. For such pride puts animals at enmity with us.

Do you see what the Lord is telling Job? Only God has absolute power and control over all creation. Leviathan is just one of many — whether Satan likes it or not! That's why the Lord wants us "hidden in Christ" — so He can protect us from Satan's wiles. [Col. 3:1-3; Rev. 12:10-11]

OLD TESTAMENT AND JEWISH INTERPRETATIONS

> *The kind man feeds his beast before sitting down to dinner.* [Hebrew proverb[138]]

The world has not always been kind to man or beast. (Even as I write this, there is a petition to ban cockfighting in Oklahoma. In cockfighting, the birds are equipped with sharp steel spurs and fight to death.) The Bible and God's people who followed His Law, stand out because they are kind to animals. The laws of kindness make people different than most of the world.

Two thousand years ago, during the time when Jesus of Nazareth, a Jew, lived, died and was resurrected, Greeks and Romans held everybody and everything, except themselves, in contempt. (I wonder if this is genetic? I know people like that.)

Max Dimont, in *Jews, God and History*, compared the Jewish and Graeco-Roman cultures. The reasons the Greeks and Romans gave for holding the Jews in contempt are instructive, if irrational. The Romans nailed people to wooden crosses and called it justice; yet expressed horror at Jewish circumcision. Romans threw defenseless human slaves to wild beasts and called it amusement; yet viewed the Jewish Feast of Passover as barbaric because lambs were sacrificed at Passover. (Never mind that the lambs were killed with merciful quickness.) Comparing the two cultures, it is the Jew who has the most compassion for less-privileged humans and for the animals:

> *The Greeks and Romans, who mercilessly worked man and beast seven days a week and called it industry, looked with scorn on the Jewish practice of a day of rest every seventh day for freeman, slave and animal.*[139]

We have a lot to thank Jews for, including one day a week as rest from work for man and beast! Thank God for those who obey His commandments, and thereby benefit every living creature.

Unfortunately, the gentile Christians and the Jews became divided. The Church lost the benefit of rabbinical teaching. Only in the latter quarter of the 20th century has an examination of our Jewish roots become acceptable to many Christians. I'm eager to learn as much as possible — especially from those who lived so long in covenant with God. Jewish people studied the Lord as an act of worship. We Christians can learn much from them. I will learn from anyone who truly knows the Lord and His truth. How about you?

The Hebrews or Jews often have a good understanding about God's plan for animals. They wrote the Book. (If you have any anti-Semitic views, take that up with God in prayer.)

A SABBATH FOR ANIMALS

The Sabbath laws required rest not only for man, but every beast on every seventh day:

> *"Thou shall not do any manner of work . . .nor thine ox, nor thine ass, nor any of thy cattle"*
>
> Ex. 20:10 & Deut. 5:14 [KJ]

> *"... but on the seventh day thou shalt rest; that thine ox and thine ass may have rest"* Ex. 23:12 [KJ]

The genesis of a seventh day of rest is when God rested after six days of creation. [Gen. 2:1-2] It became a law for all. The only "work" permitted is what is necessary to relieve an animal's suffering or tend to its need. It would be cruel to prohibit feeding animals or saving their life or health. Cruelty to animals is biblically prohibited.

It's a good law. Labor laws and Sunday closing laws find their origin in Biblical principles. At one time in our history, a day of rest for laborers (and their working animals) in the United States was the norm. When oxen and horses pulled our wagons, plows, and carriages, this meant rest for them. In recent years, the practice has greatly eroded.

The worker, the athlete, and the animal who does not take regular time to rest, will get sick, wear out or burn out. Strength must be recovered by periods of rest. It is wickedness to work man and beast without rest. As we move away from the Lord, we tend to work ourselves and others to death!

KINDNESS TO ANIMALS

The Hebrew consideration of animals is based a number of commandments. Jews are taught to praise God as the One who satisfies all living creatures, and for giving food to the beasts and the birds. [Ps.145:9-16 and Ps. 147:9] Based on the verse, "I will give grass in thy fields for thy cattle, and thou shalt eat and be satisfied," [Deut. 11:15] the rabbis have taught for thousands of years that:

> *It is forbidden for a man to eat before he has fed his animal because the animal is mentioned first.*[140]

This duty is also supported by the verse:

> *A righteous man has regard for the life of his beast, but the compassion of the wicked is cruel.*
>
> Prov. 12:10 [NASV]

Out of the same consideration, rabbis also legislated that "a man is not permitted to buy animals unless he can properly provide for them."[141]

God's compassion for animals is evident. Farmers are prohibited from muzzling an ox as it threshes grain. [Deut. 25:4] A few mouthfuls of grain rewards and energizes a working animal, and doesn't harm the farmer. From this admonition comes the principles that a worker is worthy of his wages [Deut. 25:4, quoted in 1 Tim. 5:18], and that acts of kindness beget loyalty and productivity. The Torah also says that one must not slaughter an animal and its young on the same day —

a recognition that animals grieve. [Lev. 22:28] "If you see the donkey of him that hates you lying helpless under its load . . . you shall surely release it with him." [Ex. 23:5] A parent bird must be released before taking her young. [Deut. 22:6-7] The Hebrew expression, "the pain of living things" would also find its basis in these verses.

Several other Scriptures promote conservation as part of man's stewardship. Grain fields must lie fallow in the Sabbatical (seventh) year so "the poor of thy people... and the beast of the field" may eat from the gleanings (grains dropped during harvest). [Lev. 25:6-7] Modern practices which leave little grain in the fields, violate this command. By implication, killing all critters which feed on crops would be prohibited, too. Farmers who leave hedge rows fallow and grain in the fields preserve many species of wild creatures.

DOING UNTO OTHERS

The Golden Rule, "do unto others as you would have them do unto you," applies to animals, in rabbinical teaching. [Matt. 7:12; Prov. 22:8; Ps. 126:5; Gal. 6:7] God's treatment of each of us will be according to our treatment of animals. This is a belief of rabbis and was the teaching of Mohammed.[142] To the rabbis, the promise of long life juxtaposed with the duty (mitzvah) of sending the parent bird away before taking the young, suggests this doctrine. [Deut. 22:6-7][143]

I find it terrible that many Christian theologians and apologists hold an opposite view. Their Cartesian theology is cruel in comparison. If God is love, and He is, then which view would be true? That's a "no-brainer," isn't it?

Left without the disciplines of the Bible, and without the power of the Lord God to change human hearts, we are often no better than the Greeks and Romans. We have much to learn from and about animals. May the Lord help us to be better disciples. Are you willing to change? I am!

CHAPTER 11

JESUS CHRIST AND ANIMALS

Behold...on the first night of Christ's life, God honored the animal creation.... Was it not appropriate that He should, during the first few days and nights of His life on earth, be surrounded by the dumb beasts whose moans and plaints have for ages been a prayer to God for the arresting of their torments and the righting of their wrongs?

Not a kennel in all the centuries, not a robbed bird's nest, not a worn-out horse on the tow-path, not a herd freezing in the poorly-built cow-pen, not a freight car bringing beeves to market without water through a thousand miles of agony, not a surgeon's room witnessing the struggles of the fox or rabbit or pigeon or dog in the horrors of vivisection, but has an interest in the fact that Christ was born in a stable surrounded by animals. He remembers that night, and the prayer He heard in their pitiful moan. He will answer in the punishment of those who maltreat them."

Dr. DeWitt Talmage[144]

Why was Jesus Christ born in a stable of all places? He was God Almighty. He came to save mankind, didn't

He? His titles include King of Kings and Lord of Lords. Why not in a palace or the best room at the inn?

Over one-hundred Old Testament prophesies point to the birth, life, and death of the Messiah which are fulfilled in the man, Jesus of Nazareth. God orchestrated the whole thing down to the last detail.

The Roman census could have fallen at another time. Mary could have given birth in a palace. Rich magi, wise men as powerful as kings, came and gave the infant costly gifts soon after His birth. Rich men and women later followed this rabbi, Jesus. Jesus chose to be born in a stable. Born among the animals. That was God's choice.

Have you considered how often Jesus the Christ is likened in Scripture to various animals? He is "the Lamb of God which takes away the sin of the world." [John 1:29] He is "the Lion of the tribe of Judah." [Rev. 5:5] He likened Himself to a hen gathering her chicks under her wings. [Matthew 23:37 & Luke 13:34] Can we find anything in these references to help us answer Mom's question?

It was no accident Jesus appeared as Savior first among the "brute creation." It was no accident the Savior came to be born in a stable, a place where beasts of burden rest. In a little town, Bethlehem. In a tiny country, Israel. He came in the flesh as a helpless baby into a mere carpenter's family. Jesus came a Jew, as one of a people despised by most of the world. God likes the helpless, the poor, the despised. Jesus is identified with all who are like that. Any time you feel helpless, poor, or despised, think about that. Any time you see an animal abused or neglected, think about that.

Noah's ark was really a huge stable. As we mentioned, it is thought to be a type and shadow of the Lord's salvation. The stable in Bethlehem was afloat in a sea of sin, a world adrift in corruption and carnality. Not a very safe place. The world has not changed much.

Artists and song writers through the ages depict animals in the stable with the baby Jesus. The stable is rarely empty of animals. Cattle and camels kneel before the baby in adoration.

Christmas crèches have sheep gazing on the holy Child. It has a ring of truth.

What other animals might have been in that stable? Donkeys, horses, goats, chickens, ducks, pigeons, dogs, and cats were common domestic animals in ancient Israel. Also, mice, spiders, sparrows, swallows, owls, bats, wasps, and fleas are often in or near stables.

Maybe wild animals came, too. I have a crèche statuette with baby birds, squirrels, raccoons, rabbits, geese, mice, deer and other baby animals all over it. Baby Jesus would have loved them all.

Animals let others know when something new happens. Perhaps the neighborhood critters came too. Maybe garter snakes, so helpful to gardeners, slithered in to pay its respects. Why snakes? Not all snakes are as bad as the Great Serpent in Eden. Many non-poisonous reptiles are handy to have around. Mom liked snakes, and so do I. They keep down the insect and rodent population. They fell like cool silk to handle, and have an austere beauty.

The Nativity scene would not seem right without adoring animals gathered around the Christ child. Not just shepherds, but their sheep. Not an empty stable, but one with cattle and donkeys sharing their abode with the baby, King Jesus.

A case can be made that Jesus is a fulfillment of the Noahiac covenant, the ultimate Ark which brings salvation to *all creatures*, not just humans. Let's see how the evidence stacks up.

IN THE WILDERNESS WITH THE BEASTS

The Gospel of Mark 1:13 records the beginning of Jesus' earthly ministry, some thirty years after His birth in that Bethlehem stable. After Jesus was baptized in water by John the Baptist, John saw God's Holy Spirit descend upon Him. Then Jesus went immediately into the desert wilderness of Judea. Why?

> *And immediately the Spirit impelled Him to go out into the wilderness. And He was in the wilderness forty days*

being tempted by Satan; and He was ***with the wild beasts****, and the angels were ministering to Him.*

Mark 1:12-13 [NASV]

In the original Greek manuscripts, the word translated "with" in the phrase "with the wild beasts" is a preposition meaning "in the midst of, amid." It denotes "association, union, accompaniment."[145] So, Jesus, at the very inception of His ministry as the Son of Man associated with animals.

Compare Adam with Jesus. (Jesus Christ is described as the last Adam in 1 Cor. 15:45.) Both the first Adam and Jesus began life with animals which were all "domestic" or tame. When the first Adam fell, the animals were divided into wild and domestic. The last Adam began His ministry in the desert with wild animals, reuniting man with wild animals. As both God and man, Jesus must have had a great relationship with the animals.

Robert F. Leslie tells of meeting a bear, whom he named Bosco, in the Canadian wilderness. The bear sat beside him as he fished, and spent days as Leslie's companion. They ate and played together, and the bear protected him from other bears. When Bosco left, Leslie was "desolated." However, he treasured that brief relationship.[146] I like to think Jesus enjoyed the wild animals, too, before He came to minister to men.

Stories of naturalists who have spent time with lions, wolves, gorillas, and other wild animals, living among or with the animals without being harmed, are now well publicized. For example, R. D. Lawrence, a Canadian naturalist, wrote on keeping wolves and rescuing injured wild animals such as mice, birds, lynx, bear, and moose.[147] He and his wife lived and developed a relationship with many of them. Jesus' being "with the wild beasts" is not so different.

How appropriate that while Jesus was being tempted in the wilderness by Satan, that Serpent of Old, other wild beasts were the Lord's companions. When the Great Serpent tempted Adam and Eve, it was in the presence of all animals. Now during the temptation of the second Adam, Jesus, animals are again witnesses.

SALVATION OF GOD

And all flesh shall see the salvation of God.

Luke 3:6, Isaiah 40:5 [NASV]

Recalling our discussion of what "flesh" means in the Scripture, we know that this phrase "all flesh" includes both humans and animals. It is not unreasonable to think: just as God ordered Noah to build the Ark for the salvation of man and animals, Jesus, the second Adam, came to construct in His body — or flesh — an "Ark" for the salvation of "all flesh." Marks's Gospel ends with Jesus' commission to all creation:

And He said to them, "Go into all the world and preach the gospel to all creation."

Mark 16:15 [NASV]

Why did Mark write "all creation?" Why did Mark not write, "preach the gospel to all mankind?" We must be careful. Since all Scripture is inspired by God, then Mark wrote by inspiration of the Lord. [2 Tim. 3:16; 2 Pet. 1:20-21]. The Bible commands us not to add to nor to take away from the Word of God. [Deut. 4:2; 12:32; Rev. 22:18-19] If we interpret "all creation" as referring only to mankind, are we not "taking away" from the words "all creation"? "Creation" includes all living creatures from amoeba to elephants and whales. What is God saying here?

God created all animals and He cares for all flesh. Jesus came to reconcile all flesh. As we discussed earlier, St. Francis must have known this when he became a peacemaker between the town and the wolf.

Jesus Christ commanded His disciples to preach the good news to all creation. The Legends of St. Francis and St. Anthony support that animals are receptive to the gospel. We must address that issue. We must explore, prayerfully, what it means to "preach the gospel to all creation." If we don't, we may miss God's will, His best.

Some Christians use Mark 16 as a basis to pray for animals to be healed. They combine the fact that gospel is for all creation, and that "believers" will lay hands on the sick [vs.18] (which does not limit healing to humans). I have used this combination, as well as Deut. 28:1-4, quoting Mark 16 in prayer, as I laid hands on my animals. The Lord has healed them, too.

Let me interject here that much of what I am writing in this book is new to me. Some of it stuns me. When uncovering new ideas, I tend to stare at them like a cow at a new gate. Since I've been researching and writing this for years now, with every new revelation, I test and question and explore the idea as best I know how. The Lord has met me at every new turn, at every new question. For example, after the troublesome question of why the New Testament seemed to say little about Jesus' relationship to animals, I found (in a rather miraculous way) this Third Century prayer attributed to St. Basil of Caesarea:

> *And for these also, dear Lord, the humble beasts, who with us bear the burden and the heat of the day, and offer their guileless lives for the well-being of their country, we supplicate Thy great tenderness of heart,* ***for Thou hast promised to save both man and beast.*** *And great is Thy loving kindness, O master, Savior of the world.*[148]
>
> (Emphasis supplied)

So these ideas are not new, but old. They've just been forgotten or hidden for a very long time. It is not unscriptural to say Jesus came to save both human and animal. In fact, as we are seeing, Scripture supports such a thesis. There is more Scriptural evidence supporting this truth than not. The main obstacle is the human ego — coupled with ignorance.

DOES THE LORD'S PRAYER INCLUDE ANIMALS?

Jesus taught us to pray, "Our Father, who art in heaven, . . . Your kingdom come, Your will be done on earth, as it is in heaven." [Matt. 6: 9-13 & Luke 11:2-4] It dawned on me one day that if I had no idea what His will in heaven was, then I would probably refuse or reject His actions in trying to bring His will to pass in my life on earth. My ignorance could block God's will in my life.

What if God's will is (and has always been) to redeem *all* life from the Fall — not just humans? If we have no concept of God's plan, is it little wonder we treat animals with a lack of care and concern?

If animals are in heaven — and we already know horses are there — and since that is a place without pain, sorrow or death, then we can pray for animals to have "heaven on earth" as well. If we know we *can* pray that way, shouldn't we?

In the Sermon on the Mount, Matthew records Jesus teaching by way of parable, or example, about not being anxious about your life:

> *Look at the birds of the air, that they do not sow, neither do they reap, nor gather into barns, and yet your heavenly Father feeds them. Are you not worth much more than they?*
>
> Matt. 6:26 [NASV]

Many people enjoy feeding wild birds. I throw birdseed on my patio and enjoy watching sparrows, cardinals, mockingbirds, cowbirds, and blue jays come feed. This habit of feeding the little birds has also brought squirrels, hawks, and owls. It has been a postcard-pretty treat on a winter day to see a red cardinal tucked in my snow-dressed holly bush. We who love to feed the birds may be an answer to the Lord's Prayer — agents of God feeding His birds.

In Luke's Gospel is a similar quote to Matt. 6:26, except the birds are identified as ravens. [Luke 12:24] Is not this also a statement about God's care for the birds? The fact that their value is less than humans is not an issue here. The fact is, they have value to God.

Jesus pointed to the Father's care of the little birds to teach us more than one lesson. Isn't it remarkable that in wilderness areas, without the interference from man, bird species usually thrive. Even in urban settings, many birds have adapted to urban sprawl.

The law office where I work is on the fifty-ninth floor. I often see a hawk soaring around near the building. I pray it goes undisturbed.

St. Francis of Assisi reportedly had a contest with a nightingale in singing God's praises. The bird won! The nightingale had much to praise God for, just as St. Francis did. The Psalmist wrote: "Let everything that hath breath praise the Lord!" [Ps. 150:6] That's everything, folks!

Why should "everything" (animals) praise the Lord, if this short life of pain is all they have? On the other hand, they have much to praise Him for when the Savior's lovingkindness and grace belong to "every living thing."

JESUS AND THE DONKEY'S COLT

Jesus chose an unbroken donkey's colt for His ride into Jerusalem. As the time came for his entry into Jerusalem a few days before His death, Jesus sent the disciples to bring a certain colt of a donkey — a colt which had never before been ridden. This is recorded in three of the four Gospels, showing its importance. [Matt. 21:1-7; Mark 11:1-10; Luke 19:29-38]

> *And as they approached Jerusalem, at Bethphage and Bethany, near the Mount of Olives, He sent two of His disciples, and said to them, "Go into the village opposite you, and immediately as you enter it, you will find a colt tied there, on which no one yet has ever sat; but untie it and bring it here. . . ."*
>
> *And they went away and found a colt tied at the door outside in the streets; and they untied it. ...*
>
> *And they brought the colt to Jesus and put their garments on it; and He sat upon it. And many spread their garments in the road, and others spread leafy branches which they had cut from the fields.*
>
> *And those who went before, and those who followed after, were crying out, "Hosanna! Blessed is he who comes in the name of the Lord; blessed is the coming kingdom of our father David; hosanna in the highest!"*
>
> *And He entered Jerusalem and came into the Temple;*
>
> Mark 11:1-11 [NASV]

There are several remarkable things about this event. First, either Jesus knew the owner and colt, or something supernatural happened. How did Jesus know where this donkey was located, and that it had never known a rider? Scripture does not say. (The willingness of the owner to release the colt on the words, "The Lord has need of it," is remarkable unless the man or woman knew Jesus.)

Jesus rode this colt which had never known a rider, a colt from a small village, into the busy city of Jerusalem. Bethany and Bethphage were small towns during the time of Jesus. Yet this unbroken, small-town, donkey's colt willingly carried Jesus on his back into the city of Jerusalem.

Those crowds were noisy, shouting "HOSANNA TO THE KING!" They were *throwing* their garments on the road in front of the little colt on which Jesus sat. Many seasoned donkeys and horses would have been terrified and spooked.

Can anyone explain how the donkey braved that much noise and motion? That young colt immediately trusted Jesus enough to let Him mount its back. The donkey must have felt a calm emanating from the Prince of Peace which eliminated its natural fears. This instant rapport is remarkable. It is a statement of the relationship which this last Adam has with animals.

This is a significant event. The One who is greater than the first Adam, greater than Noah, greater than St. Francis, greater than any animal trainer who has walked the earth, rode that colt. Jesus (or if you prefer His Hebrew name, Joshua or Yeshua) is like His name. "Jesus" means "the Lord who saves, who brings Shalom, the peace and wholeness of God." This colt is evidence that Jesus is Lord and Prince of Peace to all creation. In an instant that nameless donkey knew Who and What this Man was. We should be as smart!

We could say Jesus was **the** "horse whisperer" and knew "donkey" language. Men and women like St. Francis and Monty Roberts are not unique, nor are they simply "products of their time." As Creator, Jesus is the ultimate communicator with animals. He was and is God.[149]

That colt not only knew Who Jesus was, but recognized His

love for all His creation. Like the animals in that Bethlehem stable, the donkey saw the One who is Love incarnate. This intelligent animal gave Jesus instant honor and obedience. This was what all creation has been groaning for, isn't it? [Romans 8:22]

The young donkey must have gladly carried its loving Creator through noisy crowds throwing strange objects into the pathway! Believing the little donkey was eager to please the Master is easy for most who know animals. Horses, dogs, cats and other animals perform tasks and tricks with obvious pleasure. I wonder if the colt knew what was ahead for Jesus? What a privilege to carry the Savior. What a burden to carry Him to His crucifixion.

Jesus began His human life in a stable, among the domestic animals. Jesus began His ministry as Savior in the wilderness among wild animals. Jesus began His journey to Calvary on a young, never-before-ridden donkey. Jesus will return as Lord of Lords and King of Kings on a horse, one day in the future. Perhaps very soon.

THE FISH WHO PAID JESUS' TAX

St. Anthony, if you recall, when he preached to those fish, spoke of a fish who paid Jesus' taxes. The account is found in the book of Matthew. Religious leaders had asked Simon Peter if Jesus paid the temple tax. Peter, without knowing the answer, said, "Yes." When Peter returned, Jesus spoke about the taxes before Peter could even tell Jesus the question. Jesus then told this professional fisherman to go fishing:

> *... go down to the sea, and throw in a hook; take up the first fish that comes up, and when you open its mouth you will find a shekel. Take it and give it to them for Me and for yourself.*
>
> Matthew 17:27 [Amplified]

Don't we all wish taxes were that easy to pay!

The miracle is how that coin got in that fish's mouth. One possibility is this fish found and picked up the coin; held it in its mouth without swallowing it; and looked for Peter to throw in that hook. Or, God could have created the coin in the mouth of the first fish Peter hooked. The first would reflect Jesus' ability to command the obedience of fish. The latter is a simple act of God. Both are miraculous. Both are possible with God.

Myself, I like the first. It is like the Lord to use animals. It is in keeping with the sacrificial service of God and His creation to man — a point we covered earlier.

JESUS SHED BLOOD — THE ULTIMATE IDENTIFICATION

Jesus identified with the animals who were sacrificed for sin:

> *For the bodies of those* **beasts [zoon],** *whose blood is brought into the sanctuary by the high priest for sin, are burned without the camp. Therefore Jesus also, that He might sanctify the people with His own blood, suffered outside the gate. Let us go forth with Him, outside the camp, bearing His reproach.*
>
> Heb. 13:11-13 [NKJ]

The Greek word for "beast" or "living creature" has an emphasis we miss in our culture. The King James Version translated the Greek word "zoon" (Strong's #2226) as "beast." It is from "zoe" (Strong's #2222). We get the terms "zoo" and "zoology" from "zoe." While the King James is not wrong, it loses something. According to Vine's, "zoon" is used primarily to denote a "living being," **"stressing the fact that life is the characteristic feature."**[150] It is the same word used in Revelation 4:7 to describe the four living creatures before God's throne — which we will discuss further on.

Do you see the implications? If the emphasis in "zoon" is life, what is the Spirit of Truth saying in Hebrews? Remember that the life is in the soul, and the soul is in the blood.

> *... and to Jesus, the mediator of a new covenant, and to the sprinkled blood, which speaks better than the blood of Abel.*
>
> Heb. 12:24 [NASV]

Abel's blood still speaks although his body is dead,

according to Hebrews 11:4 & 12:24. That means Abel is alive and well in eternity Is the Lord saying in Hebrews that, while the bodies of these sacrificed animals are dead, they still live?

Jesus spoke of Abraham as alive and not dead in John 8:56-58 and Luke 16:19-31. Their spirits are alive. They are connected to the Source of all Life, God Himself.

Jesus identified with the animal sacrifices. The lives of these sacrificed animals are connected to Jesus Christ. He chose to die, to be sacrificed as the Lamb of God, where animals were sacrificed. Jesus gave Himself to save humans, — just like every animal sacrificed since Adam and Eve. This Second Adam loves and identifies with animals — especially animals who die sacrificially. How like God that is. I want to be like Jesus.

JESUS HEALS ANIMALS AND THEY KNOW HIM

Animals know the Lord as Healer. Many of my animals have shown this sensitivity to His healing power. I frequently hear testimonies of God healing animals. The Catholic and Episcopal churches have had blessing services for animals for a long time. An increasing number of ministers pray for animals. I've even heard reports of animals being raised from the dead after prayer. Our God is a healing Savior for both man and animal.

A few years ago, on my radio program, a veterinarian and a children's minister (who owned a dog) were my guests. We discussed animal heroes and how Jesus heals our animals. The veterinarian shared a story of another vet she knew who was a new Christian. He'd not developed the habit of praying for animals. During an operation on a dog, the dog's heart stopped. The vet was frantically attempting to get medicine to try to stimulate the heart into beating again, afraid he'd lost the dog.

At the time, the vet's office was being remodeled, and a workman there asked if he could pray for the dog. Distracted, the vet agreed. The worker prayed a short simple prayer. The dog revived. The vet was astonished — and elated. From then on, prayer became a regular part of this vet's practice. I wonder how many veterinarians have experienced similar answers to prayer? I know many pet owners have.

My Siamese, "Kitty," loved the presence of the Lord and knew Him as her healer. She had a dramatic healing in a Kentucky woods. Kitty liked to go walking with me. (Some cats like walks.) So one spring day, I took her to a state park. A trail went up over small cliffs near the lake. At the top, Kitty explored while I sat and talked to the Lord. I noticed some insects buzzing her. When I approached, I realized they were ground hornets or wasps. We both ran. When we stopped at the bottom of the cliffs, Kitty's little head and face were covered with bumps! They were swelling, causing her pretty blue eyes to swell shut.

Instantly I realized Kitty could go into shock and die from the hornet venom. Faith arose strongly in me. I pointed at her and commanded her to be healed in the name of Jesus. In seconds the swelling went down and the bumps disappeared. Kitty looked at me with those wonderful blue eyes as though to say, "Gee, thanks! Isn't Jesus great! I knew you'd take care of me." When in need, Kitty came to me for prayer like bears come to honey!

Gretchen, our German shepherd, developed a tumor-like growth on her lip. The Lord led me to curse the tumor and call it healed by faith. However, it grew bigger. Some friends, seeing it, were alarmed at its size. I felt to keep calling the tumor gone, according to Romans 4:17 & Heb. 11:1-3. (I don't deny the tumor was real; it is just that faith calls those things that are not into being. Obviously you don't need faith for what you can see, touch, taste or hear.) After several days it dropped off and a bloody place was left. I asked the Lord to cauterize the spot and the bleeding stopped. Later, I checked Gretchen's lip and could not even locate the place where the tumor was.

Earlier when Gretchen was about two years old, she had a kind of doggy "myasthenia gravis," which caused her to stumble and be unsteady on her feet. The poor dear seemed confused as to why her body would not cooperate with her. I sought the Lord for her healing. He told me that my prayers would not heal her. Technically, she was Mom's pet. The Lord required Mom to pray for her. I had not known Mom to pray for healing before, so I wanted to panic. (This disease was progressive and fatal. Healing seemed to require a lot of faith. I had never observed Mom exercising that level of faith, but I had experienced such faith.) I cried and argued with the Lord, but He knew what He was doing. Not only did Mom pray, but every time the phone rang, she enlisted others to pray for Gretchen's healing. Our phone rang a lot. Half the town and out-of-towners, too, must have joined Mom in praying. Gretchen got well and stayed well many years. I learned a lesson in trusting the Lord in others.

What Scriptures would a person use to petition the Lord for healing an animal? You don't have to quote Scripture to get answers. God loves His animals. I do it to build my faith, as much as to remind God of His promises. Jesus is the Word [John 1.1] and the author of faith [Heb. 12:2]; and faith comes by hearing the Word. [Rom. 10:17] Praying the Spirit, i.e., tongues, builds faith. [Jude 20] The Lord often requires faith to do His work. [Mark 6:1-5] Verses which I meditate on for faith, before I pray for my animals, include these:

> *Now it shall be, if you will diligently obey the Lord your God, being careful to do all his commandments which I command you today, the Lord your God will set you high above all the nations of the earth. And all these blessings shall come upon you and overtake you, if you will obey the Lord your God. ...* ***Blessed shall be ... the offspring of your beasts, the increase of your herd and the young of your flock.***
>
> Deut. 28:1-3 [NASV]

> *And whatever you ask in My name, that will I do that the Father may be glorified in the Son. If you ask Me anything in My name, I will do it.*
>
> John 14:13-14 [NKJ]

> *Have faith in God. Truly I say to you, whoever says to this mountain, 'Be taken up and cast into the sea,' and does not doubt in his heart, but believes that what he says is going to happen, it shall be granted to him. Therefore I say to you, all things for which you pray and ask, believe*

that you have received them, and they shall be granted you.

Mark 11:22-25 [NASV]

My veterinarian friend uses Mark 16:15-18 when she lays hands on sick animals for healing. Whatever Scriptures are used, we know the Lord watches over His Word to perform it. [Isaiah 55]

You may have an account of the healing or miracle relating to an animal. Such stories abound. Several magazines, such as the Readers Digest and Guideposts, regularly run stories about animals which have been rescued, protected or healed miraculously.

It would be interesting to gather more Bible verses which have played a part in the healing or protection of our animal friends. I wonder if heaven has a video-room where we can view things that happened, so we can review such stories. I never tire of hearing them.

GOD CARES

Jesus cares for our animals. The animals know it. His redemption from the curse is broad. His blood was shed for redemption of all His creation. His love is far greater than we imagine. How foolishly arrogant to think the God, who lovingly made every living creature, would care only for man.

There is a God-ordained kinship between all living things, as J. Allen Boone observed.[151] Most people treat animals far below their capacity, as inferior and sub-human. Yet animals have character, intelligence (which is difficult to define or measure), and accomplishments. Such people ridicule those of us who treat animals like friends. They refuse to think a "mere animal" can understand us, even read our minds and intentions quicker than we do.

How very poor in joy are those who have never been friends with an animal. Those who become friends with animals are the richest people I know. They have been blessed. Have you never observed the *joie de vivre* (joy of living) which animals display?

Any time I've had a rough day, I can count on my animals to make me laugh and relax. They enjoy life. They care enough to work at getting me to join in the joy. Daily they teach me how to live better.

Cultivate a friendship with an animal, if you haven't already done so. If you are faithful and patient, you will be rewarded beyond measure. Prepare to be humbled in the process. Animals are both more forgiving and know more of real dignity than most of us think. Jesus is their Lord and Savior, too. He gave great gifts to us in His animals.

Observe them. Pay close attention. They will teach you — shout at you silently — of the really important things, of the care and plans the Lord has for all His creatures.

Animals are worthy of God's love and care. Animals, wild and domestic, have served humans, even with their lives. The dogs and other animals daily assist humans to health and better lives. Remember the story of Old Soap and the account of the gray eagle guiding the lost hiker? What about the dolphins, badgers, wolves, and others which have aided humans in the ocean and in the wilderness? Balaam's donkey fought an angel for her master. What about my grandmother's stray dog which gave its life for her? What about an AIDS patient who wanted to kill himself after receiving that diagnosis, but, his cat wouldn't quit loving him; that cat was the only friend who did not withdraw from him. That cat not only stayed, but drew closer not fearing his dread disease.

There are many animal heroes. Most are unsung heroes. They know the Lord. They serve His commandments of love, faithfulness, honor and courage. Their reward must be more than this life offers.

Jesus, like the Adam He is, includes them in His plans. He came to them, in the stable and the wilderness. He came for the animals, too. Do you see? Is the puzzle taking shape now?

CHAPTER 12

WHAT PARTS DO ANIMALS PLAY?

As the heavens are higher than the earth, so are My ways higher than your ways and My thoughts than your thoughts. ... My word that goes out from my mouth: It will not return to me empty, but will accomplish what I desire and achieve the purpose for which I sent it.

Isaiah 55:9 & 11 [NIV]

"But this is wondrous strange! There are more things in heaven and earth, Horatio, than are dreamt of in your philosophy." *Hamlet,* Shakespeare

What would this life — or heaven — be like without animals? Imagine it: no bird songs or the sound of wings. No warm, fuzzy puppies or playful kittens. No doe-eyed cows; no milk. No aquariums with rainbow-colored fish. The earth is populated with living creatures — from the tiniest amoebae to the massive whales. What would this earth be without living things — from plankton to giant sequoia trees?

Why didn't the Lord make us all machines? Evidence surrounds us that God made few machines. It is fallen man who "loves" machines more than animals, I think.[152] Have you ever wondered why? I have, and I know that I am not alone! Without answers, don't we sit in darkness, ignorant of the stupendous beauty and plans which surround us?

> *Thou art worthy, O Lord, To receive glory and honor and power;*
>
> *For Thou hast created all things, and for Your pleasure they are and were created.*
>
> *Rev. 4:11 [KJV]*

It gave God pleasure to fill this earth with life. He certainly chose to make a huge number and variety of living things. Some estimate there are in excess of 1,000,000 animal species numbering over 10^{33} (as in 10 followed by 33 zeros) animals living. Researchers are still adding to that list a thousand species per year![153] That doesn't count plant life.

Devices are not as interesting as living things. Machines are useful and the thrill of technological innovation is fun. But no machine compares to life. Living things have infinitely more diversity, flexibility, creativity, and other desirable qualities. Can a computer paint a Mona Lisa or a Sistine Chapel scene? Machines don't greet me at my door and clown until they make me laugh. No machine has voluntarily sacrificed its "life" for another being. Only living things can love you, forgive you, trust, you, and be a faithful friend.

Besides other good reasons, that is the core answer: machines cannot love and don't form relationships. Our living loving Creator didn't want robots. God is love. His very nature made Him create other lovers. Machines cannot love you. God made living things to form loving relationships. The earth is truly rich with lovers living in harmony — in spite of sin's ravages:

> *The intricate and extensive web of animal life exhibits millions of creatures living together harmoniously, attacking one another only out of the necessity to eat.*[154]

What fun He must have had making all living things! I believe the Lord would have made the living creatures even if He'd never made us humans.

Mom knew that God is love, and she knew God's love for all

creation. Her favorite Bible chapter was 1 Corinthians 13, Paul's amazing description of love. People and animals were drawn to her. Mom treated all animals, wild and domestic, like potential friends. She fed black widow spiders on a bet, and protected snakes from humans who would kill them. 1 John, chapter 4 could have been written with Mom in mind.

Quite frankly, in spite of my life-long experience with animals, I had no idea the depth and width of God's love for all living creatures and their roles in His creative plans, until well along in this book.

TAKING ANIMALS FOR GRANTED

It is easy to ignore the familiar. We are so accustomed to animals working for us, we take them for granted. Animals have served the Lord, cooperating with humans since the Fall of Adam. Animals provide many services to man, in peacetime and in war.

Besides providing meat for our tables, they have worked for us. From ancient times, oxen and horses plowed our fields and hauled our wagons and carriages. In some places, it was (and still is) elephants, camels and llamas working as burden bearers. Dogs, cats, ferrets and others have killed rodents, guarded and rescued people and possessions. Dogs and horses help herd our flocks and cattle. Dogs and pigeons carried messages through enemy lines during war, and performed other heroic tasks. Today, dogs and other animals are service-trained to aid the disabled — the blind, deaf, paralyzed, and mentally ill. In truth, most animals love to work![155]

Many people today are starved for physical affection. "Pet-able" pets like dogs, cats, even horses, readily give us something loving to touch. Medical research has confirmed that babies and adults who are never touched can have severe emotional and physical health problems. (And yet, pets were never meant to replace married love. Also, animals cannot fulfill the loneliness that people have without a personal relationship with the Lord. The animals would cringe at the absurdity of the thought.)

Studies have proven that people who keep a touchable pet

live longer, healthier lives. Stroking a dog or a cat lowers our blood pressure. Pet owners recuperate from surgery and illness faster. In today's America many live isolated because of age, health, or single life styles. Our animals and I made sure Mom got touched many times a day. Now, as a single working adult with plenty of good friends, there are still days when the only loving touch I receive is from my animals. Pets provide needed companionship.

Parents keep pets because children learn lessons of responsibility, unselfishness, patience and forgiveness from caring for animals. C. W. Gusewelle wrote that some study the lives of saints to learn about forgiveness, "And some of us keep dogs."[156]

Animals are good for us! It is little wonder that the pet industry is a multibillion dollar business. Animals are not gods, but they are gifts from God to us. Praise the Lord for His good gifts, the animals.

LOVING IS HEALTHY

Animals are healthier for us than machines. Farmers don't love their tractors the way most used to care about a good team of horses or oxen. Computer games, and cyber-pets don't lower your heart rate or lengthen your life.

I wonder how many are saved from suicide because a dog, cat, bird, or horse loves them? Even death has come easier because a loving pets would not leave the side of a master or mistress. God loved us enough to surrounded us with lovers of all kinds and sizes! Look around you at the furry, feathered and fuzzy friends you have yet to make.

Yet, a cautionary word is needed. While God gave man dominion over all life on this planet, He did not mean for animals to be mere slaves. Your attitude about animals may be a test. Those who think animals are as disposable as a plastic toothbrush miss God's plan entirely.

When my parents gave me a puppy or pony, I became responsible for that animal. If I neglected or abused it, my parents would have punished me, even taken it away from me. That is Biblical. Nowhere does the Bible say that animals are enslaved, valueless, or mere disposable commodities.

A now-retired Tulsa pastor repeated this story on radio: A man liked the song of the mockingbird. Finding a baby bird, he caged it outside his dwelling so he could hear the bird whenever he liked. A few days later he saw the momma bird feeding the baby. The next day the young bird was dead. The man spoke with a noted ornithologist about the incident. The ornithologist told him that mockingbird mothers have been observed feeding their captive babies poison berries. It is as though the mockingbird believes a quick death is more desirable than slavery.

Many animals cannot handle captivity. They die or become depressed, even infertile. The joy of living is killed by useless, boring captivity. What a lesson!

ANIMALS AS ENTERTAINERS

Other animals thrive on entertaining humans. Have you ever had a pet "clown" to make you laugh? If you have watched circus animals perform or Sea World's Killer whales, porpoises, walruses, seals, sea lions, and otters act, then you know the delight of animal entertainers. For centuries, circuses used trained animals, although it's a dying art (largely because of animal rights activists). It is not "art" if the training is cruel or the activities cause many injuries, but the best animal trainers are not cruel. In truth, you cannot get the kind of performances you want with cruelty!

According to trainers and other observers, performing animals clearly enjoy their work — entertainment is a type of work. Examples are trained bears, mules jumping from up to 30 feet into a diving pool, skunks which "drag-race," and squirrels which water ski.[157] These animals perform not out of fear, but love!

Doggie sports are recreational. Besides obedience training and trials, doggie Frisbee, diving, and a freestyle dog dancing are growing dog sports. Begun in California in the 1970s, dog relay races, called "Flyball," have been spreading. Owners are as avid as "soccer moms"![158]

My mom's show dogs always seemed to enjoy themselves, strutting their doggie stuff before judges!

The body language of working and performing animals shows they enjoy it. Many of us love Sea World and zoos where animal acts are provided. It is obvious the trained animals like more than the food and affection from their trainers. Well-treated animals clearly enjoy their work.

Is that surprising? The Bible begins with God working six days. Then God gave Adam the job of tending the Garden of Eden. It stands to reason God would also give meaningful work to animals. Inactive animals show signs of boredom, even depression.

After Mom's death and my return to a law practice, her poodle, Samson, never quit grieving. He couldn't handle being left alone without human and canine company for long days. The fact that animals have emotions is accepted today. Counseling is available for emotionally disturbed dogs and cats, and medicines for their mental illness, too.

Zoos and animal breeding programs have been dispensing with cages and jail-like pens as fast as they can, opting for enclosures which emulate natural habitats as closely as possible. Innovative changes improve the mental and physical health of captive animals. They respond with behavior more like their wild relatives. One benefit is more successful breeding programs. It's more fun to observe animals who are contented and healthy.

ANIMAL TEACHERS, TOOL USERS AND ARTISTS

God's creatures are remarkable. From earliest recorded records to date, the study of animals has produced life-lessons for the observant open-minded human.

> *No animal is an island unto itself; animal societies are astonishingly well-developed when we consider the general lack of conflict among different species even amidst the most adverse conditions for survival. The only enemies animals have are hunger, cold, and the predatory survival instincts of other species. Often, in fact, one*

> *species will help another, and some animals will even endanger their own lives for the sake of rescuing another.*[159]

Man has no monopoly on creativity. Animals are creative, too. Consider the Bowerbird which creates an elaborate bower of plants and flowers to attract his mate. (Smart men know most women like flowers!) The Bowerbird truly "says it with flowers!" Chimpanzees, other primates, and elephants have painted canvases which art experts have found beautiful.[160] A dolphin has done paintings, standing on his tail with brush in mouth — and the zoo commands high prices for the art![161] The songs of certain birds, like the nightingale, are touted as musically exquisite. The song of the whales is hauntingly beautiful — recordings of whale songs are popular. The "dances" of certain birds and other animals speaks of artistic expression. Isn't creativity a mark of the Creator?

From birds to monkeys, tool-usage is common. Birds drop stones to break eggs, nuts and other encased goodies. Seals use rocks to crack mussel shells. The beaver is an admired master engineer in making dams and canals.[162] Our animal friends are quite resourceful. It's little wonder the Lord God bragged to Job about the animals!

Saying these animals are "acting out of machine-like instinct," is like saying someone from a different culture and language group has no intellect because you cannot communicate with them. Absurd! People who say such things have never lived closely with animals and observed them honestly.

Most ancient cultures considered animals to possess many human attributes, including wisdom and foolishness, intelligence and stupidity, honesty and deceit, loyalty and unfaithfulness, wit and humor. The ancients also believed animals could communicate. Jesus, and other rabbis, delighted in teaching by parables — many included animals.

> *"Animal Tales" that "stories in which animals are the principal characters, with the plot revolving around them . . . [are] found at all culture levels in all periods."*[163]

While the statement above is addressed to the Hebrew culture, it is true worldwide. Aesop's Fables from ancient Greece, India's Pilpot, and other cultures, used animals as the "stuff" of lessons for life. My mother read to me Aesop's Fables and other animal stories. Now I realize some of their significance.

From stories such as the turtle and the scorpion, to the fox and the hare, many have learned moral and character lessons. Many are clearly fictional, although usually have some resemblance to animal behavior. Yet, each has a kernel of truth.

Remarkably, the Bible contains few, if any, "fables" of imaginary or fantastical animals. The Bible is history and prophesy of things to come. The Bible animal stories are told as historical events. Only a few passages are allegorical, e.g. portions of Revelation.

Rabbinical teaching, following the Biblical admonition to learn from the animals, includes this commentary:

> *Had the Torah not been given to us for our guidance, we could have learned modesty from the cat, honesty from the ant, chastity from the dove and good conduct from the cock.* [Erubin, 100b[164]]

Animals seem to know their purpose and roles, and they seldom trust people who treat them like slaves or furniture.

Western Christianity has a schizophrenic view of animals: a St. Francis attitude on the one hand, and a Descartes/B.F. Skinner arrogant cruelty on the other. Neither side trusts the other. Frankly every animal I've known votes on the side of St. Francis, by responding to kindness and avoiding brutality.

A chief problem with the Descartes side is the belief that: "The Bible says man is superior to every other creature because 'man was created in God's own image.'" Some Christians get very upset if man's superiority to animals is challenged. It is as though an identity crisis occurs.

Personally, I think it is exciting that the meaning of being "made in the image of God" is "up for grabs." I have confidence that God's definition is far more wonderful than man's.

Scientists still explore the unknown frontiers of animal

behavior and intelligence, but there is plenty of data to prove that animals think, create, relate, and love. Animals have character and creativity. Humans have no monopoly on those abilities or attributes. Nor are the useful arts limited to man.

WHAT MUST WE LEARN FROM THE ANIMALS?

The Lord planned that animals would enrich our lives. Those who love animals are vastly the richer for it. God entrusted Adam with a stewardship over this earth and the animals in it. It was a healthy assignment. We have much to learn from them. Many of us miss the important lessons the Lord wishes us to grasp.

Animals show us truth. Most animals are amazingly honest and discerning. They are amazing judges of character. Most seem to know instantly if a person can be trusted or not. I have learned to trust my animals' judgment of people and other animals.

Animals can show us the nature of God. Many animals are models of the Lord's character qualities: love, unselfish caring, faithfulness, devotion, patience, humor, joy, grief, anger, goodness, gentleness, kindness, self-control, and intelligence. Did you know skunks are better at family relationships than most humans?[165] Without these important lessons, no man, woman or child is truly successful.

I never consciously applied Jesus' Golden Rule (i.e., do unto others as you would have them do unto you), to animals. [Matt. 7:12] It was and is practiced by such as St. Francis of Assisi, Noah, Monty Roberts, native American Indians, and Bedouin sheiks who raise wonderful horses and camels. Among "primitive" peoples in Africa, South America, and Asia are those who treat all life as a great kinship and all animals as "brothers and sisters" to man. Researching Mom's question has opened my eyes to amazing possibilities about human-animal relationships.

Wise humans in every culture have learned all life is interconnected. When we humble ourselves and listen with the heart and mind to the living things around us, we can learn much about what really counts. Often our own purpose comes in focus. Like Balaam's donkey, there are animals who will love us enough to take our beatings so we can live.

May God show us, you and me, how to learn from His animals. May we know the joy of living and the curiosity which keeps life eternally interesting which animals have. To learn to live in harmony and mutual assistance, with unselfish respect for all creation, is a great goal. God gave us role models. We have looked at some already. There are more who are unknown and unheralded. Some are our neighbors.

DISCERNING ANIMALS

This study made me realize how Mom may have come by her incredible discernment of human character. Mom could "read" a person's character within minutes of meeting them. She was rarely wrong. That has become useful to me in business, in choosing friends, and in dating.

Various accounts report that most, if not all, animals have a keen ability to read people's thoughts and motives.[166] When a stranger approaches, most animals will size them up very quickly. There are even accounts of wild animals hiding long before hunters enter their territory — as though they read the hunters' minds as the humans decided to come killing.[167]

We are all mentally and emotionally naked before God — just as Adam was before the Fall. [See, Heb. 4:12-13; 1 Chron. 28:9; 2 Chron. 16:9; Ps. 94:11a; Ps. 139:2]. It makes sense that God would gift animals in tune with Him with insights into humans around them — for the animal's safety and service. It seems that the Holy Spirit's gifts of discernment of spirits, word of knowledge, and word of wisdom mentioned in 1 Corinthians 12 are not limited to humans. We seem to be mentally naked before some, if not all, of the animals as well.

Animals are remarkably in tune with humans they love. Consider an account of American pilots stationed in England during World War II who befriended a starving stray dog. "Bomber Dog" became a mascot who saw pilots off for each bombing run. One pilot became the dog's special friend. During one run, the dog suddenly became unusually dejected. Bomber Dog's friend was shot down and thought to be dead.

For ten days the dog didn't eat, continually watching the sky toward Germany. The captain then began recording the dog's actions. For six months Bomber Dog's behavior fluctuated from playfulness, to terror, to melancholy. At the last, the dog hid, shaking in misery. A few days later, Bomber Dog came out, exploding with joy. He barked as though he was trying to tell the men something. Then he raced out to the main entrance, and enthusiastically greeted an army truck. The truck carried his pilot.

The pilot's account of his escapades of danger and escape, hope and hopelessness behind enemy lines matched — day by day — the dog's moods.[168]

Recently I was told that during the Vietnam war, a American soldier's hound dog began baying (howling) strangely one night. His family felt to pray. The soldier's letter which arrived later told of his being under heavy enemy fire at the exact time his dog was sounding the alarm.

There are many accounts of animals returning home across hundreds of miles unknown territory, following their humans to locations where the animal had never been. Other accounts tell of animals sensing imminent danger or their owner's death, even at a distance.[169]

Frankly, these accounts make sense. We've examined Bible accounts of animals serving humans at the Lord's command. They need God's supernatural gifts sometimes.

As mentioned earlier, many believe animals "talked" before the Fall of Man. Some believe the communication confusion after the Tower of Babel [Genesis 11] may have affected man's understanding of the animals' language as well.

St. Francis' ability to communicate with animals appears to be more than legend. Some people say they "read" animals' minds or communicate telepathically. This study has proved to me the concept is not necessarily unbiblical.

I don't know whether I've had such an experience or not. It's not something easy to prove or disprove. I admit to a desire for freer communication with animals. Love wants more.

Some seem to have enjoyed a communication with animals which approaches what Adam had. Such communication is not easy for humans. Trainers work on it more than most. Vicki Hearne's words are apt:

> *[M]ost of animate creation doesn't answer as loyally and with as much respect for ... the human landscape as dogs, cats and horses do. It is then the sacredness of answering, for a tribe as lonesome and threatened ... as ours is, that makes animals matter.*
>
> * * *
>
> *The animal trainer's version of Genesis...must continue to be...a picture of Adam and Eve leaving Eden accompanied by the few species who chose to share their lot, to accept human fate*
>
> * * *
>
> *...[W]e need [to do our part in] ensuring that animals are not denied their fundamental rights. This is a right that can be and indeed is violated continuously, ...but is unalienable. This is ...the right from which all others follow, for them and for us, the right to be believed in, a philosophical right to freedom of speech, the right to say things the philosopher has not taught them or us how to say.*[170]

I find J. Allen Boone's books interesting because he said he successfully bridged the language gap between animals and humans which Adam's Fall produced. He credited the silent-movie dog, Strongheart, a German shepherd, for this feat. An accomplished dog in police and war work, the dog was the first famous canine movie star. In caring for the dog Boone was instructed to: (1) speak to Strongheart as an intelligent person; (2) never "talk down" to him like a "dumb animal" or "dog"; and (3) daily read something worthwhile to the dog. Prayer with the animal is also suggested.[171] Boone's record of his experiences with animals challenge me.

Key elements cited by those who have had a two-way

conversation with an animal include: treating the animal as your equal, not as an inferior being; and being totally honest. God gave animals the ability read our hearts. They are rightly alarmed at arrogant superiority, deceit and meanness.

> *When the communication starts, incredible lessons can begin. The differences offer exciting new vistas into another life. Just as it can be fun to learn and explore a different human culture, the world of each animal and its society, can be explored.*[172]

I have always treated animals as persons and the rewards have been great. Animals have been my friends and teachers. Their body language can eloquently speak their thoughts. When I listen to the heart of each animal, I see my Lord.

Yet as I have researched and written this book, I have been challenged. Frankly, I had no idea what rich revelation this study would produce. I am humbled that the good Lord would entrust such a project to me. I am not worthy. I do not have the relationship with animals which God has shown me is possible. Frankly, the Adam-St. Francis relationship with animals is still beyond me. I feel like a child looking through the window of the candy store — with treats still beyond my reach.

J. Allen Boone summarized four essentials to worth-while living which he learned from animals in this credo: (1) Respect all life; (2) Be understanding and tolerant; (3) Never forget every living thing has a purpose, a particular needed job to do in God's plan; and (4) Whenever possible, lend a helping hand.[173] That sounds pretty Biblical to me.

AN ORCHESTRA OF PRAISE

All creation was made to sing the song of the universe, to extol the Creator God with all their being. (We humans often are either out of tune or absent.) The Lord conducts this living orchestra. The Master brings out the best from each. The results are splendid harmonies too glorious for words.

From psalms and church hymns we learn that praising God is something everything was created to do. Listen to creation's songs. Hear the eternal music, the praise of everything which loves life.

> *Praise the Lord! Praise the Lord from the heavens! ... Let them praise the name of the Lord, For He commanded and they were created. He has also established them forever; He has made a decree which will not pass away. Praise the Lord from the earth, Sea monsters and all deeps; Stormy wind, fulfilling His word; Mountains and all hills; Fruit trees and all cedars; Beasts and all cattle; Creeping things and winged fowl; Kings of the earth and all peoples; ... Let them praise the name of the Lord!*
>
> Psalm 148 [NASV]

We could learn to worship from the dog. The ancient Greek word for "worship" is "*proskuneo.*" It is a compound word which may mean "like a dog." It is used in passages describing the worship God desires, like John 4:23-24 & Rev. 4:10. Dogs "kiss" their owner's hands and fawn or prostrate themselves before their masters. Every dog I've known is a natural at praise and worship!

Whether I was gone five minutes or five months, my dogs greeted me enthusiastically. They want to be wherever I am. They watch me with adoring eyes and seek my approval in everything. Dogs respect authority, and adore masters who love them and care for them. When I think how they outdo me in worship, I'm ashamed! I am determined to improve. How about you? We can learn from dogs.

Healthy animals display an exuberance. They enjoy life! Isn't that a form of praise? As an animal lover, I've felt a warm glow inside watching my animals work and play in health and happiness. God must feel the same way.

By loving to please me, my animals praise me. The same principle works for praising the Lord. When I am enjoying doing the things God called me to do, I feel His pleasure. When His creation glows with health and harmony, He must repeat, "It is good!"

THE CHALLENGE

Through writing this book even to this point, my understanding of animals' importance in God's plans has deepened immensely. Some truths have hit me like an explosion! I have fallen more in love with Jesus, my Lord and Master.

My prayer is that you, too, have been challenged. I pray you accept God's grace and choose to change. We need what God would give us through the animals. There are animals all around us as gifts. The Lord is faithful — as His animals demonstrate to us. Let's take His hand, and allow Him to lead us into wonderful adventures of life and learning! Hallelujah! Let everything which has breath praise the Lord! The good news, the gospel, is for all creatures!

Praise God from Whom all blessings flow;
Praise Him all creatures here below;
Praise Him above ye heavenly hosts;
Praise Father, Son and Holy Ghost.[174]

CHAPTER 13

ETERNITY: TWO DESTINATIONS

I have been warned not even to raise the question of animal immortality, lest I find myself "in company with all the old maids." I have no objection to the company. I do not think either virginity or old age contemptible, and some of the shrewdest minds I have met inhabited the bodies of old maids. Nor am I greatly moved by jocular enquires such as "Where will you put all the mosquitoes?" — a question to be answered on its own level by pointing out that, if the worst came to the worst, a heaven for mosquitoes and a hell for men could very conveniently be combined.

C. S. Lewis[175]

Your courage and wisdom in reading this book, puts you above the crowd. The C. S. Lewis quote above humorously treats a topic many avoid — that of animal immortality. Actually many avoid the topic of their own mortality.

"Eternity!" "Immortality!" From ancient times, people have speculated about what lies beyond this life. Like Shakespeare's *Hamlet,* some long for death and yet fear what lies beyond this life. What does lie beyond for us? Are we immortal? Or are we destined to be forgotten — merely worms' dinners? What lies beyond the door of death? If we cannot answer these questions for ourselves, how can be hope to address them for our animals?

WHAT WE BELIEVE

According to popular polls, some ninety-percent of Americans believe in God. The overwhelming majority of Americans believe in heaven. A lot less believe in hell. Most believe — or hope — they are going to heaven when they die.

Americans are now poly-cultural and have many non-Judaic-Christian beliefs or religions. "Heaven" and "hell" mean different things to different people and in different religions. Thus, the meaning of these poll results is in question.

The culture of tolerance has influenced many churches to adopt some non-Biblical, usually Eastern, doctrines. There are important distinctions between Western Christianity and Eastern religions:

> *The real issue is one of metaphysical absolutes, or ground-beliefs. The East – ... Indian traditions in particular – does not honor the same ultimate values as does the West. By and large, the East claims finality for unity, consciousness, eternity, simplicity, soul. The West, in contrast, claims finality for love, plurality, community, diversity, complexity, time, individuality, separateness. When the East claims that All is One, it means just that. All is Brahma. This positions exalts unity over community, knowing over loving, eternity over time.*
>
> *But the God of the Bible incarnates himself in time and in an individual body. ...unity is no more absolute than is plurality, since God is both! ...God will be all in all, but he is also the God of eternally preserved individuals. ...It all flows from so simple a biblical claim as "God is love" (1 John 4:16). Love demands the plural.*
>
> *Jesus' project in our fallen history was to bring about reconciliation, an eternal conversation between man and God, not an absolute identification.... Such "news" goes beyond the ... mystical practice ... born in the valley of the Indus river ... The God of Israel and the Church is primarily concerned about loving community, and loving*

> *conversation between man and God. You and I, as persons, will be held forever distinct in the loving regard of God himself.*[176]

Again, this book answers Mom's question from a purely Biblical viewpoint — as much as I am capable of doing so.

What are your absolutes? What are your images of eternity? Do you have an image of heaven? Or hell? Why do you believe what you believe? What is the source or authority for your beliefs? Do you know the truth?

Many scholars and saints have written about eternity. Some have raised tough questions about the images the Bible gives us. Space is too limited here to address such questions. There are many books which provide well-reasoned, Biblically-sound answers.[177]

THE REALITIES OF HEAVEN AND HELL

The terms *heaven* and *hell* bring up a number of issues. First, what are the meanings of these terms? Are they merely "conditions" or are they real places? What is heaven like? Is it boring pleasantness where you sing and play harps all day? (That's the picture I had as a child.) What is hell and who is consigned there?

Another issue no sane person would avoid is: how can we be sure we have a ticket into heaven and insurance against hell? Eternity is a very long time. This present life is indeed short. Can I ensure that my loved ones, including my pet (or pets) go to heaven with me? What about hell — do animals go there, too? Can I help them avoid hell?

Are you wondering why we have to discuss negative things, such as hell? Look at it this way. If you saw a driver speeding toward a washed-out bridge, wouldn't you shout a warning? Hell is a reality that deserves a warning shout. Hell is an eternity of "living death."

TRUTH IS LOVE

There is an old saying: "Love without truth is license; truth without love is brutality." We need to be honest with ourselves and others. The Bible is abundantly clear that heaven and hell are spiritual realities. If we love each other we cannot ignore the bad, or wrap the truth in soft lies. Someone will get hurt.

Good parents teach their children that fire is real, will burn you, and can kill. If we fail to teach a child these lessons, we fail in loving them. If we fail to show others that un-repented sin has eternal fiery consequences, don't we also fail in being loving?

The Lord God is a good Parent. Just as He directs us how to come home to Him and to heaven, He places warning signs about a fiery hell all through Scripture — and requires each of His children to warn others. Love compels me to be a realist about heaven and hell. The Bible is clear that everyone not joined in loving relationship to the Living God, is unprotected.

I learned a lesson in protection one day when I was walking with our pets. Accompanying me were Mom's two dachshunds, Choc and Kinder, along with my Siamese, Kitty. I felt a bit like a shepherd that day. Kitty and Kinder always stayed with me. Choc, on the other hand, was a law unto herself. Choc got out of my sight often and into trouble just as frequently. That day was no exception.

I was sitting for a few minutes on the creek bank near a railroad overpass. Suddenly, Choc came floating past *in the water*! Her short legs were unable to fight the strong current. It pulled her toward the underpass where it was swifter and turbulent. Her face was frantic. I felt helpless — envisioning a drowned dog. I called to the Lord for help, praying in the Spirit.

Suddenly the current brought the dog near the bank where I could grab her. I'm not sure Choc learned her lesson that day, but I learned one: Stay close to the protection of the Master Shepherd and don't be off doing your own thing!

WHAT DOES THE BIBLE SAY?

Because my readers' information and beliefs may be diverse, this chapter will look briefly at what the Bible says about eternity — and it says quite a lot. There are two poles in Christian doctrine about this life and the next: (1) one emphasizes that this life is temporal, and its pleasures will detour one to hell, as in *Pilgrims Progress*; (2) the other holds that the good things of this earth are proofs of a good and gracious God and heavenly blessings, which is popular today in most churches. Both have merit.

I encourage you to stop reading a moment and make a few notes of what you believe about heaven and hell. Do you know if your beliefs line up with the Bible? Check out the references I cite here. Check out the words *heaven, hell*, their derivatives and synonyms in a Bible concordance and Bible dictionary. Pray for accurate images and beliefs. Ask the Lord Jesus to help you. If praying to Jesus is uncomfortable, simply ask your Creator to show you the truth.

HEAVEN IS — WELL, HEAVENLY

There are more than 700 references to heaven in the King James Bible. That's about seven times more references to heaven than to hell. Jesus referred often to the "kingdom of heaven" — especially in the Gospel of Matthew. If repetition emphasizes a point, then the Bible spotlights heaven.

Heaven is often plural, as in Gen. 1:1 — although you can't always see it in translations. There are at least four heavens described in Scripture. (1) The sky or atmosphere is one. [Gen. 8:2] (2) Outer space is another. [Gen. 1:14-18] (3) The "third heaven" appears to be the highest and God's current throne or residence. [2 Cor. 12:2 & Rev. 4:1-11] (4) Lastly, this earth and its heavens will be destroyed by fire on the "day of judgment and destruction of ungodly men" [2 Peter 3:4-7, 11 & 15; Rev. 20:11; Isa. 66:15; Daniel 7:9; Heb. 12:26-29; Haggai 2:6.] and, at that time a new heaven and earth will be created. [Revelation 21:1; Isa. 65:17; 66:22; & 2 Pet. 3:13]

When Bible-believing Christians refer to heaven, we tend to combine the heaven where God's throne is now with the "new heaven and earth" which will be created after the last judgment. We think of heaven as where the "dead in Christ" are with the Lord, now and for eternity. [2 Tim. 4:16] Wherever the living God sets up His throne is heaven to us — in this age or the next.

HEAVENLY VISIONS

From ancient times to date, people have had visions of, or visits to, heaven. The list includes heroes of the Jewish and Christian faith. Jacob saw angels coming and going into heaven. [Genesis 28:12] King David described heaven's splendor and music in psalms. [Psalm 8:3; Psalm 19] Isaiah saw God on His throne. [Isa. 6] Ezekiel saw God's form, His throne, and heard His voice. [Ezek. 1] Paul of Tarsus saw indescribable things in the third heaven. [2 Cor. 12:1-4]

Hebrews describes the heavenly city and some inhabitants, including Jesus. [Heb. 12:22-29] John described heaven and its inhabitants in vivid detail. [Rev.4-5 & 19-22] Even today, people have visions or dreams of heaven. Many are remarkably similar. Similarity in unconnected accounts lends credibility to such experiences.

Heaven is also called *paradise*. The repentant thief, crucified alongside Jesus, was comforted by Jesus with this promise: "Today you will be with Me in Paradise." [Luke 23:43 NASV] Paradise is used to describe heaven in 2 Cor. 12:4. The Tree of Life is there — a renewed Eden. [Rev. 2:7]

The word *paradise* derives from a Greek word, with origins in ancient Persia.[178] There is a similar word in Hebrew. This word was used for the Garden of Eden [Gen. 2:15 & 3:23]; and also gardens or parks of great beauty. That may be why Paul and John used it to describe heaven, a place of indescribable beauty and spiritual bliss. One of the enjoyable things about gardens are the flora and fauna — the beauty of things living together in harmony.

The last chapters of Revelation describe new heavens and a new earth coming at the end of this age. God's centerpiece is a city, the new Jerusalem, built by God and made of incredible wealth and beauty. Its foundations are precious stones. Its gates are huge pearls. The streets are pure gold. It is a cube some fifteen hundred miles on each side. That's some piece of real estate!

HOME

Although God's presence is everywhere, heaven is His throne. In heaven we will be with Him forever — without the hindrances of this mortal flesh. It will be home. I will never again be separated from the Lord of Love and Life. That excites me so much I can hardly contain the joy!

To me, the most wonderful thing about Heaven is the Lord Himself. I will have a clear, unobstructed look at the Lord God — Father, Son, and the manifold Holy Spirit — face to face. Until I'm fully satiated, I will gaze at Him, and "drink in" His presence. His voice, like the sound of many waters, will be such music to my ears — unmuffled by this earth's sinful clamor. [Rev. 1:15] I will hug and touch my heavenly Daddy and my Jesus — in awe and honor. Waiting for that day requires His grace.

THE LIGHT

The light in heaven will be marvelous. "The Lord is my light and my salvation," Psalm 27:1 says. Heaven is illuminated by the very being of God the Father, and the Son. [Rev. 22:5] God is pure light with no darkness at all! [1 John 1:5] I have experienced this Light in a measure, and it is impossible to describe. Jesus *is* light. His light is the energy which *is* life. [John 1:1-4; & 8:12] His presence, this Light, feels to me like being immersed in pure, liquid love.

NO MORE CURSE

There is no curse in Heaven. [Rev. 22:3 & Zech. 14:11] God will:

> *... wipe away every tear from their eyes. Death is gone for good – tears gone, crying gone, pain gone – all the first order of things gone.* Rev. 21:4 [TMB]

Imagine what that means. To be sorrow-free and pain-free forever. To never lack for any good thing. The very air is life. There is no tiredness or weariness of heart, mind, or body. Everything is crystal clear and clean. We will think, understand, do things, and feel good — all without effort. Everyone loves everyone, for the royal law of love governs everything. [James

2:8] There is something in heaven for everyone. Real, everlasting pleasures and joys. [Ps. 16:11]

LIFE AND TRUTH

God's plan made Jesus the Way, "the ticket"or "the key," to entering heaven. [John 14:6] Jesus died and was resurrected to give us eternal life, abundant life. [John 10:10; 11:25; & Heb. 2:9-15] Those who confess and obey Jesus as Savior, pass from spiritual death into life. [Rom. 6:23; & John 3:14] Death is defeated and is no more. [1 Cor. 15:54-56; & Rev. 21:4] Life fills heaven.

He is Truth. [John 14:6] Truth is the atmosphere of heaven. There are no hidden agendas, no selfish thoughts or unholy ambitions. In the pure presence of God and His Christ, all you ever want to do is whatever pleases Him.

Far from boring, heaven is a place of unfettered and unmarred creativity. Our Creator God loves to work and to do new things! [Prov. 8:30; Isaiah 42:9; 43:19 & 48:6-7] Like a body in perfect health, all work together in harmony. Everything is beautiful, perfect, and good.

I realize to some this may sound trite or simplistic. Describing Jesus and His heaven to some people is like describing a sunset to a person born blind, or beautiful music to a person born deaf. Such things must be experienced. That's the case for me anyway.

If this is true for you, simply ask the Lord to open your eyes and ears. That's His part of this message. [Prov. 20:12] Only our Lord Jesus can open the eyes of the blind and the ears of the deaf. He is more than willing to do so.

OTHER WITNESSES OF HEAVEN

Through the ages, Christians have described their visions and dreams about heaven or their visits to heaven. When Mom was dying, I asked her if she saw heaven and Jesus. She nodded, "yes." Numerous books describe such experiences.

Others have written "inspired imaginings." From the 13th

century, we have Alighieri Dante's *The Divine Comedy*. In the 17th century, John Milton's epic allegorical poems, "Paradise Lost" describes hell, and "Paradise Regained" describes heaven. C.S. Lewis wrote *The Great Divorce*, an allegory about heaven and hell. *Pilgrim's Progress,* written by John Bunyan from an English jail, is an allegory of Adam's offspring traveling toward heaven and the difficulties encountered along the way.

Heaven is a real place. Heaven is a place where God is very present. Therefore it's a place filled with all God is: light, eternal life, love, wisdom, truth, goodness, peace, joy everlasting, beauty, music, grace, and every good and wonderful thing possible. There are several good books on heaven which are informative if you wish to learn more.

HELL, THE ULTIMATE TORMENT

If Heaven is real, then it only makes sense that there is a real hell. Jesus referred to hell in His teaching. He described it as a place of everlasting torment where the inhabitants are "gnashing" their teeth.

> *The real existence of hell is irrefutably taught in Scripture as both a place of the wicked dead and a condition of retribution for unredeemed man.... The nature of hell is indicated by the repeated reference to everlasting punishment (Matt. 25:46); everlasting chains (II Thess. 1:8); the eternal fire (Jude 7); the pit of the abyss (Rev. 9:2,11); outer darkness (Matt. 8:12); the wrath of God (Rom. 2:5); second death (Rev. 21:8); eternal destruction from the face of God (II Thess. 1:9); and eternal sin (Mark 3:29).*[179]

Hell is the absence of all that heaven is, just as darkness is the absence of light. [Matt. 8:12; 22:13; 25:30] There is a "horror of darkness." [Gen. 15:12] Such darkness can be felt. [Exo.10:21] Hell has chains of black heavy darkness forever. [2 Pet. 2:4; Jude 6 & 13] Hell is a place for those who want nothing to do with Light and Truth, with God. [John 3:19; & 12:35-46] Hell can be understood as the total absence of all the benefits of the Light. It is the absence of the Lord's influence for good.

I once meditated on the Scriptures which described hell. It was instructive if unpleasant. The Bible describes hell as a "lake that burns with fire and brimstone, which is the second death." [Rev. 21:8] In hell, they swim in flames. It is not solid, but rather like "residing" in the Sun.

Human skin contains the most nerve endings in the human body. The pain of a burn is the most excruciating pain. Hospital burn units know. Residents of hell are in constant unrelenting burn pain. The consequences? They would never be able to stand being touched — no hugging, no kissing, no hand-holding. Starved for affection, but unable to endure being touched, the torture would be double — both physical and emotional.

Burning matter can be noisy. The roar of the fire, the popping and crackling of the "fuel" would be horrible. There would be no peace, no quiet, no pleasant sounds.

Brimstone smells like rotten eggs. In hell, you'd lose your appetite pronto. With burned, brimstone-filled mouths, nothing could be eaten without pain. Brimstone is nauseating, too. Inhabitants feel hunger gnawing at their insides, while nausea and pain prevent eating and drinking — if these were available.

Hell's inhabitants are thirsty. But fire and water don't mix. In Luke 16, Jesus told of a certain rich man and poor Lazarus. The rich man died and went to hell, and begged Abraham to send Lazarus across the chasm that separated Hell from Paradise to give him just a drop of water. Abraham couldn't do it. There is no relief there.

WHO INHABITS HELL?

The Bible is clear that the eternal hell is the place for the wicked. It's where rebels against the Lord reside. In a sense, hell is God's eternal prison for evil, mean persons. A list of those destined, if they do not change their ways, includes:

> *... the cowardly and unbelieving and abominable [depraved] and murderers and [sexually] immoral persons and sorcerers [practicers of magic arts] and idolaters and all liars, their part will be in the lake that*

burns with fire and brimstone, which is the second death.

Rev. 21:8 [Amp.]

But without [heaven] are the dogs and those who practice sorceries (magic arts) and impurity (the lewd, adulterers) and the murderers and idolaters and every one who loves and deals in falsehood — untruth, error, deception, cheating.

Rev. 22:15 [Amp.]

Hell does not exist to frighten sinners into serving God although some preachers make it sound as though it does. "Hellfire and brimstone" preaching leaves me cold. I cannot imagine someone serving God because that person was terrified of Him. I wouldn't want to give my heart to the Lord Jesus if He tried to frighten me into serving Him.

At the same time, I recognize that sometimes people are like the proverbial Missouri mule — you have to beat them over the head with a club to get their attention. Pain, or the threat of it, is a great attention getter.

Jesus wooed me with gentle strength, patient love, and delightful humor. Although I ignored Him for years, enjoying the transitory pleasures of this world and serving other gods, He persisted in love until I returned to Him. There were times I felt hopeless and worthless. I even wondered why my animals loved me. Now I know that even then Jesus valued me and kept believing in me.

The Lord God is no respecter of persons. [Acts 10:34] He treats all of us the same. The real God is loving, patient, kind, humble, not easily provoked, longsuffering, unfailing, and One who does not think evil. [1 Cor. 13] It is a false Christ who would be cruel and oppressive.

God loves us so much He sacrifices the lives of animals who love us in order spare us. He sent His own Son to die for us as the ultimate act of unselfish love. The God described in the Bible is Love, Truth, Wisdom, Righteousness.

Along with love and wisdom comes justice. He had to

satisfy the demands of justice when man broke the laws of God. Hell satisfies that judgment. Both those who choose right and those who do not (rebellious, evil people) receive their just rewards. Some receive in this life; some in the next.

No loving father enjoys having to discipline a child. Somehow, if we could feel the Creator's pain because of what we have done, I suspect we'd know real hell. I know when I have realized the pain and trouble I've caused the Lord (and others) by my mistakes, it has hurt. I'm glad to know that pain now, so I have a chance to change my ways! Search the Scripture and thoroughly study the character of the Lord God. I challenge you to find one act of clear-cut, unprovoked meanness on God's part recorded in the Bible.

HELL — ARE THERE ANIMALS THERE?

The Bible tells us that hell's foremost prisoner is an *animal* — the Great Serpent, Satan. [Rev. 20:10] Also, it will be the future home of the Beast. This Beast is described in Revelation 13:2 as being like a leopard, with feet of a bear and mouth of a lion. Hell was prepared for God's adversaries. [Matt. 25:41] The principals destined to be there are the Great Serpent Satan, the Beast, the False Prophet, Death and Hades. [Revelation 19:20-21; 20:11-14]

Since we know animals have spirits, Job's description of the place or places of death includes both human and animal:

> *The departed spirits tremble under the waters and their inhabitants. Naked is Sheol [hell or the nether world] before Him and Abaddon [Destruction] has no covering.*
>
> Job 26:5-6 [NASV with footnotes interwoven]

ETERNAL JUDGMENT — GOD'S JUSTICE

Isaiah, Jeremiah, Ezekiel and other Bible prophets lived during times when ancient Israel and their neighbors worshipped of all kinds of gods. These idolatrous practices included orgies of sexual license and cruelties to children and animals. People gave lip service God's commandments, but they did whatever pleased them. Isaiah wrote:

> *Thus says the Lord, "Heaven is My throne, and the earth is My footstool. But to this one I will look, To the one who is humble and contrite of spirit, and who trembles at My word.* ***But he who kills an ox is like one who slays a man; He who sacrifices a lamb is like the one who breaks a dog's neck; He who offers a grain offering is like one who offers swine's blood****; He who burns incense is like the one who blesses an idol. As they have chosen their own ways, And their soul delights in their abominations, So I will choose their punishments, And I will bring on them what they dread.*
>
> Isaiah 66:1-3 [NASV]

Archeological evidence has shown that in Israel or Palestine, ancient idol worship included human sacrifice — some babies and children — and many animals, both clean and unclean. Bestiality and other cruelties to animals were part of this.

These bear little resemblance to the animal sacrifices discussed in earlier chapters. God's sacrifices restored a man's relationship to God and His Creation broken by sin (if only for a limited time). Killing was never designed to afford humans any amusement or to be mere ritual. God instituted rules ensuring that the killing of sacrifice animals was swift and painless, and very messy. There was no pleasure intended in sacrifice.

These sacrifices helped mankind understand the cost of sin and the price of peace with God. Man was to contemplate the animal's innocence and value each time a sacrifice was required. To make any sacrifice to God, it must be with the right kind of animal and done in the manner God prescribed, or it was an abomination to Him.

Dumb animals[180] (meaning speechless, not brainless) have stood by as silent witnesses while mankind behaved badly through the ages. I believe passages, such as 2 Peter 2:12 & 16 and Jude 10, describe corrupt evil people and contrast them to "dumb" animals. (Not all translations carry this meaning, since some translators have Descartes' philosophy.)

If I understand the Greek text correctly, such Scriptures mean some people behave worse than speechless animals. Animals know better by instinct. It does not fit with the whole of Scripture to consign all "dumb animals" to this life alone, nor to the same fate as human brutes described in these passages. There are too many Scriptures to the contrary.

The subject of judging and judgment is a huge topic in the Bible. When I was just out of law school, I served as an administrative law judge. During this time, I had committed my life to the Lord; therefore I was interested in what the Bible said about being a judge. It says a lot! Especially the points about being just, and not showing partiality to rich or poor. [Gen. 18:25-26; Exo. 23:1-9; Deut. 16:18-20; Lev. 19:15]

> *God will surely judge both the righteous man and the wicked man, for a time for every matter and for every deed is there.*
>
> Ecclesiastes 3:17

God Himself is the Judge over all the earth. [Gen. 18:25; Ps. 50:6; Heb.12:23] The Lord is Judge, Lawgiver, and King, and that is how we must know Him for full salvation. [Isa. 33:22; Matt. 25:31-46; James 4:12]. He is the Judge over the living and the dead [Acts 10:42; 2 Tim. 4:1; & 1 Pet. 4:5] and knows and judges the secrets in our hearts. [Rom. 2:16] At the last judgment, the Great White Throne judgment, everything will be judged and separated into hell or the new heaven and earth. [Rev. 20-21]

God is a just and fair God. First He gave us the law, the commandments. The law is "genetically" programmed within every human. These commandments were written in our consciences when the first Adam ate of the fruit of the tree of the knowledge of good and evil.

A just judge applies the law to those accused of breaking it. To invent new rules when the accused stands before the judge is unfair and unjust. That's why the Bible says that where there is no law, there is no sin or transgression. [Rom. 4:15] God holds the world accountable because of the law. It's because of the law that the knowledge of sin comes. [Rom. 3:19-20] Those who keep the law, whether they know what is right through hearing God's word, or simply because of their conscience, they are counted as righteous (or in covenant with God) and are rewarded. [Ps. 58:11; Rom. 3:25-29] Those who don't keep the law, are subject to the penalty of sin, which is poverty, sickness and eternal death. [Rom. 3:10-18; 6:23; Deut. 28; Rev. 20:13-15.]

No human has been able to keep the full letter of God's law, since Adam's Fall. That's why Jesus came. He becomes the Way home.

DO "BAD" ANIMALS GO TO HELL?

A classified ad in *Times-Gazette,*[181] Ashland, Ohio, said, "*Damnation* puppies, 8 weeks old, $45." In spite of this, I don't think there are a lot of animals in hell.

We have already established that animals have souls and spirits. They show their ability to make moral and rational choices. Observant pet owners have seen their animals act either defiant or guilty when disobedient. Animal trainers understand this.

All of us who spend time with animals have been bitten, scratched, stepped on, thrown off, knocked down, or otherwise injured by these animals. But such injuries are nearly always accidental (without malice) on the part of the animal, unless the animal is protecting itself or someone else. If you have a good relationship with the animal, that animal is usually profoundly sorry that you were hurt.

Most animals are good — just like people. Some are good because it's as natural to them as breathing. I've seen animals suffer unspeakable cruelty and still offer love and forgiveness to the person hurting them. Animals often love people as Mother Teresa loved — without prejudice and without being repelled by a person's condition. Such animals don't care if you are unwashed, covered with putrid sores, or dying. They still give love. If there's a heaven for such saints as Mother Theresa, surely God has rewards in eternity for loving animals.

On the other hand, some animals would rather bite than love. Anyone who has lived and worked with animals knows there are a few truly "bad" or evil animals, just as with humans. Some turn bad. They may turn bad because of severe abuse from humans. Some are subjected to hell-on-earth. Some may go bad for other reasons.

Usually people and animals "go bad" by choice. The Bible says all of us have broken God's Laws, and we all are criminals deserving of punishment or imprisonment. God, being just, must judge all according to our deeds. Sin is often the easier choice. Sins are like weeds which pop up voluntarily, then take over. Good character, like good crops, takes cultivation. Being good demands work. It's impossible without help from God — which is called grace.

While many wish to avoid issues regarding a place of eternal punishment, I am too much of a realist to do so. The matter becomes personal to me. If my dog can go to hell for a bad attitude, doesn't the same apply to me?

Just like the human arena, the animal world has its bad characters. Adam's Fall was influenced by an animal — the crafty serpent. I believe that the Bible teaches that certain animals will go to hell — just as certain people will.

I base this in part because God's judgment falls on both man and animal in this life. Earlier, we ascertained that judgment came on animals *and* humans in Nineveh before Jonah arrived. The domestic animals such as cattle, were subject to judgment and responded to Jonah's preaching with fasting and repentance just as the humans did.

Before Moses led the Children of Israel out of Egypt, the Egyptian animals suffered and died from the plagues right along with their owners. At the same time the Hebrews and their animals remained untouched. [Exo. 8:17; 9:1-12, 25-26; 11:4-7; 12:29-32] Pharaoh's army with their horses were destroyed in the Red Sea when they went after the Children of Israel. [Exodus 14-15]

Everything that breathed (humans *and* animal) was destroyed when the land of Canaan was given to Abraham's descendants. [Deut. 7:1-2; 20:10-20; Joshua 6:21]

Let's clarify what is meant when referring to bad or evil

animals deserving of eternal punishment. This does not refer to animals which injure or kill to protect themselves, to protect others, or their territory. It does not refer to animals reacting in fear, or killing to eat. It does, however, refer to the rare animal which intentionally hurts or tries to kill humans or other animals out of pure meanness, out of bitter, unforgiving hatred or "just for sport."

This is the animal bent on injuring and hurting others, as does the Serpent in the Garden, Satan. They are (or would be) killers. Fortunately there are few of them.

Are there consequences for animals who are truly mean, or are killers because they enjoy killing? In Matthew 25:31-46, it says that the Son of Man will judge all nations, dividing them into "sheep" and "goat" nations. Those who were kind to strangers, prisoners, and the destitute are sheep, and those who were not are goats. The former are to be with Jesus in eternity; the latter burn in hell. We already know from the examples of the judgment in the Old Testament, that a judgment on a nation is a judgment on men, women, children, and *animals*.

The Bible does not say there are any excuses or defenses available in the last judgment. We cannot stand before God and say, "The devil made me do it" or "It's my parents' fault," or "It's the environment I grew up in." Nor can any animal, I dare say.

But faced with a clear choice some animals — like those in Nineveh at Jonah's preaching — change. Some call this *retraining.*

When my brother gave Gretchen to Mom, I took account of her enormous size and large teeth. I knew if that large German Shepherd showed the least sign of aggressiveness, if she could not be retrained, I'd have her put down, no matter how much I loved her. I could not risk the destruction that a ninety-pound dog could do. This is a difficult but necessary choice when you love animals. Animals that get in the habit of hurting people and won't quit, must be destroyed. Again, such animals are small in number. Most of the time, the problem is lack of or wrong training and human error.[182] God's big on retraining us! He'd rather save than destroy any day.

Heaven and hell are real. Both humans and animals will be consigned to one or the other in the last judgment. As a lawyer, in a country where the founding fathers based our system of laws on the Bible, I have an appreciation for justice. In our judicial system we see rewards for good behavior and punishments for evil. Could it be any different with God?

There is nothing hidden from the Lord Judge of all. In the end, no matter what heaven or hell you or any animal experienced on earth, our present choices determine our eternity. God is just in all His judgments. The Lord created all things to be good. He will cleanse all things in the last judgment to restore Paradise.

The words, "Jesus came to save that which was lost," takes on new meaning, doesn't it? [Matt. 18:11]

CHAPTER 14

THE RESTORATION OF ALL CREATION

A stork that was present at the song of a dying swan told her 'twas contrary to nature to sing so much out of season; and asked her the reason of it. "Why," says the Swan, "I am now entering into a state where I shall be no longer in danger of either snares, guns, or hunger: and who would not joy at such a deliverance?"[183]

The warm Indiana morning was green with life when my father asked me to join him in a drive to the county incinerator. Doc had put a client's old dog to sleep as I recall. This dog had entered a stage when pain was more common than comfort— and romps in the fields were only a memory.

The incinerator was out in a hilly area. Doc took dead animals there. It was the safest way to check any disease the animal might have had. I climbed into the front seat of Doc's car. I was only a child. Going anyplace with my busy father was a treat. His car was his mobile veterinary clinic out of which he doctored farm animals.

Immediately I began asking questions. My parents never discouraged my questions. Often their answers were to give direction on how I might find the answers myself. (I still love asking questions.) As we drove down the country road, I studied my father's tanned, intelligent face. As I did, an interesting question popped into my head.

"Where is this dog now?" I asked him.

"Its body is covered with a tarp in the trunk," Doc answered.

"Did this dog go to heaven? Are there animals in heaven?" I wanted to know.

Something like surprise flickered swiftly across Doc's face. He paused. Doc was a deep thinker, but I don't recall him talking about God. A quiet, shy man, Doc was a man of few words. His interests were more in science, history and world events. I knew him to be honest. I could trust anything he said.

"I'm sure there is a heaven for dogs," he told me.

The answer came in a matter-of-fact way. It filled my young heart with confidence and peace. I was satisfied that there was a heaven for animals. Doc said so. I imagined a heavenly meadow with dogs playing with joy.

As children, my brother and I held funerals, with Mom's help, for our little furry or feathered friends. Doc's words completed the picture for me. There was something more than this brief existence for them. A promise of a beautiful place with endless comfort and pleasure for my animal friends was a certainty. Doc said so. Therefore, I never again thought about the issue of animals going to heaven — until Mom asked all those ministers her question.

AN AFTERLIFE FOR ANIMALS?

Throughout history, people have believed in an afterlife for animals. Ancient Chinese and Egyptians killed both servants and animals of their deceased wealthy masters and buried them in the same tomb. They believed the masters needed and wanted the animals in the next life. (They believed they could "take it with them." Talk about keeping the same lifestyle!)

We should be repulsed by the idea killing servants and animals just because their master died. Yet we can sympathize with the hope of an afterlife for all of them. The servants may have been willing to die with the prospect of the afterlife more attractive than this life. Whether they joined their master or mistress in Paradise or in Hades is the question! The animals had no choice. Some animals choose to die when their human master dies, but that is different than being killed for that purpose!

The belief that there is an afterlife for humans and animals is common today among those of many religions and philosophies. Books and magazines discussing animals' importance in our lives, line the shelves of bookstores and libraries. Pet-loss became a hot topic in the 1990s.

As adults, we generally re-examine things we were told as children. Believing alone does not make a thing so. Otherwise, Santa Claus would arrive in every good child's home with presents on Christmas, this world would have already ended, and politicians would never be guilty of lying. What is the truth? Is there a reliable source?

Was Doc stating a truth by inspiration or was he telling me a fairy tale, like Santa Claus coming down the chimney on Christmas morning? What in my childhood was truth and what was fiction? Could that have been the living God putting words in Doc's mouth? Does the Bible back up Doc's statement? Or does the Bible disprove his reply? Whether Doc believed what he said or not, something in him moved him to speak those words to his child.

ANIMALS GRIEVING

We know by observation that animals grieve over the loss of loved ones. It is well documented that both domestic and wild animals grieve, some to the point of death or suicide, over the loss of a loved mate or master.[184] Mom and I observed our animals grieve over such loss.

A statement of Arthur Schopenhauer, the German philosopher, sounds good, but is really not worth much:

> *Animals have these advantages over man: they never hear the clock strike, they die without any idea of death, they have no theologians to instruct them, their last moments are not disturbed by unwelcome and unpleasant*

ceremonies, and no one starts lawsuits over their Wills. Animals hear about death for the first time when they die.[185]

How would Schopenhauer explain some behavior of animals relating to time and death? For example, could he explain the tales I've been told of pets which act strangely just days and hours before their owner dies?

Or, the film clip of a hippopotamus rescuing an antelope from death? The antelope, fleeing from a pack of wild dogs, ran into a river where she was seized by a crocodile. The crocodile let her go when the hippo charged. The hippo nudged the impala up the river bank, helped her to her feet, and opening its huge mouth, repeatedly breathed warm air on the stunned impala before leaving her.[186]

Or the geese who clearly are upset at the death of a mate? Or Koko the gorilla who grieved when her kitten was killed? What about the dying cat who managed to find a human to feed her while she was pregnant, and hang on just long enough to wean her kittens before expiring?[187]

What about the Syke terrier, Greyfrier's Bobby, a shepherd's dog, who in 1858 followed his master's funeral procession and stayed by the grave until 1872 when the dog died?[188] In Scotland, the Greyfrier's churchyard has a statue inscribed with a tribute to the dog's faithfulness. Consider the 7-year-old Siamese cat who quit eating when her dying master lost his appetite two days before he passed on; the cat died 18 days later.[189]

Mom's toy poodle certainly appeared to understand when Mom had passed on. Samson quit going to her side of the car, looked very sad and a bit confused as to how to treat me, now that I was the #1 human in his life. Who would not hope the Lord rewards such love in eternity!

Now we come to the crux of Mom's question. What is the will of the Creator God? What is heaven really like? Who is there? Are animals included? What animals? Is there a resurrection for our earthly animal friends, as the Bible says there is for human believers? Or does heaven contain no earth-born animals? Do you pray the Lord's Prayer, asking, "Your will be done, Your kingdom come, on earth as it is in heaven" as I do? If we believe He hears and answers, what are we asking? We need to know.

CHRISTIAN THEOLOGY IS A HISTORY OF MIXED BELIEFS

In earlier chapters we saw that a half-dozen ministers gave Mom as many different answers. Christians' viewpoints are a mixed bag of beliefs about animals in heaven. In spite of the prevailing theology, people have clung to the idea that animals are in heaven. For example, an Inquisition[190] document describes "beautiful groves with singing birds," although this rural image of paradise was frowned on by church leaders in the twelfth and thirteenth centuries.[191]

The Dominican, Thomas Aquinas, and the Franciscan, Bonaventure, did not believe there were animals in heaven.[192] (Consider the irony that a disciple of St. Francis did not believe animals went to heaven.) These beliefs are expressed in Dante's description of heaven in his Divine Comedy,[193] as pure light; no animals dwelt in that pure light, only redeemed human spirits and God. This is in keeping with their belief that animals lacked souls.

The Reformation saw new theologies — which included animals in heaven. Believing the Lord would purify the earth and heavens in the last judgment, Martin Luther taught that everything in the original Eden would be in the refashioned heaven and earth: "all creatures most beautiful," even insects and unpleasant creatures will be transformed and fragrant.[194] There is hope skunks and stink bugs will smell beautiful.

Puritans and other ascetic reformers, however, retained something of Aquinas and Bonaventure. The hereafter was viewed to be a purely spiritual realm, without much resemblance to this material world.[195]

John Wesley, the Anglican priest and the father of Methodism, held a God-centered or theocentric view of heaven, like most reformers, but Wesley made a very strong argument for animal immortality.[196] He must have known and loved dogs. The Lord has always had His witnesses. Some shine as one lone candle in a great darkness.

ANIMALS IN HEAVEN NOW

As wonderful as space ships might be, Jesus doesn't return to earth in a mechanical contraption. John foresaw that Jesus, as the Messiah, the King of Kings and the Lord of Lords, will return in the flesh mounted on a white horse. [Rev. 19:11-21] I picture the Lord returning to earth as a conquering hero — on a magnificent stallion which looks something like Pegasus. (Pegasus was a winged white stallion of Greek mythology and favorite of the Muses.) Whatever the horse looks like, it will be a magnificent scene!

I am glad the Lord loves horses since they have been such special friends to me. Beautiful horses put a song in my heart. They are as refreshing as the mythical waters Pegasus's hoof print was said to bring. I agree with Trish (Chapter 2), that heaven would not be heaven to me without horses.

THE WONDERFUL CHERUBIM

The beings in heaven which may be most important to Mom's question are the cherubim. (Cherub is the singular of cherubim.) Many artist have portrayed cherubim as babies with wings. Biblical cherubim are **not** cute little baby angels. What do cherubim really look like?

The prophet Ezekiel is our main source of information. He had several visions which included cherubim. Ezekiel first saw cherubim at the river Chebar. [Ezek. 1] Then he saw the "glory of the Lord" arrive at the temple at Jerusalem on a cherub or cherubim. [Ezek.9:3] The cherubim were in a great storm, flashing with lightings, with glowing metal in the midst of it. Wheels whirled and above was the throne of God. Pretty exciting!

Ezekiel's cherubim had human form but four different faces. Each had a man's face, with a lion's face on the right and an ox or bull's face on the left. All had an eagle's face. In Hebrew thinking, the ox, eagle and lion, combined with man, symbolized strength and wisdom.[197] The cherub's legs were straight, but its feet were like a calf's hoof, and looked like burnished bronze. They had four wings, with human hands under the wings. They covered themselves with wings. Their whole body, hands, wings and wheels, were full of eyes all around. Ezekiel always saw the cherubim connected with whirling wheels, as though they were part of each other.

Archeological findings of figures in the Near East have led some to conclude cherubim look like winged sphinxes.[198] This does not fit with accounts in the Bible. Sphinxes have a lion's body, a human face and two wings.

THE PURPOSE OF CHERUBIM

What purpose do cherubim have? David sang about the Lord riding on cherub's wings. [2 Sam. 22:11 & Ps. 18:10] King Hezekiah acknowledged that the Lord dwelt among cherubim. [2 Kings 19:15] Ezekiel saw the Lord above or in the midst of flying Cherubim. [Ezek. 1 & 10] God stationed cherubim with a flaming sword at the entrance to the garden of Eden after Adam's Fall. [Gen. 3:24] The prophet Ezekiel saw a cherub put his hand into fire, and put coals of fire into the hands of an angelic man to scatter over Jerusalem in judgment. [Ezek. 10:6-7] In addition, the glory and presence of the Lord is associated with cherubim:

> *Then the glory of the Lord went up from the cherub to the threshold of the temple and the temple was filled with the cloud, and the court was filled with the brightness of the glory of the Lord. Moreover, the sound of the wings of the cherubim was heard as far as the outer court, like the voice of God Almighty when He speaks.*
>
> Ezek. 10:4-5 [NASV]

This many-eyed, fireproof immortal is intimate with the Almighty. Cherubim are beyond any ancient Icarus[199] or modern science fiction spacecraft! Cherubim guard things holy and precious to God, like a good watchdog. Cherubim have to be pure spirits to stay close to the Almighty; He is pure Light and a consuming fire! [Ps. 27:1; John 1:1-9; John 14; 1 John 1:5; Heb. 12:29] (Mortal flesh cannot handle the presence of God any more than we take vacations to the sun.) Cherubim must be breathtakingly magnificent. Holiness is beautiful. [Exo. 15:11]

Huge images of cherubim were fashioned of gold and placed

over the ark of the covenant in the holiest place in Moses' tabernacle. In this ark were the tablets given to Moses, written by the Lord. On top of the Ark was the "mercy seat." Two gold cherubim were on either side of the mercy seat, covering it with their wings. There the Lord God spoke with the high priest. [Exo. 25:18-22; 37:7-9] This same ark was brought into Solomon's temple built in Jerusalem about 950 B.C. Also, images of cherubim were embroidered on the tabernacle curtains and later put on the temple walls. [Exo. 26:1; 1 Kings 6:29]

REPRESENTATIVES OF ANIMATE CREATION

The origin of the Hebrew word for "cherub" is unknown, and so its meaning is unclear. *Vine's Complete Expository Dictionary*[200] says something significant for our question:

> [Cherubim] *"are regarded by some as the ideal representatives of* ***redeemed animate creation****."* (Emphasis added)

Vine's goes on to say the presence of cherubim, at the gate of the Garden of Eden, is a promise that "redeemed men, restored to God on God's conditions, would have access to the Tree of Life." As animals were sacrificed to spare Adam instant death, so animals guard and guide the way to the Tree of Life. How fitting! This is another piece of the answer to Mom's question.

John described living creatures in and around the throne of God which sound much like Ezekiel's cherubim. [Rev. Chapters 4 & 5] It is unclear whether John saw four different beings or one kind with four faces:

> *..And in the center and around the throne, four living creatures full of eyes in front and behind. And the first creature was like a lion, and the second creature like a calf, and the third creature had a face like that of a man, and the fourth creature was like a flying eagle. And the four living creatures, each one of them having six wings, are full of eyes around and within; ...*

Rev. 4:6b-8a [NASV]

These beings are always heard saying, "Holy, Holy, Holy is the Lord God Almighty!" They say "Amen" when "all creation praises Him Who sits on the Throne, together with the Lamb of God." [Rev. 5:13-14] These are the same living creatures or "beasts" which say, "Come!" to the four-horsemen of the Apocalypse which begins the final judgments, the end of this Age. [Rev. 6]

Think of it. This world began with animals. Adam was spared by the sacrifice of animals. God uses cherubim, the representatives of animate creation, both to guard the way to Life and to herald the End of this Age. That's a fit honor for "animate creation" which has suffered and sacrificed for man. Animals announce the destruction of all that deals out suffering and death to man and to animals. Wow.

The six-winged seraphim, which stand above the Lord God appear to be different beings, with different functions. [Isa. 6] Yet these living beings also proclaim: "Let everything that has breath praise the Lord!" [Ps. 150:6.]

REAL OR MYTHICAL?

Some will say these cherubim are mythical beings. No one in the Bible who saw them described them as such. Men may use metaphors to try to describe unearthly beings, yet all accounts treat cherubim as real.

As I mediated on these cherubim, several things struck me. First, the images of human-animal combinations are found in other religions and cultures, like the Greek Pan and centaurs. Secondly, although cherubim appear similar to some mythical beings, they differ greatly in character and purpose. There is nothing of the fickleness and cruelty of other gods, who care little for man. Cherubim are holy and loving servants of the living God.

ANIMALS, GOD'S COMPANIONS

What is relevant to our study is that the Lord of heaven is intimate with and enjoys other living beings, not just humans. Cherubim, as "ideal representatives ...of redeemed animate creation," combine human and well-known animal attributes. The ox is strong, useful in work, and is domesticated. The lion is intelligent, regal, powerful, and beautiful. The eagle is smart, farsighted, and a magnificent master of the winds. God clearly likes to have more than just human types near Him. Amen!

To approach God is to approach cherubim. These servants of God are constantly in His presence. When I think of the Lord surrounded by cherubim, it reminds me of how my animals love to stay close to me. To visit my home is to visit my animals. They greet you, check you out, and stay with me, if permitted, while you visit. I've never had a loved animal which didn't follow me around. My cats have supervised the writing of this book. My stallion, Rebel, turned loose when we picked blackberries, would follow and eat handfuls! Pete, our parakeet, flew around the house following us.

If cherubim are heaven's animals, then they are like our earthly animal friends. Cherubim follow the Lord God and stay as close to Him as possible, serving Him and loving Him. Sounds like heaven to me.

PETER'S VISION OF HEAVEN

Are you good at taking a hint? The apostle Peter had an interesting vision of animals which may hint at the answer to Mom's question.

> *Then he became very hungry and wanted to eat; but while they made ready, he fell into a trance and saw* ***heaven opened*** *and an object like a great sheet bound at the four corners, descending to him and* ***let down to the earth****. In it were all kinds of* ***four-footed animals of the earth, wild beasts, creeping things, and birds*** *of the air. And a voice came to him, "Rise, Peter; kill and eat." But Peter said, "Not so, Lord! For I have never eaten anything common or unclean." And a voice spoke to him again the second time, "What God has cleansed you must not call common." This was done three times.* ***And the object was taken up into heaven again.***
>
> Acts 10:10-16 (NKJ) (Emphasis supplied)

The main purpose of Peter's vision was to prepare him to accept non-Jews as disciples of Jesus the Messiah. But is there more to learn here? Why did the Lord show Peter "animals of the earth" brought from and taken back up into heaven? Why didn't the Lord simply show Peter various animals on earth?

Is it possible these animals had once known life on earth and were now residents of heaven? That is implied by the vision. Was Peter's vision metaphor or reality? If real, then heaven already has earthly animals of all kinds.

THE EVIDENCE BUILDS

Now we have Biblical evidence that animals are already in heaven — horses, cherubim, beings like oxen, lions, and eagles. Also, there are Peter's animals: "all kinds of four-footed **animals of the earth**, wild beasts, creeping things, and birds of the air" which came down from heaven and were taken up there again.

In the preceding chapters, we have examined 1) creation 2) naming of the animals, 3) the Fall and its implications, 4) the covenant God made with Noah and all land animals of every species; (5) Job and other passages; and (6) Jesus of Nazareth. The Scriptures in these chapters more than hint at a hereafter for animals. What else is there? Lots more!

ISAIAH'S VISIONS OF NEW HEAVENS AND EARTH

The prophet Isaiah, who lived some 27 centuries ago, had several relevant visions. Isaiah's visions are Messianic prophesies which Christians believe refer to the Lord's Second Coming, the end of this age. Consider this passage:

> *For behold, **I create new heavens and a new earth**; And the former things shall not be remembered or come to mind. ... The wolf and the lamb shall graze together, and the lion shall eat straw like the ox; and dust shall be the serpent's food. They shall do no evil or harm **in all My holy mountain**, says the Lord.*
>
> Isa. 65:17 & 25 [NASV]

Note that there are **new** heavens and **new** earth, but not **new** animals. Isaiah saw familiar animals — wolf, lion, serpent — with changed natures and metabolisms.

In a later passage, Isaiah repeats almost the same thing:

And the wolf will live with the lamb, the leopard will lie down with the goat, the calf and the lion and the yearling together; and a little child will lead them.

The cow will feed with the bear, their young will lie down together, and the lion will eat straw like the ox.

The infant will play near the hole of the cobra, and the young child will put his hand into the viper's nest.

They will neither harm nor destroy on all my holy mountain, for the earth will be full of the knowledge of the Lord as the waters cover the sea.

Isa. 11:6-9 [NIV]

Eternity contains earth's animals.

This is confirmed by several modern Christian leaders. Billy Graham quotes Rebecca Springer's vision of heaven,[201] telling of a kitten which predeceased a child and greeted her when the little girl died just weeks later. Jesse Duplantis reports seeing horses, dogs and large cats in heaven.[202] Roberts Liardon, taken to heaven by Jesus as an eight-year-old, wrote:[203]

Jesus and I continued walking. As we went over a few hills, I noticed more things. I saw all kinds of animals, every kind you could think of, from A to Z. Sometimes people have questioned this, but if you think about it, why should there not be animals in heaven? The Bible talks about horses in heaven, so why would God only have one kind of animal?

How can one argue with that logic?

A dear friend of mine, named Mozelle, told me of a similar vision of heaven. Some years ago while Mozelle lived in Monroe, Louisiana, she saw a vision of Jesus beside a stream of bubbling water. On the grassy bank beside Him were smaller animals of various sorts. They were on Jesus' right, a place of honor. Included was a snake! The snake surprised Mozelle, since she doesn't like snakes. Soon after receiving the vision, she shared it with someone. As it turned out, that person had a deep need to know that there are animals in heaven. Mozelle felt she was given that vision for that person. Perhaps it was for readers of this book as well.

Since the Fall of Adam, the earth has experienced nothing like Isaiah's harmony. Few have tasted such harmony since, although remnants of it are all around us. Areas of untouched wilderness seem to reflect great harmony at times. Yet many species feed off of other life forms. Some even will kill and eat their own species. Cats and bears use sharp claws and teeth, and vipers are yet dangerous to children.

Some may be bothered by the thought of wild animals making heaven. Wolves, snakes, and the big cats like lions and tigers, injure or kill people and domestic animals. Others don't like dogs because they or someone they love has been badly hurt by a dog. Bulls, pigs, and horses have injured and killed also. Chimpanzees have cannibalistically attacked their own.[204] I don't care to see centipedes in heaven — at Jesus' feet or anywhere else. (I must have been frightened by a poisonous one as a child in Louisiana.)

Dogs, wild animals, snakes and centipedes will be in the new earth. The Lord will change all of us — animals and people — so we will get along. He'll remove our fear of such animals, and theirs of us. Heaven is harmony and love. However difficult that is to imagine, it's true.

It should not surprise us that there is redemption for snakes and other "dangerous" animals. The Lord is able to redeem anything He created, if they'll let Him. The choice lies with each creature, both human and animal. That should give us hope. We will all be changed. It is not clear what we'll all be like in heaven — only that we will recognize one another. Since God can change human natures, reforming snakes should be easy.

Some theologians call Isaiah's vision "millennium" passages — referring to a thousand-year period described in Revelation 20. This isn't supported by Scripture. The passage in Isaiah 11 follows a description of the Messiah — full of the Spirit, judging the earth in righteousness and faithfulness. Isaiah's prophesies track Revelation 21, covering the advent of a new heaven and earth. Logically, the description of the animals returning to the pre-Fall vegetarianism and harmony would follow that last judgment.

Isaiah foresaw a "new heaven and earth" — God's promise that animals will be restored to an Eden-like state. I'll bet heaven is better than the original Garden. God's always doing new things. [See Isa. 42:9; 43:19; Jer. 31:22 & 31; & Ezek. 36:26]

CREATION'S EAGER EXPECTATION

Next to the Isaiah passages, Romans 8 is the best known "proof text" that animals go to heaven. Let's take a look:

> *Now if we are [God's] children, then we are heirs — heirs of God and coheirs with Christ, if indeed we share in his sufferings in order that we may also share in his glory. I consider that our present sufferings are not worth comparing with the glory that will be revealed in us.* ***The creation waits in eager expectation*** *for the sons of God to be revealed. For the* ***creation was subjected to frustration****, not by its own choice, but by the will of the one who subjected it, in hope that the* ***creation itself will be liberated from its bondage to decay*** *and brought into the* ***glorious freedom*** *of the children of God.*
>
> *We know that the* ***whole creation has been groaning*** *as in the pains of childbirth right up to the present time. Not only so, but we ourselves, who have the firstfruits of the Spirit, groan inwardly as we wait eagerly for our adoption as sons, the redemption of our bodies. For in this hope we were saved.*
>
> Rom. 8:17-24a [NIV] (Emphasis supplied)

What does this passage mean? In Adam's fall, death affected all this earth. Why would we omit all *creatures* affected by death in Christ's redemption and restoration?

> *This earth's poets, philosophers, scientists, face to face with death with a capital D, – in every crushed ocean shell, in every rotten log, in the very minor keys in which the voices of beasts and birds are pitched, seem never to get a*

glimpse of the bondage of corruption in which all creation is groaning; but talk in sprightly ways of "progress," of "evolution"! How far from understanding the creation around them are human beings all, – except Spirit-taught Christians![205]

The groaning of creation started with human sin. The war between good and evil continues. Technology and the increase in knowledge (predicted by Daniel 12) has served two extremes: one enables us to better care for humans and animals, while the other empowers us to destroy each other and creation.

It takes righteousness to heal and bless a land and its life forms.[206] [Deut. 28; Prov. 14:34; 2 Chron. 7:14]. Francis and Edith Schaeffer believed Christian stewardship over this earth means our gardens and lands should be the most artistic, beautiful and fruitful.[207] Agnes Sanford taught that our daily prayers should include the earth and all life around us.[208] Righteousness treats all life as a sacred trust, deserving of care and prayer. This has been the practice of many great Christians.

DO ANIMALS CEASE TO BE?

If animals cease to be after they die, then what does the passage from Romans 8 mean? Where is their freedom? Their restoration? What logic or reason could separate man from animals after death? How can it be that our animals might never know liberation from frustration and decay? Is that God's Truth or man's lie? If animals cease to be after death why would all creation be "groaning for the revelation of the Sons of God"?

Now although we who are in Christ are new creatures, yet God has left our bodies as the link with the present "groaning" creation. Meanwhile, how "the bondage of corruption" appears on every side! ... Every decaying carcass of poor earth-creatures speaks of the "bondage of corruption." What ruin man's sin has effected throughout the creation, as well as upon himself! It was God's good pleasure that, when man sinned and became estranged from his God, all creation, which was under him, should

> *be subjected to the "bondage of corruption" along with him, in decay and disease, suffering, death, and destruction, everywhere, – of bondage, with no deliverer.*[209]

KING SOLOMON'S WISDOM

King Solomon was both the "playboy" and a wise man. Solomon asked what the difference was between humans and animals. We studied the passage when looking for Bible proof animals have spirits [ruwach]:

> *I said in my heart with regard to human beings that God is testing them to show that they are but animals. For the fate of humans and the fate of animals is the same; as one dies, so dies the other. They all have the same breath, and humans have no advantage over the animals; for all is vanity. All go to one place; all were from the dust, and all turn to dust again.* ***Who knows whether the human spirit goes upward and a spirit of animals goes downward to the earth?***
>
> Ecclesiastes 3:18-21 [NRSV]

God does test us to see what is in our hearts. [Deut. 8] Will we treat all God's creation as our disposable toys? Or respect other living things as equal to us? It is a test which each human faces.

What is the answer to Solomon's last question? The Spirit of the Lord inspired Solomon's question for a reason. I think the answer is implied.

Paul's words in Romans 8 answer Solomon's question, don't they? All creation was "subjected to futility" or "frailty" (Amplified), and "bondage to decay" or "corruption." John Wesley said:

> *But will the creature, will even the brute creation, always remain in this deplorable condition? God forbid that we should affirm this; yea, or even entertain such a thought! While "the whole creation groaneth together" (whether men attend or not) their groans...enter into the ears of him that made them.... [H]e knoweth their pain,*

> *and is bringing them nearer and nearer to the birth which shall be accomplished in its season. ...* ***the whole animated creation ...'shall be delivered'*** *(not by annihilation; annihilation is not deliverance) 'from the' present 'bondage of corruption, into' a measure of 'the glorious liberty of the children of God.'*[210]

Wesley and Newell's beliefs are further substantiated by the Apocryphal Book of Wisdom: "... because God did not make death, and he does not delight in the death of the living." [1:13][211] "Living" is a term not limited to humans, as the next verse proves: "For He created all things that they might exist..." [Wis. 1:14]

> *Each species, to put the matter succinctly, is a masterpiece. It deserves that rank in the fullest sense: a creation assembled with extreme care and genius. ... If DNA helices in one cell of a mouse ... were placed end on end and magically enlarged to the same width as a piece of wrapping string, they would extend for about 600 miles... How all that genetic information translates into a fully functioning organism is still partly a mystery. The lesson to be drawn is that the life-forms around us are too old, too complex, and too valuable to be carelessly discarded.*[212]

What the Lord created in delight has not ceased to be His. Would it not be more surprising for our Great God to extinguish their existence than to restore them? Why would anyone think that loving God would not want all His masterpieces to be restored to their former glory throughout eternity? What foolish thinking! I begin to understand why Paul said that the wisdom of men is foolishness to God! [1 Cor. 1:18-30]

> *Every creature in the forest is mine, the wild animals on all the mountains.*
>
> *I know every mountain bird by name; the scampering field mice are my friends.*
>
> *... All creation and its bounty are mine.*

Do you think I feast on venison? Or drink draughts of goats' blood?

Spread for me a banquet of praise, serve High God a feast of kept promises.

Ps. 50:10-14 [TMB]

REDEMPTION AND RESTORATION

The good news is that God plans to redeem and to heal all His creation — not just mankind. While man bears the responsibility for this earth, we are powerless to cleanse our own sin let alone the effects which have contaminated the earth like a massive plague. Our need for a savior, a redeemer, extends beyond human need and out to the whole earth. Only our Creator has the ability and will to redeem, restore, and recreate what we have messed up.

Luke's record of the Apostle Peter's sermon given soon after Jesus' ascension back to heaven puts "the cure" in simple terms:

Repent, then, and turn to God, so that your sins may be wiped out, that times of refreshing may come from the Lord, and that he may send the Christ, who has been appointed for you – even Jesus. He must remain in heaven until the time comes for God ***to restore everything****, as he promised long ago through his holy prophets.*

Acts 3:20-21 [NIV] (Emphasis supplied)

Peter's sermon is a wonderful promise, isn't it? We can do something. Repentance and turning to God will bring the Messiah, the Christ, who will "restore everything." The New Revised Standard Version calls it "the universal restoration that God announced" and Weymouth translates it "the reconstitution of all things." It means restoring of a thing to its former state or place.[213] I like that.

The Greek word for "restore" is "*apokatastasis.*" It means "reconstitution" or "restoration" in health, home or organization. *Thayer's Greek-English Lexicon of the New Testament* says it is "the restoration of not only the true theocracy but also of that more perfect state of (physical) things which existed before the fall, Acts iii.21."

What does "all things" mean if not everything? Jesus said that the prophet Elijah will return (as Malachi 4 says), and God "will **restore all things**." [Matt.17:11; Mark 9:12] This is from the same root word for "restoration" used in Acts 3:21.

It is reasonable to believe all animals will be restored or "reconstituted" in the new earth. "Restored" does not mean "replaced." That must mean God will take the scattered DNA of each life form and remake each being anew. Hallelujah! There is hope for creation in its futile fragility. It will be set free in new life.

> *Regardless of how both the Church and her enemies have ill-treated or been ignorant of the message of the Bible, one thing is certain.* **The whole tenor and thrust of the Bible is toward salvation and healing,** *not only of individuals, but of families, nations, and countries – indeed,* **of the very land itself**. *The Bible demands personal responsibility on all levels of life and calls for a level of commitment to care for life unmatched by any other major religious writing in history.* ***
>
> *As a matter of fact, the sixth Commandment says, "You shall not murder" (Exodus 20:13, NIV). It does not say, "Do not murder people," but, "Do not murder," which includes any selfish taking of life. ..... including an animal, flower or tree.... Every act of cruelty to animals, as well as to other human beings, is offensive to the Creator of all beings.*[214]

Why? Look at the phrase in Roman 8:21: "because creation itself also shall be delivered from the bondage of corruption, into the liberty of the glory of the children of God."

> *The "liberty of the glory of the children of God" awaits Christ's second coming. How blessed it is to know that into that glorious liberty, creation, which has shared "the bondage of corruption," will be brought along with us!*
>
> *Contrast the state of creation now with the Millennial order described in Isaiah 11.6-9: The wolf dwelling with*

the lamb, the leopard with the kid; the calf, the young lion, and the fatling together, and the little child leading them.[215]

It's ironic that many Christian theologians believe that redemption extends to all creation, but still aren't sure if the animals we know and love have an afterlife:

Redemption extends to the furtherest corner of the physical realm. ... this earthly kingdom is the same as the kingdom of heaven, the world of the coming age, the coming redeemed creation (Rom. 8:21).[216]

This is echoed in Eastern Orthodox circles. Consider the words of Vladimir Lossky:

Man is not a being isolated from the rest of creation; by his very nature he is bound up with the whole of the universe . . . In his way to union with God, man in no way leaves creatures aside, but gathers together in his love the whole cosmos disordered by sin, that it may at last be transfigured by grace.[217]

GROANING IN TRAVAIL

Paul's statement in Romans 8:22, that all creation "groans in travail" is not new. The prophet Jeremiah spoke of the earth and of a land mourning, and as a result, humans, animals and everything living in them suffering and disappearing. [Jer. 4:27-28; 12:4 & 11; Hosea 4:3] I am not alone in wondering if that isn't part of what causes earthquakes and other natural disasters — just as a boil erupts to free the body from poison.

God gave creation, all the animals, creeping things, birds, fish and flowers the task of groaning as in "travailing." So all living things join with human believers to groan "and travail" together. This speaks of pregnancy, of childbirth. Such groaning is to produce LIFE, ETERNAL LIFE. Paul travailed until Christ was formed within the disciples. [Galatians 4:19] We need to do the same. God's servants have this privilege. [Ps. 48:6; Isa. 53:11; 66:7-8; Micah 5:2-5; John 16:21-22]

...the Spirit does not take us out of sympathy with

groaning creation, but rather supports us in such sympathy! ....No one should feel as tender as should the child of God toward suffering creation. No one should be as gentle. Not only should this be true about us as concerns unsaved people: as Paul says, "Be gentle, showing all meekness toward all men," but, I say, we should be tender and patient toward all animals, for they are in a dying state – until our bodies are redeemed.

* * *

Thus, then, does the Christian become the true connection of groaning creation with God! He is redeemed, heavenly; but his body is unredeemed, earthly. ...Thus the believer and the whole creation look toward one goal – the liberty of the coming glory of the sons of God![218]

"Groaning in travail" is unfamiliar to many Christians. I dare say it is incomprehensible to a nonbeliever. Yet, it is a part of true intercessory prayer. Jesus groaned in the spirit before He raised Lazarus from the dead. [John 11:33] Saints through the ages wrote of groaning in prayer. I believe Mother Theresa of Calcutta understood such groaning.

I am willing to groan with creation until Christ is formed in myself and others. Until we bring down God's glory. Until my Lord Jesus returns in the flesh bringing in the new heaven and earth. Until all are free from the death and decay of this world. How about you? Are you willing to travail with creation? If so, tell the Lord about it. He'll teach and empower you to do His will. Together we can bring down heaven on earth.

THAT PLAN AND ORDER OF REDEMPTION

Is it not logical and reasonable that the Creator would include in His plan of redemption all that was subject to death at human hands?

For since by a man came death, by a man also came the resurrection of the dead. For as in Adam all die, so also in Christ all shall be made alive.

1 Cor. 15:21-22 [NASV]

God's plan of redemption has an order of restoration. "For as in Adam all die" included all living creatures; therefore, "In Christ all shall be made alive," is also inclusive. Jesus Christ is the resurrection and life! [John 11:25] He alone has the power of indestructible life! [Heb. 7:16 NASV & Weymouth] Glory!

In Romans 8, Paul made three points about creation. First, God Himself subjected all creation to the effects of Adam's sin. Second, God will liberate creation from decay when His purpose is fulfilled. Third is that this is a saving hope. A hope not given for us alone, but given to all creation. In the revelation of us as "sons of God," we get to take creation into glory. It pays to be a child of God.

Restoring something well takes careful planning, skill, and time. God's plan and order of redemption are found in the Bible. It is most fully detailed in the New Testament letters to the early church. (It is easy to miss some details unless you are asking the right questions.)

In I Corinthians, Paul addressed the issues of resurrection. Apparently, some challenged whether there is a resurrection of the dead — including Jesus' resurrection. What Paul wrote is relevant to Mom's question:

> *But each in his own order: Christ the first fruits, after that those who are Christ's at His coming, then comes the end, when He delivers up the kingdom to the God and Father, when He has abolished all rule and all authority and power. For He must reign until He has put all His enemies under His feet. The last enemy that will be abolished is death.*
>
> 1 Cor. 15:23-26 [NASV]

I always read that passage as referring exclusively to humans, but is that what it means? Paul's own words belie that assumption.

Paul left us great insights into God's plans for His creation. Paul had first-hand knowledge, since he visited heaven. He was "caught up" into heaven and heard unspeakable things. [II Cor. 12:2] Compare these two translations of Ephesians 1:7-10:

It is in Him, and through the shedding of His blood, that we have our deliverance – the forgiveness of our offenses — so abundant was God's grace, the grace which He, the possessor of all wisdom and understanding, lavished upon us, when He made known to us the secret of His will. And this is in harmony with God's merciful purpose for the government of the world when the times are ripe for it — the purpose which He has cherished in His own mind of ***restoring the whole creation to find its one head in Christ****; yes, things in heaven and things on earth, to find their one Head in Him.*

[Weymouth] (Emphasis supplied)

This you can tell the strength of his power at work in Christ, when he used it to raise him the dead and to make sit at his right hand, and heaven, far above every sovereignty, authority, power or for domination, or any other name that can be named, not only in this age but also in the age to come. He has put all things under his feet, and made him, as the ruler of everything, the head of the church; which is his body, ***the fullness of him who fills the whole creation.***

[Jerusalem](Emphasis supplied)

God's plan is to restore everything in and through Christ Jesus. We are destined for a huge celebration. The universe will explode with restoration. The foolishness of human thinking will be exposed and God's great wisdom revealed. God will be most happy when His precious creation is restored in full!

This quote from the introduction to *Witness; Endangered Species of North America* has eternal relevance.

We belong to the natural world; it does not belong to us. The interconnectedness of life, in the present instant as well as through time, illuminates our place and our rightful relationship with other species here are on earth. Can we find our place in the world as human beings if we devalue the rest of life? It is part of who we are.[219]

Can we find our place in heaven, if we devalue the rest of life? If we do not become fully "Sons of God," members of the mystical Body of Jesus Christ, doing our part in the restoration of all creation, don't we lose part of what we are?

OUR PETS

Does the Scripture say anything about the resurrection of animals we've known? Yes, I believe it does.

> *And He is the image of the invisible God, the first-born* ***of all creation****.*
>
> *For by Him* ***all things were created****, both in the heavens and on earth, visible and invisible, whether thrones or dominions or rulers or authorities —* ***all things have been created by Him and for Him****.*
>
> *And He is before/existed prior to* ***all things****, and in Him* ***all things*** *hold together.*
>
> *He is also the head of the body, the church; and He is the beginning, the* ***first-born of the dead****; so that He Himself might come to have first place* ***in everything.***
>
> *For it was the Father's good pleasure for all the fulness to dwell in Him*
>
> *and through Him to* ***reconcile all things*** *to Himself, having made peace through the blood of His cross; through Him, I say,* ***whether things on earth or things in heaven.***
>
> Col. 1:15-20 [NASV] (Emphasis supplied)

I have read this passage hundreds of times, yet never before considered its application to animals going to heaven. I did the same with other Scriptures. I know I am not alone. All the ministers I've heard preach do the same. Yet "all creation" and "all things" cover more than the human race. Our pets and the entire animal kingdom are covered by this phrase.

Considering the marvelous complexity of life, the variety and inner-connectedness of it all, it makes more sense that God would restore, rather than destroy. To give an analogy, an art or antique collector would never think of discarding any damaged piece that could be restored. Why would God discard precious living animals when He is well able to restore?

The plain words of Colossians are "all creation" and "all things." Just as Noah took every kind of animal into Ark, so Jesus will restore, will reconcile, and will raise from death "all things." All was made in, by, for and through Him.

"All" covers humans and animals, insects to elephants, trees to flowers, springs and oceans, mountains and meadows, amoebae and atoms, sun, moon and stars. The Living Lord will restore the damaged DNA of this universe in a glorious new creation. The blood that Jesus shed on the cross, is for all created things. Things both on earth and in heaven. Wow! That's enough to shout about. I have a Bible-based hope that my Shamus, Kitty, Gretchen, Samson, and many others will be there. What an awesome God!

CHAPTER 15

HOPE OF RESURRECTION!

Her imagination made her wonder if in fact there were any animals to be found in Hades. . . .

No, Heaven would be filled with animals, for it would not be Heaven without them, while in Hell it would be one of the things one longed for and could not have.[220]

Does the Bible say more? Does it say how the Lord will populate His new heaven and earth? Will He create new animals or resurrect some of the ones who have already lived? We have been seeing the pieces come together. For animal lovers, heaven just wouldn't be heaven without their animal friends. We have hope.

"Because of the hope laid up for you in heaven of which you previously heard in the word of truth, the gospel/good-news," were Paul's opening words in Colossians 1:5. The Scriptures we've examined already give us good news! These are pieces of the puzzle — pieces that give hope.

HEAVEN WILL MAKE US HAPPY!

Mom's wisdom that "God is love, and if it isn't love, it isn't God" is a fair test of theological doctrines in my experience. An anecdote which William F. Buckley, Jr., a hero of intellect to our family, wrote about his faith as a Catholic, illustrates this test:

> *I would most like to visit Heaven because it was there I would be made most happy. I gave Fr. Sharkey's exegesis: He had been approached some weeks earlier, he told us, by a devout elderly woman who asked him whether dogs would be admitted into Heaven. No, he had replied, as there was no scriptural authority for animals getting Heaven. "In that case," the lady had said to him, "I can never be happy in Heaven. I can only be happy if Brownie is also there."*
>
> *"I told her" – Fr. Sharkey spoke with mesmerizing authority – "that if that were the case – that she could not be happy without Brownie – why then Brownie would in fact go to Heaven. Because what is absolutely certain is that, in Heaven, you will be happy." That answer, I am sure, sophisticated readers of the Esquire dismissed, however intelligently, as Jesuitical. Yes. But I have never found the fault in that syllogism.*[221]

Neither have I, friend. Besides, there is far more scriptural authority for animals going to heaven than the good Fr. Sharkey realized. We could stop right now, I believe, and have proved our case. But there is yet more.

GLORIFIED BODIES

Bible teaches that believers (those in covenant relationship with God through their Messiah, Jesus) shall receive new "glorified" bodies and live with the Lord eternally "in glory." [Rom. 8:23; 2 Cor. 5:1-10; Col. 3:4]. Jesus described Himself as "the Resurrection and the Life," to Martha before raising her brother Lazarus from his grave. [John 11:25].

Consider this promise of heaven:

> *But there's far more to life for us. We're citizens of high heaven! We're waiting the arrival of the Savior, the Master, Jesus Christ, will transform our earthly bodies into glorious bodies like his own. He'll make us beautiful and whole with the same powerful skill by which he is putting*

everything *as it should be, under and around him.*

Phil. 3:20-21 [TMB]

FROM DEATH TO RESURRECTED LIFE

If human believers will be glorified, i.e., get new immortal bodies, through Jesus Christ, what about animals? Will they get new bodies, too? Consider this statement from Psalms:

> *O Lord, how many* and *varied are Your works! In wisdom You have made them all; The earth is full of Your riches* and *Your creatures . . . When You take away their breath [ruwach], they die and return to their dust. When you send forth Your Spirit* and *give them breath [ruwach], they are created; and You replenish the face of the ground. May the glory of the Lord endure for ever; may the Lord rejoice in His works....*
>
> Psalm 104:24, 29b-31 [Amplified]

These verses (previously discussed in Chapter 4) concern animal life, not human. Notice the order in which these statements are made: First, the death of animals; then "They are created" and "You replenish the face of the ground."

I used to wonder if the Psalmist had things a little backward. Doesn't "dying" comes before "give them breath, they are created"? Why would the Lord inspire the psalmist to write in this order?

If this is a repeat of creation described in Genesis 1 & 2, it is not in the right order. But what if it is looking forward to the new heavens and earth? If it describes the restoration of all things in Christ Jesus in the next life, then it is written correctly. First death, *then* a new creation. First is the "taking away" and afterward comes the "restoration" or "resurrection" or "replenishing." This Psalm logically describes a progression from death to resurrection.

It fits with other verses. Consider Psalm 102:25-26, as it quoted in Hebrews 1:10-12 [NASV]:

> *And, "Thou, Lord in the beginning didst lay the*

foundation of the earth, And the heavens are the works of Thy hands;

They will perish, But Thou remainest; And they all will become old as a garment, And as a mantle Thou wilt roll them up; ***As a garment they will also be changed [allasso]****. But Thou art the same, and Thy years will not come to an end.*

What will be changed? Who are "they?" What do the "foundation of the earth" and "the heavens" refer to? They will perish. But that is not the end. They will be changed.

Why would the Lord change the "foundation of the earth" and "the heavens" like an old garment? The only thing that makes sense is that he needs a new habitat for his creation — one that can bear His own Presence — those [Psalm 104] recreated animal spirits referred to in Psalm 104.

Is that what Ps. 102 is really saying? Read in conjunction with Psalm 104, Romans 8, Colossians 1 and other passages, it is a reasonable interpretation. The breath (or spirits) taken when animals die, are with God. [Eccl. 3] In the fullness of time, God will destroy this earth and its heavens with fire and create new ones. [2 Pet. 3; Isa. 66:15; 2 Thess. 1:7] Then the Spirit of the Lord, which worked with God in the original creation, will breathe life into these dead animals and replenish the new earth and heavens. All animals, including extinct species, have hope.

EVERY EYE SHALL SEE JESUS!

In the book of Revelation, John gives an interesting salutation to the churches which adds support to this thesis:

John to the seven churches which are in Asia: Grace to you and peace, from Him who is, and who was and who is to come;

And from Jesus Christ, the faithful witness, ***the first born from the dead****, and the ruler of the kings of the earth. To Him who loves us and released us from our sins by His Blood,*

....to Him be glory and dominion forever and ever. Amen.

*Behold, He is coming with the clouds and **every eye will see Him**, even those who pierced Him...*

Rev. 1:4-7 [NASV] (Emphasis added)

Rev. Jack Van Impe discussed this Scripture on his television show.[222] I don't know if it was live or pre-recorded.

The subject of discussion was whether or not animals go to heaven. Arguing that animals *do go* to heaven, Rev. Van Impe cited this Scripture, stating the phrase "every eye" includes animals because animals have eyes.

DEATH, WHERE IS YOUR VICTORY?

To me, one of the most powerful Scriptures to support our premise of animals being resurrected, is in Paul's writings. The Apostle Paul wrote his letters to the Corinthian church to address wrong teaching about the resurrection. Some leaders were stating there was no resurrection. If so Jesus Christ never rose from the dead, and we who believe in Jesus are deceived and without hope.

Paul offered several arguments against this teaching in I Cor. 15. Ponder some of Paul's words with Mom's question in mind:

But someone will say, "How are the dead raised? And with what kind of body do they come?"

You fool! That which you sow does not come to life unless it dies; and that which you sow, you do not sow the body, which is to be, but a bare grain, perhaps of wheat or of something else. But God gives it a body just as He wished, and to each of the seeds a body of its own.

***All flesh is not the same flesh, but there is one flesh of men, and another flesh of beasts, and another flesh of birds, and another of fish**. There are also heavenly bodies and earthly bodies, but the glory of* *the heavenly is one, and the glory of the earthly is another. There is one glory of the sun, and another glory of the moon, and another glory of the stars; for star differs from star in glory.*

So also is the resurrection of the dead. It is sown a perishable body/in corruption, it is raised an imperishable/in incorruption; it is sown in dishonor, it is raised in glory; it is sown in weakness, it is raised in power; it is sown a natural body, it is raised a spiritual body. If there is a natural body, there is also a spiritual.

So also it is written, "The first man, Adam, became a living soul." The last Adam became a life-giving spirit. However, the spiritual is not first, but the natural; then the spiritual. The first man is from the earth, made of dust; the second man is from heaven.

As is the earthly, so also are those who are earthy; and as is the heavenly, so also are those who are heavenly. And just as we have borne the image of the earthy, we shall also bear the image of the heavenly.

Now I say this, brethren, that flesh and blood cannot inherit the kingdom of God; nor does the perishable inherit the imperishable. Behold, I tell you a mystery: we shall not all sleep, but ***we shall all be changed (allasso),*** *in a moment, in the twinkling of an eye, at the last trumpet; for the trumpet will sound, and the dead will be raised imperishable, and* ***we shall be changed (allasso).***

For this perishable must put on the imperishable, and this mortal must put on immortality.

But when this perishable will have put on the imperishable and this mortal will have put on immortality, then will come about the saying that is written, "Death is swallowed up in victory. "O Death, where is your victory? O Death, where is your sting?"

The sting of death is sin, and the power of sin is the law; but thanks be to God, who gives us the victory through our Lord Jesus Christ. Therefore, my beloved brethren, be steadfast, immovable, always abounding in the work of the Lord, knowing that your toil is not in vain in the Lord.

1 Cor. 15:35-58 [NASV plus Greek additions]

Why did Paul speak of God giving each living being a body as He chooses "and to each of the seeds a body of its own"? The meaning, taken in context, seems to be that seeds of immortality — of resurrection — are in all living beings. Is there any other rational explanation? This is at least a fair interpretation.

Paul does not limit "dead" to humankind. Rather he describes how each kind of living thing has different "flesh." Both in Greek and Hebrew the words most commonly translated "flesh" mean the "body" or by extension the "self." [223] The Greek word used most in the New Testament, including in this passage, is "*sarx*." It refers to meat stripped off an animal, as well as the "body" or "soul" or "spirit" of man or beast.[224]

When Paul wrote of "different kinds of flesh" (sarx) in I Cor. 15, he specifically mentions animals.

Some commentators say this passage means: because all animals are flesh they will perish eternally. [Ps. 49:12 & Isa. 40:6] In truth, all flesh, both animal *and* human, will perish like dry grass in a prairie fire when the Lord returns. [Isa. 40:6 & 1 Pet. 1:24] Only those with the imperishable seed of regeneration will live again, raised from the ashes of destruction to eternal life. [1 Pet. 1:22-25; 2 Pet. 3.] The Bible doesn't limit "flesh" to humankind. Why exclude animals?

There is no Biblical basis to exclude animals from having "seeds of resurrection" to receive spiritual, glorified bodies. Isn't it a better interpretation to ascribe to the Creator enough love and power to raise animals along with redeemed humans? God is love. Why would He exclude His living loving creatures?

In the above Scripture, Paul also contrasts the "glory of the heavenly" and the "glory of the earthly" bodies. Why? Does Paul wants us to understand that while the temporary, mortal body is perishable, weak, and dishonored, God's "glory" is heavy with splendor like that of sun and stars? That the "seeds of glory" lie within every earthly body God created? It makes sense to me.

This means each mortal — human and animal — can be raised in incorruption, in glory, in power, a spiritual body. This would never make sense if we did not know (as Paul knew) that both animals and humans have *nephesh,* i.e., souls, and *ruwach,* i.e. spirits. The flesh "returns to earth," but the spirit either "ascends" or "descends" — as Ecclesiastes 3:21 says.

LIGHT — THE ENERGY FORCE

What are "spirits"? God is a spirit. [John 4:24] God is light, and He dwells in blazing light. [1 John 1:1; 1 Tim. 6:15-16; Ps. 104:2; Dan. 7:9] Jesus, Word of God, is Life in which is Light. [John 1:3] People, dead in sin, are in darkness, but after rebirth or salvation, people become children of light. [Isa. 60:1-3; Acts. 26:18; Eph. 5:8; James 1:15] This light-energy has actually been measured in nonbelievers, "born-again" Christians, and Spirit-filled Christians.[225]

Remember the cherubim? Only pure spirits, purified by holy fire, are able to withstand the intense fire and light of God's being.

Every living creature has a "glory" in the sense of "splendor" or "light."[226] "Light" is energy. All living creatures have an energy force we call "life." It leaves when they expire. When death extinguishes the light, where does that energy go? Don't you think it goes back to God, its source?

If different kinds of natural flesh have their own "glory" then it makes sense that animals also have within them the "seed of glory," "the seed of resurrection." We can interpret Corinthians 15 as including all creation without straining interpretive rules.

1 Corinthians 15:51 & 52 say "we" shall be "changed." Paul's "we" could include "all flesh" – just as Nivevah's judgment included all humans and animals. "Change" in this verse is the Greek word "*allasso.*" It means to "make different, to change," "to exchange one thing for another," "to transform." If all the dead will be "raised imperishable" then animals change as well. It's a rational interpretation — perhaps the only one, in light of the whole Bible.

Paul's argument also addresses the issue of death. If animals are not resurrected, where is the full victory over death which the Bible's God promises? Death would be victor, if we who love them never see our animal friends in the hereafter. The swan's dying song would be for naught. God would violate His covenant with Noah and the animals.

It maligns God character to limit Him to resurrection of humans alone. It limits His love, His compassion and His power. I'm sure no one can make such a case from the Holy Bible.

I believe these Scriptures fully answer Mom's question. It took me a years of work and research to answer it, but it was worth every effort. Her question deserves a proper answer. It has blessed and changed me. I pray it blesses you as well.

TWO POSSIBILITIES; TWO CHOICES

Frankly, I did not start this book with any other design than to answer Mom's question. But the answer has raised important issues. One is, how do you and I ensure our animals will get to heaven? Is anything required of us?

Ensuring that our animals get to heaven is something Scripture doesn't spell out clearly. I think that's very smart of God.[227]

I like to take the easiest way, but I'll choose the hard way if that's the only one ensuring success. The Lord knows me — and you.

From what I have learned in this study, I believe there are two possible ways our animals get to heaven. One of them depends solely on you and me. Romans 8 and other Scriptures we have studied, support this theory — Sons of God take creation, those under their stewardship, with them.

This way is illustrated by C. S. Lewis in his novel, *The Great Divorce.*, which allegorically contrasts hell and heaven.[228]

In Chapter 12, Lewis described a lady in her eternal body. She is preceded by a great entourage of spirits heralding her. She was greatly honored. Accompanying her were dozens of animals. When the visitor asked about the animals, the angel guide replied:

> *Every beast and bird that came near her had its place in her love. In her they became themselves. And now the abundance of life she has in Christ from the Father flows over into them.*[229]

The Great Divorce may be truth. It is our love, our salvation, our revelation as "Sons of God" (men and women) which determine if our pets go. We are their tickets to heaven!

C. S. Lewis further supports this when he wrote that because his dog and cat lived together and appeared to enjoy it, one of man's functions may have been to restore peace to the animal world; and if man had not sided with Satan, we might have succeeded to an extent unimaginable.

If that is the case, then for our dog (or cat or horse or bird) to make heaven, we must become and behave like "Sons of God." Our rightness with God ensures that our animal goes with us. Our stewardship to our animals is to believe on Jesus, repent, and obey Him. If it depends on you for your pet to live in eternity, will you do it? Will you risk the alternative?

The second possibility is that, like humans, each animal has a choice. Noah's ark is an example. The animals came to Noah to enter the ark. Wild animals and tame, they gathered to God's call. No man captured them or forced them to come. They were chosen and they chose to come. I see this as an archetype of animals coming to Jesus to enter heaven. Because God calls all creation to redemption and to restoration, animals come voluntarily. Those who do not come, perish.

I think of homeless strays, cats and dogs, or even wild animals, that have chosen human friends. Some have chosen us as companions and protectors. Some animals have protected and served us freely and willingly. Like my grandmother's stray dog chose her and protected her. Others have served and protected their own and other species with apparent compassion and faithfulness. The living God is just and righteous. He must reward such good choices.

What if your dog (or other pet) is eligible for heaven, but you are not? If that animal loves you, won't it miss you? Will you cause your animal additional grief because you miss heaven?

The choice is given to all flesh. The call has gone out.

FRESH WITNESSES

Now that we have Bible proof your dog (or cat, horse, lizard or bird) has a decent chance to go to heaven, let's look at a few anecdotes and some more questions.

PUPPIES IN HEAVEN

The Tulsa newspaper reported that a three-year-old boy, Ben, had a near fatal accident. His heart stopped on the way to the hospital. Ben was in critical condition with brain swelling, on a ventilator. When the awoke — lots of folks were praying he would — he told his mommy that he saw Jesus, and that there were puppies in heaven. Ben got to play with those puppies. His mother was surprised, for they'd never had a dog, and Ben had always been afraid of dogs.[230]

Heaven has puppies to play with — puppies which cure a little boy's fear of dogs. Isn't that like God! Ben's story is also a reminder of how fragile this life is. How quickly we can be gone!

"RAINBOW BRIDGE" ANECDOTES

When their pet dies, many people say they feel peace and a strong belief the animal is in heaven. Years ago, a man in a prayer group I attended, experienced the Lord's comfort after his dog died. Jesus gave him a dream in which his dog was in heaven playing at the Lord's feet. This man was a Kentucky coal miner, a family man, and a devout disciple of Jesus Christ. His experience was not unique.

A little girl named Jennifer of Las Vegas, Nevada, wrote me about her puppy, Misty. Jennifer hopes her experience will "help those who have lost their beloved pets, to give them faith and hope." Jennifer wrote:

> *In October of '95, my puppy Misty died. She had drowned. I was so upset, ... I ... thought she would not go to heaven. So I prayed to God for peace.*
>
> *Well, after I cried myself to sleep, I dreamed a wonderful dream. I went up to heaven ... With me was my*

angel . . . When I got up to heaven, I was greeted by God. I ran and gave him a big hug, and when he looked me in the eyes, I felt peace and he told me, "Everything is going to be all right." He then showed me around. It was so beautiful, flowers ... clear lakes... trees with fruit ... made of gold and silver.

God and I passed over a big hill,... There I saw what I wanted to see more than anything in the world — Misty. She ran from a group of other animals, which all were playing... She ran into my arms, and kissed me over and over again. I must have spent hours with her in the flowers playing. While sitting there with her,... I saw millions of animals. Everyone's dead pet was there. ... I felt very peaceful and happy . . . So now I know that our pets go to heaven. ...

I said "good bye" to Misty and she just looked me in the eyes ... like she was telling me, not good bye but "see you soon."

... Yes, you feel sad for losing a lost pet, but ... there's nothing to worry about. They're with God in heaven.

A few weeks after receiving Jennifer's letter, a client in North Dakota told me her sister had lost her beloved cat in an accident. Broken-hearted, this sister prayed for comfort. She too dreamt. Her dream was remarkably like Jennifer's. She saw her cat in a field of animals — animals awaiting the arrival in heaven of their human friends.

Some argue dreams are mere subconscious longings. Ben's case disproves that argument. The boy was not dreaming. He was unconscious and afraid of dogs. He was clinically dead or dying. There is only one logical explanation: it was real. Jesus and those heavenly puppies actually appeared to Ben.

These experiences are like the popular "Rainbow Bridge" story:

There is a bridge connecting Heaven and Earth. It is called the Rainbow Bridge because of its many colors. Just this side of the Rainbow Bridge, there is a land of meadows, hills and valleys with lush green grass.

When a beloved pet dies, the pet goes to this place. There are always food and water and warm spring weather. The old and frail animals are young again. Those who are maimed are made whole again. They play all day with each other.

There is only one thing missing. They are not with their special person who loved them on Earth. So each day they run and play until the day comes when one suddenly looks up! The nose twitches. The ears are up. The eyes are staring. And this one suddenly runs from the group.

You have been seen, and when you and your special friend meet, you take him or her in your arms and embrace. Your face is kissed again and again and again, and you look once more into the eyes of your trusting pet.

Then you cross the Rainbow Bridge together, never again to be separated.[231]

Heaven is for animals, too. God gave them to us as gifts and teachers — as witnesses to the Lord's grace and glory.

But ask the animals, and they will teach you, or the birds of the air, and they will tell you; Or speak to the earth, and it will teach you, or let the fish of the sea inform you. Which of all these does not know that the hand of the Lord has done this? In his hand is the life of every creature and the breath of all mankind.

Job 12:7-10 [NIV]

SAMSON'S "HOMEGOING"

A few years after Mom passed on, her little poodle Samson started having seizures. Prayer and a special diet prolonged the little guy's life, but I knew his time with me was short. One evening he began having seizures again. The next morning Samson could not walk with me even a few hundred feet. Since I had prayed for the Lord's grace and wisdom, I knew He would help me.

As I looked to the Lord, Jesus gave me a sense that Mom and Gretchen (Samson's German shepherd "best friend" who'd died years before) were coming to escort Samson home to heaven. This image gave me grace to take fifteen-year-old Samson to the vet for his last time.

Losing Samson was harder than any previous loss. Maybe it was because he was Mom's. I found myself very tearful. However, the "sense" of Mom and Gretchen coming for Samson gave me comfort. It also set up a longing for heaven within my own heart.

I live in comfort and joy looking forward to what is ahead! My faith is doubly blessed, for it is grounded on the Bible and His personal word to me. Now I can say: Yes, Mom, dogs *do* go to heaven.

The Lord holds a special place in eternity for animals who have fulfilled His purpose in this life. Loving is the highest calling of God. The animals who have shown His unconditional love and forgiveness, His patience and faithfulness, surely have a place close to the throne room of God. Samson loved us. He was a ray of sunlight all his days.

THE PUZZLE COMPLETED

As I was writing this book, I found these words in one of Mom's notebooks. I do not know if they are original or copied from another, but I wept as I read them for they are so like Mom:

Looking at Life Through Rain Spattered Glass

Rain spattered glass blurs the images into gentle shades.
It is like taking off a strong pair of eyeglasses.
Things become fused into each other.
Nothing is quite so clear.
The edges are not sharp.
(Perhaps that is the way we were meant to see things.)

And yet there is a beauty about un-blurred images —
a cleanness, a sharpness.
However painful reality may be,
it is somehow worth it to see one clear image,

than a thousand imperfect pieces.
Being shown the lumber and cement,
the paint and the candelabra,
and even the master plan,
is never quite the same
as seeing the cathedral.

Do you see how the pieces to Mom's question have come together? Do you see the "cathedral?"

Yes, Mom, dogs do go to heaven!

Perhaps not all dogs, but good dogs go. So do all the animals who have chosen or been chosen to grace God's new heavens and earth. God has a plan and place for them — just as He did on the Ark during the Great Flood.

Some may say that the idea of animals in heaven is like wearing "rose-colored glasses" — one big fantasy. However, God's reality is usually better than any dream. Life, real life, is something about which we can be joyously excited! The *joie de vivre* for a believer is a "joy-of-eternal-life!" Eternity with the Creator who Loves all creation is beyond comprehension. What a trip!

I want to be there. To be sure there is no chance of missing it, I keep my heart close to the Lord's heart, trusting Him and obeying His loving orders found in His Holy Bible.

I hope to take many people and animals along with me. Heaven would not be heaven without all of you. Please be sure you come, too.

Your pet's life may depend on it.

Old Blue died and he died so hard,
I dug the ground in my back yard.
Lowered him down with a silver chain,
Every link I did call his name.
Blue, oh Blue, You good dog, you.

When I get to heaven, I know what I'll do.
I'll take my horn, And I'll blow for Blue.
Blue, oh Blue, I'm a' comin there, too.

U.S. (southern) folk song

PRAYER OF PRAISE AND ADORATION:

We acclaim you, holy Lord, glorious in power. Your mighty works reveal your wisdom and love. You formed us in your own image, giving the whole world into our care, so that, in obedience to you, our Creator, we might rule and serve all your creatures. When our disobedience took us far from you, you did not abandon us to the power of death. In your mercy you came to our help, so that in seeking you might find you. Again and again you called us into covenant with you, and through the prophets you taught us to hope for salvation.

Father, you loved the world so much that in the fullness of time you sent your only Son to be our Savior. Incarnate by the Holy Spirit, Born of the Virgin Mary, he lived as one of us, yet without sin. To the poor he proclaimed the good news of salvation; to prisoners, freedom; to the sorrowful, joy. To fulfill your purpose he gave himself up to death; and, rising from the grave, destroyed death, and made the whole creation new.

And, that we might live no longer for ourselves, but for him who died and rose for us, he sent the Holy Spirit, his own first gift for those who believe, to complete his work in the world, and to bring to fulfillment the sanctification of all.

1979 Book of Common Prayer,
Eucharistic Prayer D, pp. 373-374
[according to the use of The Episcopal Church]

ENDNOTES

1 *Wall Street Journal,* 12/9/96, p. B1.

2 The "scientific method" is simply defined as following these steps: (1) obtain information, facts or data by observation; (2) classify them into categories; (3) form a working hypothesis or theory about the data; (4) conduct experiments, under controlled conditions, to test the hypothesis; (5) if confirmed, the hypothesis becomes a theory or principle of science; (6) other scientists attempt to verify or disprove the results, especially with regard to its value in prediction; and (7) long established theories are accepted as "natural laws" until disproven. M. Winokur & Ruckes *General Biology* (Littlefield, Adams & Co. 1967), p. 2.

Legal proof has similarities to the first three steps of the scientific method. However, while both seek truth, the lawyer's task is to seek a judgment as to what happened in the past — a past which obviously cannot be repeated in a "test tube." The lawyer's tools of reconstructing a model of what happened sometimes relies on science, but recognizes the weakness of both science and of eye-witnesses in predicting what really happened. Both sides of a legal dispute collect evidence and develop hypotheses about the past event. Both lawyers match principles of law to the facts and present the case to the court or jury as convincingly as their skills and the evidence permits

3 The oldest animal protection society in the world is the Royal Society for the Prevention of Cruelty to Animals (RSPCA), founded in 1824 by Rev. Arthur Broome and Richard Martin. It was founded at a time when brutality to animals was common and therefore they were ridiculed and scorned. See Vida Adamoli, *The Dog That Drove Home, The Snake-Eating Mouse, and Other Exotic Tales from the Animal Kingdom,* [St. Martins Press, 1991], (Published in Great Britain under title *Amazing Animals*), p. 183. The U.S. S.P.C.A. was founded in 1866 by philanthropist Henry Bergh.

4 See chapters 1 & 2 of Rousas John Rushdoony, *The Institutes of Biblical Law* [The Presbyterian & Reformed Publ. Co., 1973] for a scholarly and provocative discussion of the First and Second of the Ten Commandments.

5 Jean Pierre Claris de Florian, France, *The Great Fables of All Nations* (Tudor Publ. Co. 1928), p. 343

6 I have been told several times that in the 19th century whalers found at least one man alive in a whale's belly – someone who'd fallen overboard a couple of days before. The whale's digestive juices made the man's skin "worse for the wear," and he was a bit crazy, but he was alive!

7 There are worldly pleasures which we shouldn't partake of, but the Kingdom of God has a lot of joy and pleasure. See Ps. 16 & John 10:10.

8 Origin unknown

9 Origin unknown

10 George Graham Vest (1830-1904); from his speech in the Senate (1884)

11 Source: *Electronic Dictionary of Quotations.*

12 Alphose de Lamartine (1790-1869), letter to John Forster (1850)

13 See Paul Drew Stevens, *Real Animal Heroes; True Stories of Courage, Devotion and Sacrifice,* [Signet Books, 1988]; Stephanie Leland *Animal Angels* [1998 Conaci Press Books]; Reader's Digest *Animals You Will Never Forget* [1969, Reader's Digest] ; *Listening to the Animals; Best Friends* [1999, Guideposts]

14 See *GESENIUS, HEBREW-CHALDEE LEXICON*, #3611, the Hebrew word for "dog".

15 See also, Ps. 68:23, I Kings 14:11, 16:4, and 23:38 which speak of dogs kept in cities who cleaned up after battle.

16 I wish it were not necessary to say that I don't condemn any person experiencing homosexual lusts. I have compassion for such people. The Bible treats all sexual sins (all sex practices outside a marriage between one man and one woman) as "sins against our bodies" and therefore worse than other sins. While many Americans today have been taught that homosexuality is "natural," the Bible treats it as an aberration, and the practice of sex with members of the same sex as sin. While all healthy humans have some sort of sexual desires, none have to be gratified outside the marriage bed. We have choices in that department. I know. While I am single and heterosexual, I live celibate – not because I have little or no desire or "sex drive," but out of choice by the Lord's grace. (So don't tell me it cannot be done!) Those failing to control such desires need compassionate help. There is no condemnation from the Lord for the person trapped in homosexuality or any other pattern of sin. God sent His own Son to redeem all humans from all sin, but one. Sexual sins are all in the redeemable category. While some sins appear harder to get loose from than others, our God is able to do what is impossible for man — when we really want His help.

17 *Gesenius, supra.*

18 J. G. Lawson, *The World's Best Loved Poems*, (N.Y.: Harper & Bros. Publ., 1927), p. 118-19

19 Author unknown

20 *Your Incredible Cat,* by David Greene [Ivy Books, 1984] Chapter on "Your Brilliant Cat" p. 24

21 Ordinary house cats have jumped would-be burglars and rapists, and sent them packing with claw and bite marks the men will never forget; They have awakened family members when lethal fumes or fire would overcome them. A family cat has warned a mother of a baby choking to death; cats have attacked or held at bay poisonous snakes traveling toward the children's rooms in a house; and demonstrated numerous other acts of genuine affection. There are documented cases of cats finding their way home, even as far as some 1,400 miles from California to Oklahoma, or to a new location of their family. See, *Mysteries of Animal Intelligence* by Sherry Hansen Steiger and Brad Steiger [Tom Doherty Assoc. Inc. 1995) and C*at Scan* by Robert Byren and Teressa Skelton [Atheneum, 1983]; and Y*our Incredible Cat* by David Greene [Ivy Books, 1984].

22 *Encyclopedia Judaica, "Cat"*

23 *The Tiger in the House*, by Dr. Carl Van Vechten, Ph.B. (Afred A. Knopf, 1920, 1936), p. 84

24 *Real Animal Heroes, supra*

25 *Tiger in the House*, by Carl Van Vechten, p. 161

26 Id., p. 93, referring to Rev. J. G. Wood, *Man and Beast: Here and Hereafter.*

27 *The American Heritage Dictionary*, [1969] p 1245

28 Frederic Skinner, [1904-1990], is known for his contributions to behaviorism Skinner founded radical behaviorism and experimental analysis of behavior. Other behaviorists, like Sigmund Freud, explained behavior by referring to nonconscious, purely mental states. Skinner instead adopted the view that "mind" is mythical. For Skinner, behavior was controlled by the environment (including the private environment of consciousness), not by internal forces. Skinner and his followers studied simple animal and human behaviors under carefully controlled experimental conditions, hoping eventually to build a complete psychology. With his famous "Skinner box.," he studied learning processes in pigeons and other animals. [Source: Grolier Multimedia Encyclopedia, 1998] A major problem with Skinner's box is that humans and animals confined in small spaces go crazy, i.e., exhibit aberrant behavior. Skinner and his followers ignore or are ignorant of Aristotle's admonition to study specimens which retain their nature and not those which have been corrupted [*Politics, I, v. 5]*. Today behaviorist say animals must be studied in natural habitant to get good data. A prison box does not produce natural behavior.

29 Daisie and Michael Radner, *ANIMAL CONSCIOUSNESS (Prometheus Books, 1989) p. 7-8*

30 "Masses" had to be literate to read, but even the illiterate were hearing Scripture from pulpits and literate laity who were talking about or quoting Scripture.

31 *The Columbia Encyclopedia, Second Ed.*, (Columbia Univ. Press, 1935, 1950), p. 531

32 *Animal Consciousness, supra, p. 8-9*

33 Id.

34 *Animal Consciousness, supra,* p. 90-91

35 See, C. S. Lewis, *The Problem of Pain*, chp. 9 "Animal Pain" [MacMillan Pub. Co., 1962, 1986]

36 Stephanie Laland, *Animal Angels,* [Conari Press 1998], p. 188

37 The Hebrew is difficult here. Some translations substitute "a strutting cock" for "greyhound".

38 Vicki Hearne, *Adam's Task; Calling Animals by Name*, [HarperPerenial, 1982, 1983, 1985, 1986, 1994] p.6

39 (Harcourt Brace Jovanovich, Pub. 1990)

40 Id. P. 159

41 Id, and see *Amazing Animals* [Time-Life Books] p. 130; & Felicity Brooks, *Usborne Science and Nature: Animal Behavior* [Usborned Publ. 1992] p. 11.

42 *Mysteries of Animal Intelligence*, p. 128-129

43 "Brave Hearts" *People*, 7/14/97, p. 106 at 108-109

44 Stephanie Laland, *Animal Angels, supra,* p. 42 & 63

45 Winkey Pratney, *Healing the Land, supra.*

46 Jack Canfield, et al, *Chicken Soup for the Pet Lover's Soul* [Health Communications 1998], pp. 225-226.

47 *Jesus the Jewish Theologian*, [Hendrickson Pub. 1995], p. 280

48 *Pictorial Bible Dictionary*, edited by M. Tenney & S. Barabas, (Zondervan, 1963, 1974), [at p. 807] and *The New Compact Bible Dictionary*, edited by T. Alton Bryant, (Zondervan Pub. 1967) at p. 563-64]

49 Winkey Pratney, *Healing the Land*, p 109-110

50 *Pictorial Bible Dictionary,* supra, p. 807

51 Id.

52 *Animal Consciousness, supra, p. 7-8*

53 See for example, Article "Talk Set on Violence, Animal Cruelty Link", *The Daily Oklahoman*, 2/2/98, p 3

54 *Pictorial Bible Dictionary*, supra, p. 807 and *The New Compact Bible Dictionary,* supra, p. 563-64

55 Cecil Frances Alexander

56 Isaac Watts, *The Works of Isaac Watts: Psalms Paraphrased* [London: 1813], p. 328

57 Carl Boberg, 1859-1940, translated Stuart K. Hine, [copyr. 1955, Manna Music, Inc.]

58 Luarentius Abstemius, *The Great Fables of All Nations* (Tudor Publ. Co. 1928), p. 207 — Italy 16th century

59 Whether your faith takes the simple words of Genesis as literal or metaphorical, is between you and the Lord. There are other authors who address these issues on both sides of the debate between creation and evolution. Here we will assume the Bible is true and operate from that assumption. How that truth is interpreted is again a matter of faith. But then so is the whole subject of this book!

60 G. Richard Bozarth, "The Meaning of Evolution," *American Atheist*, Feb. 1978, pp. 19, 30, is quoted by John D. Morris, Ph.D. in *The Young Earth* as saying:

Christianity has fought, still fights, and will fight science to the desperate end over evolution, because evolution destroys utterly and finally the very reason Jesus' earthly life was supposedly made necessary. Destroy Adam and Eve and the original sin, and in the rubble you will find the sorry remains of the son of god. Take away the meaning of his death. If Jesus was not the redeemer who died for our sins, and this is what evolution means, then Christianity is nothing!

This statement is partly true, i.e. evolution is contrary to the Bible. However, science is neutral, like electricity. Science's uses can be very influenced political and religious politics. "Science" helps some and hurts others. Jesus Christ's death at the hand of political and religious leaders illustrates that principle.

61 Have you thought about the philosopher's debate on which came first, the chicken or the egg? The Bible answers this. God made a mature world. (This throws a monkey wrench in dating the Beginning. Created last, Adam himself couldn't verify if the first cow was five minutes old, or five years old.)

62 My intellectual heritage was challenged by my encounter with the God of the Bible when I became a committed Christian. I had to choose and chose to believe the Bible, letting the Lord be my source of knowledge, wisdom and understanding. [Proverbs 1-8] I've learned since that many scientists are challenging the facts and logic of the evolutionary theories and evidence which used to support it. See, John David Morris, Ph.D. *The Young Earth*, [Master Books, 1994]; Henry M. Morris and Gary E. Parker *What is Creation Science?* [Master Books, 1982 & 1996]. There is a vigorous debate among scientists, including Christian scientists, about the evidence about a "young earth." See Alan Hayward, Ph.D. *Creation and Evolution*, [Bethany House 1985]. Only the good Lord knows the truth.

63 Bartleby Nash and Ptolemy Tompkins *Mother nature's Greatest Hits; The Top Forty Wonders of the Animal World*, (Living Planet Press, 1991) pp. 30-32

64 Somehow if the proof is ever all in from science, my gut feeling is that the Bible will come out as a book as accurate (albeit often in metaphor) as a record of scientific truths, as it has been shown by archeology.

65 F. F. Bosworth, *Christ the Healer*, [Fleming H. Revell, 1973], p. 115

66 Hugh Ross, *Fingerprints of God: Reasons to Believe*, cited in Winkey Pratney's *Healing the Land*, (Chosen Books, 1993), p. 60.

67 Healing the Land, supra, Chapter 6, "Three Life Exceptions to the Natural Law"

68 *Healing the Land;* supra, p. 60

69 Henry David Thoreau, *Walden,* [Houghton Mifflin Co, 1906], pp. 250-252

70 *Healing the Land*, supra, p. 72

71 See *Mother Nature's Greatest Hits*, supra; A.B.C. Whipple *Critters; Adventures in Wildest Suburbs*, [N.Y.: St. Martin's Press, 1994; Karen Gravelee, *Animal Societies* [Venture Book; 1993]; David Attenborough, *The Trials of Life*, [Little, Brown & Co. 1990]; Dorothy Hinsaw Patent, *How Smart are Animals?* [Harcourt Brace Jovanovich, 1990]; and *Amazing Animals*, [Time-Life Books, 1990], for a few titles on animal behavior and intelligence which shows the remarkable variety and complexity of the fish, bird and land animal world.

72 *Wall Street Journal*, 1/5/99, p. A1 & B5

73 See, R. J. Rushdoony, *The Institutes of Biblical Law, supra,* p. 124-126.

74 Adrian Room, *The Naming of Animals,* (McFarland & Co., 1993)

75 *Adam's Task, supra,* pp. 47-48

76 R. J. Rushdoony, *The Institutes of Biblical Law*, [The Craig Press, 1973], (p.

124-126) discusses naming. He also, as part of his interpretation of the Sixth Commandment (You shall not murder) speaks of God's laws relating to animals, including insects, and our relationship to them and the earth at pp. 255-262. He covers hybridization, bestiality, and man's attempts at being god over creation. See also, W. Pratney's *Healing the Land,* supra, for discussion of animals, plants and insects in God's order and plan.

77 Charles Darwin, quoted from *Evolution in Science and Religion* by R. A. Millikan, [New Haven: Yale University Press, 1927], at p. 60. I was told before he died, Charles Darwin repented of his advocacy of a Godless world and his theory of evolution. His writings belie a true atheism..

78 For examples, see *Amazing Animals* [Time-Life Books]; & Felicity Brooks, *Usborne Science and Nature: Animal Behavior* [Usborned Publ. 1992]; and *Mysteries of Animal Intelligence* supra.

79 *Mysteries of Animal Intelligence*, supra

80 Id., pp. 1-7, 122-124

81 *The Man Who Listens to Horses*, by Monty Roberts [Random House, 1996, 1997]

82 See Paul Tarchtman's article in *The Smithsonian*, "The Horse Whisperer; Legendary Trainer Buck Brannaman.." Buck Brannaman is a Wyoming cowboy who taught Robert Redford to handle horses with "Brannaman's touch" for the movie, "The Horse Whisperer." The two men's techniques are both are based on language – horse language. The article also references J. Allen Boone, *A Kinship With All Life.*

83 Raphael Brown, trans. *The Little Flowers of St. Francis*, [Image Books; Doubleday, 1958], p. 76-77

84 Id., pp. 88-91; 320-322

85 Id., pp. 131-133

86 Id., pp. 131-132

87 Id. pp. 131-133

88 See for example, Beatrice Lydecker, *What The Animals Tell Me* [Harper & Row; 1977], who writes of her experiences of being able to share or experience animals' "feelings, thoughts, direct factual information, memories, and past experiences." She wrote that she is a practicing Christian and denied that her "gift" of talking to animals was occult or supernatural. p. xi Her anecdotes are remarkable, but not incredible.

89 Sermons of John Wesley, Sermon 60, p. 440

90 Id.

91 For example, the Lord told Elijah that He was commanding the ravens to bring Elijah food during the time Elijah was hiding from King Ahab during the drought. 1 Kings 17:4-6. There are other examples of the Lord communicating directly with animals, but one is enough to disprove that particular point.

92 Many believe Satan was an archangel, and use Isaiah 14:12-15 and Ezekiel 28 as proof texts. Having searched Scripture, this author found no link between these Scriptures and the verses actually describing Satan or the Devil.

93 *Adam's Task, supra,* pp. 47-48

94 While some think God has since fallen down on the job, let's just address the first crime here.

95 *Mother Natures Greatest Hits, supra,* p. 72, 78-79

96 For evidence of grief in the death of an elephant see Cynthia Moss' *Elephant Memories: Thirteen years in the Life of an Elephant Family*; and Jeffery Mousssaieff Masson & Susan McCarthy, *When Elephants Weep.*

97 "Koko," a gorilla who was taught human sign language at the California Gorilla Foundation. Koko asked for a kitten for her birthday. Later, after Koko had bonded with it, the kitten was accidentally killed. Koko behaved with actions showing grief. When her trainer asked Koko questions about death, Koko sobbed, and signed "Sad/frown" and "sleep/cat." In sign language, the gorilla communicated that she understood death and could understand on her own mortality. F. Patterson & E. Linden, *The Education of Koko*, (N.Y.: Holt, Rinehart & Winston, 1981); & Jane Vessels, "Koko's Kitten," *National Geographic,* v.167, #1, P.110.

98 Carl Anderson, "The Obstreperous Owls of Hammel," *Animals You Will Never Forget*, (Reader's Digest, 1969), p. 109.

99 *Encyclopedia Judaica*, "Animals, Cruelty To"

100 Please refer to the *Encyclopedia Judaica* and other rabbinical literature for a more complete view of these lessons.

101 Jews have been persecuted from time immemorial, and undoubtedly will be until the Messiah returns to rule and judge all men. Perhaps it is because they will always be different, God's chosen ones, set apart for service to Him and His world. If you do not love God, you will not love His people. The Bible states clearly that those who fellowship with God, soon bear His presence and character. Those who love evil, hate the light of God's presence. Therefore they hate those who carry His light. Things haven't changed. (Christians, too, are persecuted; in fact, more have been killed for their faith in the 20th

century than in all the time since Jesus lived.) We can learn much about God from those who have spent centuries studying Him and His law.

102 *Encyclopedia Judaica*, "ANIMALS, CRUELTY TO" The Jewish laws regarding killing animals are the kindest available. Slaughter houses in the U.S. are supposed to kill by humane methods, i.e. be quick. (Packing houses don't always obey the laws.) This was based on Biblical, "kosher" laws. The Jewish methods are motivated by consideration for the animal. Jewish law requires the knife to be exceedingly sharp and without the slightest notch. The killing blow is to be swift, and the animal must be bled immediately. Such bleeding would ensure a quick painless death. According to the rabbis, in the verse, "I will eat flesh, because my soul desires to eat flesh" [Deut. 12:20], the Hebrew word for "desire" has a negative connotation. Meat eating should be in moderation, so few animals would be killed. Proverbs 23:20-21. God's attitude toward His animals is one of mercy.

103 William Shakespeare, *Merchant of Venice*, Act V, Scene I, Portia

104 Charles Dickens, *Tale of Two Cities*

105 See Introduction, *Listening to the Animals: To the Rescue* [Guideposts, 1999]

106 *Compton's Interactive Encyclopedia, "Dogs"*

107 Susan Chernak McElroy, *Animals As Teacher & Healers*

108 id., p. 54-55

109 See *Animals As Teacher & Healers*, supra; *Listening to the Animals: To the Rescue*, supra; *Chicken Soup for the Pet Lover's Soul [1998, Jack Canfield, Mark Vitor Hansen, Marty Becker and Carol Kline]*, for examples.

110 *Animals As Teacher & Healers, supra.*

111 *The Great Fables of All Nations, supra,* pp. 429-430.

112 There are also numerous stories of animals, dogs and cats particularly, who have shown up at a time of human need, only to leave or disappear when the need is over. How do they know? Are they sent by God, like four-footed angels?

113 In *Real Animal Heroes,* [Signet Books, 1997] editor Paul Drew Stevens identifies organizations which grant awards to animals that have demonstrated heroic courage, devotion and sacrifice for humans and other animals. Included are stories of cats, dogs, dolphins, horses, mules and pigs.

114 *Man's Search For Meaning* quoted in *Chicken Soup for the Soul, condensed version*

115 J. Martin Kohe, *Id.*

116 *Real Animal Heroes,* supra, pp. 32-36

117 Vicki Hearne, *Adam's Task; Calling Animals By Name*, p. 153, 157-158

118 From Xenophon, the ancient Greek who is the "father of training," to modern trainers, all agree that genuine training occurs only when an animal is understood; when communication is established, through respect and listening to the animal.

119 *William Shakespeare, Merchant of Venice*, Act IV, Scene I, Portia's speech

120 *In Healing the Land*, Winkie Pratney discussed the harmony of nature and evidence that (1) animals do not fear death, as man does; and (2) both humans and animals when attacked and badly injured, feel no pain initially. Chapter 7, "Nature, Soft of Foot and Fur" especially pp. 97-101

121 Malachi prophesied the messenger of the New Covenant would come. [Malachi 3:1]

122 That is surely what Jesus addressed in Matthew 5:33-37, concluding that we should let our "Yes" be "Yes" and our "No" be "No" — without fancy oaths or vows.

123 This is **not** to say I am for governments legislating what religious beliefs their citizens must profess. Only God has that right. Only God is all knowing and wise enough to have such a right. The First Amendment rights of freedom of religion were bought with the lives, fortunes and families of the founders of this nation. I strongly believe in this right to believe what you wish without government interference. (Separation of church and state is another issue.)

124 For a good discussion, see the chapter on "Crazy Horses" in Vicki Hearne, *Adam's Task, supra*, especially at pages 145-146, where she quotes from William Steinkraus' book *Riding and Jumping* – Steinkraus was a renowned horseman and trainer. While I have not read Ms. Hearne's book *Bandit: Dossier of a Dangerous Dog*, about a pit bull which injured or killed. In it, I understand, this trainer addresses issues of truly bad animals, and those who have behaved badly without necessarily being truly mean or evil.

125 This is confirmed in *Gesenius' Hebrew-Chaldee Reference to the Old Testament,* p. 146, Strong's #1320.

126 Let me repeat that I approach evidence as a lawyer. The scientific arguments and debates about Creationism vs. Evolution rage about us. I believe scientists are just as likely as lawyers to utilize or manipulate the evidence to support their personal biases or the case they wish to make. As in trials, what such debates usually comes down to is, not the unprovable "scientific facts" about our origins and the history of the earth, but what you

are willing to believe. To acknowledge the evidence of Creation science, point to the God of the Bible. That requires facing God's commands and claims.

127 I recall from my college studies learning of archeological evidence of huge sophisticated cities dating at least 3000 or 4000 years before Christ, in India, and in South or Central America, and that the engineering of the massive stones which comprise the pyramids so that they fit air-tight is still beyond our modern technology. Human skill and knowledge must have been much higher the closer you get to Adam. What they were able to do, technologically, had to have been destroyed in the Flood or later cataclysmic events. (That race of giants had giant brains, too.) However, technological skills don't teach us much about how they got along with each other.

128 See Agnes Sanford's *Creation Waits*, [Bridge Publishing, Inc./Logos Int'l.

129 See *Encyclopedia Judaica* "Animals, Cruelty to" & "Dietary laws"

130 *Healing the Land*, supra, pp. 97-101

131 Rabbi Yechiel Eckstein, *What Christians Should Know About Jews and Judiasm*, [Word Books, 1984) p. 53

132 *Judiasm*, (Washington Square Press; 1963), p. 8

133 See the *Open Bible*, introduction to Book of Job; & *Pictorial Bible Dictionary*, [Zondervan Publishing House, 1964] p. 433

134 David Greene, *Your Incredible Cat*, [Ballantine Books, 1984], p. 85-88

135 Stephanie Leland, *Animal Angels*, [Conari Press, 1998], p. 100

136 Adele von Rust McCormick, & Marlena Deborah McCormick. *Horse Sense and the Human Heart*, [Health Communications, 1997], pp. 33-46

137 "Saddle Therapy" *Chicken Soup for the Pet Lover's Soul*, [Health Communications, Inc. 1998], p. 123.

138 *Cat Scan*, at p. 45

139 Max I. Dimont, *Jews, God and History* [1962] p. 111

140 *Encyclopedia Judaica*, "Animals, Cruelty to"

141 *Encyclopedia Judaica*, "Animals, Cruelty to"

142 My Muslim neighbor told me that their prophet Mohammed taught that a man who mistreats a dog, no matter how religious, will be denied heaven; and one who is kind to a dog will be rewarded with access to that paradise.

143 *Encyclopedia Judaica*, "Animals, Cruelty to"

144 From *The Immortality of Animals and the Relation of Man as Guardian From a Biblical and Philosophical Hypothesis* by ED. Buckner, A.M., M.D., Ph.D., [George W. Jacobs & Co. 1903], at pages 62-63

145 *Thayer's Greek-English Lexicon of the New Testament*, [Baker House, 1977], Strong's #3326, p. 402

146.*Animals You Will Never Forget,* [Readers Digest, 1969], pp. 81-85

147 *The Zoo That Never Was*, by R. D. Lawrence, [Holt, Rinehart & Winston, 1981]

148 Attributed to St. Basil of Caesarea, prayer A.D. 370 (*The Washington Daily News, April 16 1971, P. 23).* Source: *Respectfully Quoted; a Dictionary of Quotations*, edited by Suzy Platt [Barnes & Nobles Books; 1993]

149 If you are either not certain or dispute that Jesus, Yeshua, is God, then I challenge you to reconsider. Only after considering the evidence fully can you defend a position of faith, of doubt, of another religion, or of atheism, with intelligence and integrity. Read the New Testament; start with John's Gospel and Acts. Jesus is Word of God, Word made flesh. John 8:58, identifies Him with the holiest name of God, the Name given to Moses in Exodus 3:14; the great "I AM." Repeatedly, Jesus is identified as the only Son of God the Father; we become God's children only through Jesus. Study the Old Testament prophesies fulfilled in the life of Jesus relating to His birth, life, ministry, death and resurrection. There are good Christian books which address this evidence. Do it before you become locked in the position of a fool – which is what the Bible calls those who do not trust and obey God — Ps. 14:1 & 53:1.

150 *Vines*, supra, "Beast" p. 53.

151 J. Allen Boone, K*inship With All* Life, (Harper & Row, 1954).

152 I like what machines can do and, like most Americans, I use lots of machines,. But, I am aware of a loss. As a office-bound, working adult, I am largely divorced from nature.

153 Warren D. Thomas, D.V.M. & Daniel Kaufman, *Dolphin Conferences, Elephant Midwives and Other Astonishing Facts about Animals*, [Jeremy P. Tarcher, Inc., 1990]., p. 17. See also, Dr. Bernard Heuvelmans, *On The Track of Unknown Animals*, third revised edition, [Columbia Univ. Press, 1955, 1995]

154 *Dolphin Conferences,* supra, p. 129.

155 See Vicki Hearne, *Adam's Task* and Jeffery Moussaieff Masson, *Dogs Never Lie About Love*, [Crown Publ. 1997] for discussions of animals loving meaningful work.

156 *Listening to Animals; Best Friends*, [Guideposts 1999], p. 82 [from C. W. Gusewelle, *The Rufus Chronicle* [Ballantine Publ. 1996]]

157 "The Last of The Politically Incorrect Country Fairs," *Wall Street Journal*, 7/24/98, p. W-1

158 "Flyball Is A Sport People Really Sink Their Canines Into," by Tony Horowitz, *Wall Street Journal*, 8/5/98, p. A-1

159 *Dolphin Conferences*, supra, p. 71

160 Desmond Morris, *The Biology of Art*, (N.Y.: Knopf, 1962), p. 151; D. Guewa & J. Ehmann, *To Whom it May Concern: an Investigation of the Art of Elephants*, (Norton, 1985)

161 *Mysteries of Animal Intelligence, supra*, pp 101-103

162 Warren D. Thomas, D.V.M. & Daniel Kaufman, *Dolphin Conferences, Elephant Midwives And Other Astonishing Facts About Animals*, p. 106

163 *Encyclopedia Judaica, supra*

164 Source: Rabbi Alexander Feinsilver, *Talmud for Today*

165 J. Allen Boone, *Kinship With All Life*, pp. 111-113.

166 See J. Allen Boone, *Kinship With All Life*, & *Language of Silence* [Harper & Row, 1970]; *Animals Tame & Wild*, edit. Gilbert & John Phelps [Topaz Publ. 1979]; Steiger's *Mysteries of Animal Intelligence, supra; "Ben Got His Man"* in *Animals You Will Never Forget*, [Readers Digest, 1969], for examples. J. Allen Boone and others have explored communication with animals and observed important things, even if their terminology and interpretations do not always appear Biblically sound.

167 *The Language of Silence*, supra.

168 *Language of Silence, supra,* p. 104

169 For examples, see Vida Adamoli's *The Dog That Drove Home, The Snake-eating Mouse, And Other Exotic Tales From The Animal Kingdom*, [St. Martin's Press, 1989]; "Hector the Stowaway Dog" *Animals You Will Never Forget, supra.*

170 Vicke Hearne, *Adam's Task, supra,* p. 264, 265, 266

171 As mentioned before, the Steigers successfully used these methods with their Rottweiler, Moses. See, *Mysteries of Animal Intelligence*, by Sherry Hansen Steiger and Brad Steiger, *supra*, citing J. Allen Boone, *Kinship with All Life*.

172 J. Allen Boone said a chemist, J. William Jean, achieved results with microorganisms which others were unable to achieve; that the man lived the golden rule, by looking for the best in and assisting the other life form to achieve its fullest expression. Millions of microorganisms visibly (under the

microscope) turned to Dr. Jean with enthusiasm. The implications are vast. *Kinship with All Life, supra*, p. 115

173 *Kinship with All Life*, p. 116

174 Bishop Thomas Ken, Doxology, 1692

175 *The Problem of Pain* (Collier Books, 1962), p. 136-137

176 U. Milo Kaufmann, *Heaven, a future finer than dreams*, [Light and Life Press, 1981], p. 13-14

177 See for example, Grant R. Jeffrey, *Heaven the Last Frontier*; and W.A. Criswell and Paige Patterson, *Heaven; Heaven, a future finer than dreams*, supra. *Heaven; Close Encounters of the God Kind* by Jesse Duplantis is another. I would also commend to the reader the sermons of Charles G. Finney, a lawyer turned evangelist in the 1800's, and Watchman Nee, the great Chinese teacher-evangelist. See also, William F. Buckley, Jr., *Nearer, My God*, [Harcourt & Brace, 1997].

178 *Pictorial Bible Dictionary*, supra, "Paradise", p. 622

179 *Pictorial Bible Dictionary*, supra, p. 346

180 Going to the Greek text, the phrase translated "unreasoning animals" or "brute beasts" is "aloga zoa". "A" is negative and "loga" is from "logos" meaning words or speech; "aloga" is "without speech." "Zoa" is the root of "zoology," and means a living being, including its spiritual life. See George Ricker Berry, Ph.D., *The Interlinear Literal Translation of the Greek New Testament*, [Zondervan, 15th printing 1974]

181 Source: *Reader's Digest*

182 I support laws which give owners a chance to prove that an animal is not mean. Giving a dog at least one bite, before they must be put to sleep, is an old rule of law. With modern training and animal intelligence studies, it makes sense to try to retrain the animal — or find out why it hurt someone in the first place. Let the owner pay damages for the injury, and spare the animal if it acted only in fear or defense. Sometimes the dog has a good excuse for biting. However, killer animals are the equivalent of human murderers. While they are not a large part of the population, the public must be protected from their ravages.

183 Luarentius Abstemius, Italy 16th century, *The Great Fables of All Nations, supra, p. 205*

184 See *Dogs Never Lie About Love*, supra, especially the chapter "Being Alone: the Sadness of Dogs"; and, *Animal Angels;* supra, pp.188-189 (about a pet cougar who refused to eat and died after the couple who'd had him his first five years, abandoned him).

185 Arthur Schopenhouer (1788-1860), quoted in Robert Byrne & Teressa Skelton, *Cat Scan;* Supra, p. 11

186 "The Hippo and the Antelope" is from *Dogs Never Lie About Love*, supra, and quoted in *Listening to the Animals; Best Friends,* [Guideposts, 1999], p. 38

187 Bert Clompus, "Cat with No Name," *Listening to the Animals; Best Friends,* [Guideposts, 1999], p 195.

188 *Dogs Never Lie About Love,* supra, p 177

189 "dr. karen on behavior & beyond" Pets: part of the family, Sept/Oct 1999 issue, p. 10.

190 Begun in 1233 AD., as an emergency device, when the Christianity in Western Europe was the Roman Catholic church, the inquisition continued until the 19th century. Originally the pope commissioned a group of Dominican priests to investigate a sect in south France. This Inquisition became, through the years, marked with torture and corruption, even though such was frowned upon by the pope. The Spanish Inquisition, was begun by Ferdinand and Isabella of Spain, to spy out insincere moorish and Jewish converts. Soon all Spaniards feared the Inquisitors. Imprisonment was common, but burning at the stake made martyrs of many.

191 Colleen McDannell & Bernhard Land, *Heaven, a History*, [Yale U Press 1988], p. 72

192 Id, pp. 84, 118

193 Id, pp. 84-85

194 Id, pp. 154-155

195 Id, pp. 172-180

196 Sermons of John Wesley, Sermon 60 *The General Deliverance* and Sermon 64 *New Creation*

197 #3742, "Cherub" *Gesenius, supra*, p 413

198 "Temple" *Pictorial Bible Dictionary, supra*, p 831

199 Icarus, in Greek mythology, escaped from the isle of Crete on wings fashioned from feathers Exuberant with flight, he flew too close to the sun, which melted the wax which held the wings together. Icarus plunged into the sea and died.

200 [Thomas Nelson, 1984, 1996], p 98

201 Rebecca Springer, *Within Heaven's Gates*, [Whitaker House, 1984]

202 *Heaven; Close Encounters of the God Kind*, [Harrison House, 1996], p 71

203 *I Saw Heaven*, [Albury Publishing, 1983, 1991], p 31

204 Jane Goodall with Phillip Berman, *Reason for Hope*, [Warner, 1999], from review in *Publishers Weekly*, 8/2/99, p 61.

205 William R Newell, *Romans Verse By Verse*, [World Bible Publ, 1938], p. 322

206 I recommend Winkie Pratney's *Healing the Land;* especially chapter 11, for a short, thoughtful lesson in ecology from a Christian viewpoint.

207 See Edith Schaeffer, *Hidden Art*, [London: Norfolk Press, 1971] & Francis A Schaeffer, *Pollution and the Death of Man* [London: Hodder & Stoughton, 1970].

208 Agnes Sanford, *Creation Waits*, [NJ.:Logos/Bridge Publishing]

209 William Newell, *Romans Verse by Verse, supra*, p 321

210 Sermons of John Wesley, Sermon 60 *The General Deliverance* and Sermon 64 *New Creation*, pp 442-445

211 *The Apocrypha*, Revised Standard Version [Thomas Nelson, 1957]

212 Introduction by E O. Wilson, *Witness; Endangered Species of North America* by Susan Middleton and David Liitschwager [San Francisco: Chronicle Books, 1994], p. 17.

213 *The Analytical Greek Lexicon*, [Zondervan Publ 1970, 1973], p. 42

214 Winkie Pratney, *Healing the Land*, supra P. 51-52

215 Newell, *Romans Verse by Verse, supra*, p 321-322

216 Colin Brown, editor, *The Dictionary of New Testament Theology*, Vol A-F, [Zondervan, 1975] p. 518

217 *The Mystical Theology of the Eastern Church*, quoted in Andrew Linzey, *ANIMAL RIGHTS; a Christian Assessment of Man's Treatment of Animals*, [London: SCM Press Ltd, 1976] at p 69

218 *Romans Verse By Verse,* supra, p. 323-324

219 Forward by Susan Middleton, in *Witness; Endangered Species of North America,* supra, p 13.

220 Barbara Cartland, *Lucifer and the Angel,* [1980, Bantam] p. 82

221 *Nearer, My God; an autobiography of Faith*, [Harcourt Brace 1997], p. 13-14

222 The date I saw this program aired was on September 18, 1996. I don't know if it was live or pre-recorded.

223 Interestingly, the Hebrew word for flesh, "*basar*," comes from a root word meaning "to be fresh," i.e., "full" or "cheerful."

224 In the New Testament, *sarx* is used also "a human being, with all our "frailty" or "human nature."

225 Harold Hill, with Irene Harrell, *How Did It All Begin? From Goo To You By Way Of The Zoo*, [Logos International, 1976], pp. 81-84. Harold Hill was an engineer. He describes an experiment where light in these three groups of people were measured. The three emitted significantly different degrees of light energy. Frankly, it is usually apparent to the enlightened eye.

226 The Hebrew term most used for the Lord and heavenly things, translated "glory" is "kabowd." It means "weight" or "heavy" in a good sense. It is also translated "honor." Poetically the term is used of the "heart" or "soul," i.e. the noble part of man. [*Gesenius*, #3519, p. 382] The Greek word used in the New Testament is *doxa* whose root means to "think" or "seem," relating to reputation. So *doxa* signifies an opinion or estimate, and therefore the honor resulting from a good opinion. Glory means:

"It is used (I)(a) of the nature and acts of God in self-manifestation, i.e., what He essentially is and does, . . . (b) of the character and ways of God as exhibited through Christ to and through believers, 2 Cor. 3:18 and 4:6; (c) of the state of blessedness into which believers are to enter hereafter through being brought into the likeness of Christ, e.g., Rom. 8:18, 32; Phil 3:21 ... (d) **brightness or splendor**, (1) supernatural, emanating from God (as in the shekinah "glory," in the pillar of cloud and in the Holy of Holies, e.g., Exo. 16:10, 25:22) Luke 2:9; Acts 22:11; Rom. 9:4; 2 Cor. 3:7; Jas. 2:1; in Titus 2:13 it is used of Christ's return.... (2) **natural, as of the heavenly bodies,** 1 Cor. 15:40, 41;" [*Vine's, supra*, "Glory, Glorious" p. 267-268.]

227 The Lord, in inspiring Scripture, is very clever. Getting to heaven is both very simple, and exceedingly difficult. It is as simple as choosing to love and live for God, to trust Jesus, like a child trusts; but requires dying daily to all our selfish, willful ways to get there, so it is impossible without God's help.

228 While C. S. Lewis reserved his opinion as to whether our particular pets would actually populate the new earth, he clearly imagined such a possibility. See *The Problem of Pain*, "Animal Pain." — Chapter 9 [Macmillan Publ. Co., 1962]

229 *The Great Divorce,* [Macmillan Publ. Co. 1946, 1974], p. 106

230 *Tulsa World*, 12/11/93, p. 1 & 3

231 *Tulsa World* 8/9/98.

ORDER FORM

Don't delay. Order Additional Books and Products Today!

Qty		Price
______	Do Dog's Go To Heaven?	$19.95
______	Signed, Limited Edition, 24" x 18" print	$125.00
______	12" x 9" Unsigned, unframed print	$25.00
______	T-shirt (s, m, l, xl) *(circle size needed)*	$22.95
______	T-shirt (xxl, xxxl) *(circle size needed)*	$23.95
______	Sweatshirt (s, m, l, xl) *(circle size needed)*	$39.95
______	Sweatshirt (xl, xxl) *(circle size needed)*	$42.95
______	Note Cards (package of 12)	$10.00

________ TOTAL

________ Oklahoma residents, add sales tax 8%
(FL, NC & IL residents add applicable sales tax).

________ Shipping and handling (OK residents $6.00 Outside of OK $7.00)

________ GRAND TOTAL

☐ Check ☐ Credit card (MasterCard or Visa) ☐ Money Order

Name ______________________________

Address ______________________________

City ____________________ State ____ Zip

Phone (Day)____________________ (Night) ____________

Credit card # ____________________ Exp. Date ____________

Name as it appears on credit card ____________________

Signature ______________________________

Mail to: JoiPax Inc., P.O. Box 701252, Tulsa, OK 74170-1252 or order by phone: **1-877-540-2872** or (918) 499-1897 *(Tulsa, OK area)*; or on our webpage at www.joipax.com

Prices subject to change. Please allow up to 6-8 weeks for delivery.

ORDER FORM

Don't delay. Order Additional Books and Products Today!

Qty		Price
______	Do Dog's Go To Heaven?	$19.95
______	Signed, Limited Edition, 24" x 18" print	$125.00
______	12" x 9" Unsigned, unframed print	$25.00
______	T-shirt (s, m, l, xl) *(circle size needed)*	$22.95
______	T-shirt (xxl, xxxl) *(circle size needed)*	$23.95
______	Sweatshirt (s, m, l, xl) *(circle size needed)*	$39.95
______	Sweatshirt (xl, xxl) *(circle size needed)*	$42.95
______	Note Cards (package of 12)	$10.00

________ TOTAL

________ Oklahoma residents, add sales tax 8%
(FL, NC & IL residents add applicable sales tax).

________ Shipping and handling (OK residents $6.00
Outside of OK $7.00)

________ GRAND TOTAL

☐ Check ☐ Credit card (MasterCard or Visa) ☐ Money Order

Name ______________________________

Address ______________________________

City ____________________ State _____ Zip

Phone (Day)____________________ (Night) ____________

Credit card # ____________________ Exp. Date ____________

Name as it appears on credit card ____________________

Signature ______________________________

Mail to: JoiPax Inc., P.O. Box 701252, Tulsa, OK 74170-1252 or order by phone: **1-877-540-2872** or (918) 499-1897 *(Tulsa, OK area)*; or on our webpage at www.joipax.com

Prices subject to change. Please allow up to 6-8 weeks for delivery.